Davidson
1973

LONGER ELIZABETHAN
POEMS

THE POETRY BOOKSHELF

General Editor: James Reeves

Robert Graves: *English and Scottish Ballads*
Tom Scott: *Late Medieval Scots Poetry*
James Reeves: *Chaucer: Lyric and Allegory*
William Tydeman: *English Poetry 1400–1580*
Martin Seymour-Smith: *Shakespeare's Sonnets*
Martin Seymour-Smith: *Longer Elizabethan Poems*
James Reeves: *John Donne*
Maurice Hussey: *Jonson and the Cavaliers*
Jack Dalglish: *Eight Metaphysical Poets*
James Reeves and Martin Seymour-Smith: *Andrew Marvell*
Gareth Reeves: *George Herbert*
Dennis Burden: *Shorter Poems of John Milton*
V. de S. Pinto: *Poetry of the Restoration*
Roger Sharrock: *John Dryden*
James Reeves: *Jonathan Swift*
John Heath-Stubbs: *Alexander Pope*
Francis Venables: *The Early Augustans*
Donald Davie: *The Late Augustans*
F. W. Bateson: *William Blake*
G. S. Fraser: *Robert Burns*
Roger Sharrock: *William Wordsworth*
James Reeves: *S. T. Coleridge*
Robin Skelton: *Lord Byron*
John Holloway: *P. B. Shelley*
James Reeves: *John Clare*
Robert Gittings: *Poems and Letters of John Keats*
Edmund Blunden: *Alfred Lord Tennyson*
James Reeves: *Robert Browning*
Denys Thompson: *Poetry and Prose of Matthew Arnold*
James Reeves: *Emily Dickinson*
James Reeves: *G. M. Hopkins*
David Wright: *Seven Victorian Poets*

[*National Portrait Gallery*

SIR WALTER RALEIGH
(Artist unknown)

LONGER ELIZABETHAN POEMS

Edited with an Introduction and Notes

by

MARTIN SEYMOUR-SMITH

BARNES & NOBLE, INC.
NEW YORK
Publishers & Booksellers since 1873

ISBN 0 389 04175 0

Introduction and Notes
© MARTIN SEYMOUR SMITH 1972

First published 1972

First published in the United States by Barnes & Noble,
New York 1003
Printed in Great Britain by Morrison & Gibb Ltd,
London and Edinburgh

CONTENTS

	page
INTRODUCTION	1
SELECT BIBLIOGRAPHY	53
POEMS	57
Christopher Marlowe and George Chapman: *Hero and Leander*	57
John Donne: *The Progresse of the Soule*	133
John Davies: from *Nosce Teipsum*	155
Walter Ralegh: *Cynthia*	175
Edmund Spenser: *Prothalamion*	195
NOTES	203

To Gladys Williamson

INTRODUCTION

In this book I have printed four important longer Elizabethan poems, and selections from a fifth. In no other age has poetry been so versatile: *Hero and Leander* is a narrative poem, an 'epyllion' ('little epic'); Davies' *Nosce Teipsum* is philosophical; Ralegh's *Cynthia* is a personal lament couched as a love elegy in the pastoral mode; Donne's *The Progresse of the Soule* is a satirical mock-epic. All were written within the space of the eleven years between 1592 and 1603; they share the same kind of vocabulary and the same general reliance upon Neoplatonic doctrine; but they have little else in common.

Hero and Leander is chosen because it is the best of all the Elizabethan narrative poems, and because Chapman's continuation of it has, until the recent work of C. S. Lewis, D. G. Gordon and M. Maclure, been seriously neglected. A study of it casts considerable light—much of which may be new for the student—on the personality and attitudes of Christopher Marlowe; and it serves as the best possible introduction to the difficult but fascinating and underrated poetry and drama of George Chapman, for here Chapman is at his most approachable.

Nosce Teipsum is almost unique in English poetry, in that it puts forward orthodox doctrine in a most attractive and original manner. It deserves to be known as second only, among the author's works, to *Orchestra*. The resemblance of Primaudaye's prose passages (several of which are given in the commentary) to Davies' verse is particularly interesting, and should provide scope for comment and perhaps argument.

Cynthia, only discovered a century or so ago, is a peculiarly 'modern' poem. Not intended by the author for publication, or perhaps even for anyone's eyes but his own, it is remarkable, two centuries before the advent of romanticism, for its exposure of the writer's state of mind. It is undoubtedly one of the most important poems of its time—a major poem—and it establishes Ralegh as a major poet: no poem of such a length states its writer's feelings as they actually occur, and thus provides a record of an intricate mind in passionate flux. My commentary provides as much help as is necessary and desirable; but the exercise of teasing out the poet's meanings—which often cannot be established with any degree of certitude (as Ralegh's chief editor has noted)—should prove an invaluable one. *Cynthia* has long demanded a much wider circulation. It should be read aloud several times as a preliminary to the attempt to elucidate its meaning.

The Progresse of the Soule is vital to an understanding of Donne's humorous, unhappy, sceptical position in the months prior to his materially disastrous marriage. Previous generations have found the poem hard to digest because of its irreverence and obvious pleasure in awkward facts or funny sexual lore. Donne here was, above all, rationally puncturing solemnity; to take the poem too seriously—this is a warning I have repeated—is to fail to enjoy it. It is a piercingly intelligent comic and satirical fragment, and there are now no serious barriers to its wide appreciation.

Prothalamion is an example of what an Elizabethan poet could do with a commission: an example of a perfect keeping of decorum— even the smuggling in of the personal complaints has its proper precedents. For Spenser the subject was trivial. He had not even met any of the people concerned. But he blew up so gorgeous a bubble out of it that when we come to try to break it, we find the transparent walls are as hard as glass.

CHRISTOPHER MARLOWE: LIFE AND WORK

Christopher Marlowe was born in Canterbury some days or weeks before 26 February 1563/4, when his baptism was registered. His grandfather had been a tanner, but his father John took up the allied trade of shoemaker. Only about twenty-four when his second child Christopher was born, he was made a freeman of the city of Canterbury in the same year. Whether Marlowe had attended the grammar school, or the famous King's School as a commoner, before he took up a scholarship to the latter on 14 January 1578/9 is not known. In late 1580 he went up to Corpus Christi College, Cambridge. Soon after this he obtained a Parker Scholarship. Matthew Parker, Archbishop of Canterbury 1558–75, had been a Scholar, Fellow and the Master of Corpus Christi, and he founded a number of scholarships to the College. That Marlowe should have been awarded one after only two years at King's School is testimony to his early academic promise, and, very likely, to a then unexceptionable and orthodox interest in theology. For it seems probable that until 1587, when Marlowe had held his scholarship for the maximum six years, he had at least announced his intention of taking holy orders.

At Cambridge he would have acquired a knowledge of logic, theology, some science and medicine, classical literature and world history. It is not clear whether he knew Greek; all his Greek sources were available in Latin versions. In 1584 Marlowe took his B.A. degree. In the spring and early summer of 1587 he was engaged abroad on government service; when he got into trouble from the University authorities for his absence, the Privy Council exonerated him: it had been reported—reads an entry in the Privy Council Register signed by, among others, the then Archbishop of Canterbury, Whitgift, and Lord Burleigh (Chancellor of the University of Cambridge)—that he had been determined to go to Rheims and to remain there; but, the entry makes clear, he was in fact on government business, and 'Their Lordships request that the rumor thereof should be allaied by all possible meanes, and that he should be furthered in the degree he was to take this next Commencement [his M.A.]. . . .'

Many English Roman Catholics, especially ones from Cambridge, went to Rheims between 1580 and 1592; so that the 'rumour' had obviously suggested that Marlowe had leanings—or worse—towards Roman Catholicism, and therefore treason. Rheims was legitimately regarded by the English government and its secret service as the headquarters of the Catholic opposition. On what business Marlowe was employed it is impossible to say—if he was not actually spying on the recusant community at Rheims by temporarily pretending to be one of them, then it is at least likely he came into contact with some of them. We may infer, however, that someone of importance had early spotted him as a person of distinction and ability. The University authorities had little alternative but to grant Marlowe his M.A.

By 10 November 1587 both parts of Marlowe's drama *Tamburlaine the Great* had been produced in London, by the Lord Admiral's Company. Whether he wrote the first part while still in residence at Cambridge or not, 1587 was a busy year for Marlowe. It seems likely that he must at least have sketched it out there, for he could not have left Cambridge before early July. It is generally thought that he also wrote his translations of Ovid's *Amores* while still at Cambridge, although they were not published then (the dates of the surreptitious editions, one of which was ordered to be burnt by order of Whitgift in 1599, cannot be established—but are not likely to pre-date Marlowe's death in 1593). The manuscript circulation of these translations would account for his already established reputation when he went to London in the summer of 1587.

There is no evidence, then, that Marlowe, now twenty-three, had yet displayed any of the irreligiosity, intemperance, cruelty of heart or proneness to violence for which he was to become notorious in the less than six years of life that remained to him.

His literary output during those years was not large by Elizabethan standards, but it established him as one of the leading playwrights and poets of his time. The chronology of his writings is by no means clear. *Tamburlaine* was first acted in November 1587, entered in the Stationers' Register (incongruously, as 'twooe commicall discourses') by Richard Jones in 1590, and published by him in octavo in 1590 and again in 1592. There was a third edition, in quarto, in 1605. None of these bears Marlowe's name, but the case for his authorship is overwhelming.

There is controversy about the date of composition of *Dr. Faustus*, Marlowe's most famous play. The consensus is that it was written in about 1592; but some good critics still put it as early as 1588/9. We know it was being performed in 1594. The earliest edition is dated 1604; two more quartos followed in 1609 and 1611. Then a series of further editions, 1616, 1619, 1620, 1624, 1631 followed; these contained a radically altered text, and presented problems that can never be wholly solved, although the late Sir Walter Greg's conjectural reconstruction (1950) went a long way towards their elucidation.

The Jew of Malta, a tragic farce that is still underrated, was written in about 1589 (the *terminus a quo* is 23 December 1588) but no edition earlier than the quarto of 1633 is extant; it was entered in the Stationers' Register in May 1594, but no copy of this edition, if it was published, has survived. It seems to have been the most popular of all Marlowe's plays.

Edward II, almost certainly Marlowe's latest complete play, was registered only a month after his death. Probably there was an edition within two or three months of registration, rushed out in order to cash in on the author's notoriety; only a part of this survives. The first full edition is dated 1594.

The Tragedie of Dido Queene of Carthage, attributed to Marlowe and his Cambridge contemporary Thomas Nashe in the first quarto edition of 1594—it is obvious enough why so much acknowledged work of Marlowe's appeared in that year, and it is testament to his high literary reputation as well as to his notoriety—was possibly written by Marlowe in his Cambridge days, as his first play, and later prepared for publication by Nashe. It is usually, and most sensibly, treated as a prentice play.

The short *The Massacre at Paris*, which exists only in an undated octavo, is certainly late Marlowe; but it is crude, violent and not up to his highest standards. However, the text we have is garbled and heavily abridged.

Marlowe's translation of the first book of the rhetorician (and nephew of Seneca) Lucan's *Pharsalia*, one of the earlier blank verse poems in the language, was probably written at Cambridge after the *Amores*. It was registered in 1593 but not published until 1600, when it was issued by Thomas Thorp, the probably piratical publisher of Shakespeare's *Sonnets*.

Apart from *Hero and Leander*, usually, and probably rightly, supposed to be his last work of all—this is fully discussed below— Marlowe wrote a few extant short poems, of which the best known is *The Passionate Shepherd to his Love*. Besides this, he wrote the beautiful untitled fragment beginning 'I walkt along a streame for purenesse rare'. Other attributions include a Latin elegy and a number of eclogues and sonnets more doubtfully his.

The few biographical glimpses of Marlowe we are able to take have inevitably suggested to critics that he was a violent, reckless, unrestrained and irreligious man. It can only be a part of the truth about him, but it must be a significant part.

Marlowe was involved, to our knowledge, in no less than four infringements of the law in one form or another; the last had no outcome because any action the authorities might have contemplated was interrupted by his death. The first case, involving homicide, was perhaps the most potentially dangerous for Marlowe, although this depends on one's view of how much weight the Privy Council would have attached to the accusations of blasphemy that were laid against him at the time of his death.

In the summer of 1589 one William Bradley, son of the landlord of the Bishop Inn in Gray's Inn Lane, asked for sureties of the peace against three men. One of these was Thomas Watson (?1557–92), Marlowe's neighbour in Shoreditch, and a fellow dramatist, poet and translator. Bradley stated that he went in fear of his life. All this was part of a quarrel with which Marlowe had nothing to do; it is probable that he became involved by accident.

One afternoon, probably the 18th, between two and three, Marlowe was engaged in a sword-fight with this Bradley. We do not know why. Perhaps Bradley recognized him as a friend of his enemy Watson, and attacked him. . . . Perhaps Marlowe recognized him as an enemy of his friend. . . . Evidence that Bradley was a belligerent and brawling character makes the first hypothesis more likely. As Marlowe fought Bradley, Watson himself came along. The record of the affair—this might refer to the truth or to a story the two survivors cooked up—asserts that Bradley now cried: 'arte thowe nowe come then I will have a boute with thee'. Marlowe withdrew, and Watson was driven to the edge of a ditch, whereupon in desperation he killed Bradley. Both men were arrested on suspicion of murder. On the next day a coroner's inquest cleared both men, and Watson was adjudged to have acted in self-defence and 'not by felony'. Watson spent five months before receiving the Queen's official pardon; but Marlowe was entitled to bail, as not having been involved in the homicide, and he soon found two sureties. He had been in Newgate for less than fourteen days.

In May 1592 Marlowe was again in trouble, although it may not have been serious: on 9 May he entered into a recognizance under a penalty of £20 to keep the peace towards the constable and the sub-constable of Holywell Street; he had used threatening language towards them.

Dr William Urry, archivist to the city of Canterbury, has unearthed evidence—full details of which are yet to come—that Marlowe was in Canterbury in the autumn of the same year, and that he fought a duel with a William Corkine, a musician of the Cathedral; this is said to have ended in 'a charming reconciliation'.

Towards the end of his life Marlowe was a guest at Scadbury of Thomas Walsingham, younger cousin of Francis Walsingham, Privy Councillor and head of Elizabeth's espionage services. This Walsingham was a patron of Thomas Watson (who died in 1592) and, later, of George Chapman. Thomas Kyd, a fellow playwright with whom Marlowe had once shared a room, was arrested in May in connection with an agitation in the City of London against foreigners; in the course of searching his apartment the agents for the Privy Council found a heretical document. Kyd, probably truthfully, maintained that this document was Marlowe's, and had got mixed in with his own papers. In fact the incriminating literature was a transcript of a book called *The Fal of the Late Arrian* by John Proctor (1549). This took up several Arian arguments— Arianism denied the divinity of Jesus Christ, holding him to be but a creature, even if the highest of creatures—and refuted each in turn. The fragment in question therefore looked more incriminating than it was; but it seems likely that Marlowe himself was interested in the arguments of the Arian heresy, which were intelligent. There is conclusive evidence that he was a free-thinker (rather than an 'atheist'), a questioner of the basic tenets of a religion that, we have to remember, was savagely enforced in his time—and by no means in accordance with its own avowed principles. This evidence is best summarized and discussed in Paul H. Kocher's *Christopher Marlowe*.

Because of what Kyd had said about him, Marlowe was apprehended by the Privy Council: on 20 May he entered his appearance, and was told to report to 'their Lordships' daily until 'lycensed to the contrary'. This was not necessarily a very serious matter. That the Privy Council did not take it too seriously is suggested by the fact that they did not arrest Marlowe as they had the less well connected Kyd. Perhaps this had something to do with Marlowe's address: the Council's first warrant had directed their messenger 'to repaire to the house of Mr Tho Walsingham in Kent. . . .' It is not even clear whether they wanted Marlowe as a witness or a malefactor.

It was at this point, some time just before or just after Marlowe's violent death on 30 May, that a rogue named Baines stepped into the picture. He handed in a note 'Containing the opinion of one Christopher Marly, concerning his damnable judgment of religion and scorn of Gods word'. The questions of the nature of Marlowe's 'blasphemies', and of his critique of Christianity and his attitude to contemporary thought are discussed below. Here it is sufficient to say that while Baines's accusations might have complicated things for Marlowe, there is again not much reason to suppose that he could not, with his connections, have got away with it. It is almost certain that the Baines who handed in this note has been correctly identified. He was well-bred scum: lawyer, crook, informer, he was hanged at Tyburn for an unknown offence only eighteen months after Marlowe's death. A man not often out of trouble, he doubtless saw some kind of advantage to himself in informing against Marlowe when he heard that he had been summoned before the Council.

On 30 May 1593, at ten o'clock in the morning, Marlowe was at Deptford Strand drinking at the 'house of a certain Eleanor Bull, widow'. Perhaps he had not returned to Scadbury after reporting to the Privy Council; although Deptford lies less than seven miles to its north-west. The three men with him, all just entitled to the status of gentleman, were bad, disreputable, but comparatively fortunate men. All of them were intimately connected with Marlowe's host, Thomas Walsingham; Marlowe's killer, Ingram Frizer, was his personal servant.

Poley was a skilful man, a cunning and successful spy, who combined effrontery with ruthlessness. Committed to the Marshalsea prison in 1583 by Sir Francis Walsingham (it is not known why; but Walsingham, as head of the secret service, was often his employer) he 'alienated the affections' of a cutler's wife, giving her 'five bankets' in his chamber, but refusing to see his own wife. He also borrowed money from the unfortunate cutler. Such a man might well fascinate the violently unconventional Marlowe. The Marshalsea affair would doubtless have amused him: by means of a gift and some cash for the lodgekeeper of the Marshalsea (his intermediary!) Poley on his release was reconciled to the cutler, but none the less continued to sleep with his wife—now at her mother's house. When the mother in 1585 discovered 'her daughter sitting upon . . . Polley's knees, the syght thereof did soe stryke to her hart. . . . She prayed God to cutt her of verie quickly. . . .' She died within a few days. Poley was a lucky man. Soon afterwards he played an important part, as a double agent, in the affair that cost Mary Queen of Scots her life: the Babington Plot. It was in connection with this that he met Thomas Walsingham. One significant remark he is known to have made is: 'I will sweare and foresweare my selffe rather than I will accuse my selffe to doe me any harm'.

No one seems to have trusted him completely—except the unfortunate Anthony Babington, of the famous conspiracy, who paid for it with his life Walsingham did not trust him, yet he secured his release from the Tower after the Plot. Poley boasted to the cutler, whom he was still cuckolding, that Walsingham was more beholden to him than he to Walsingham—and that Walsingham had contracted venereal disease in France. He seems to have been particularly unfortunate for poets: probably he was the Poley who was set to 'catch advantage' of Ben Jonson when he was imprisoned—Jonson mentioned him in a poem, equating him with a spy—and in 1595 he was trying to expose a book by the Jesuit Robert Southwell, soon afterwards burnt. He disappears from view in 1601. His lifestory is one of duplicity—but of the kind of duplicity that interested Marlowe, which is why I have detailed it at some length. As F. S. Boas says: 'He is the very genius of the Elizabethan underworld'.

Nicholas Skeres, the other witness to Marlowe's death, is a more obscure figure. He seems to have been associated with a friend of Chapman's and Marlowe's, the poet—highly thought of by many contemporaries—Matthew Roydon, in 1581/2. He was also probably mixed up, with Poley, in the Babington Plot.

Ingram Frizer, the killer, was a less impressive crook than Poley. He seems to have made a living by cheating various dupes. He, too, had been associated with Skeres, who probably at one time had substantial funds. His master was Thomas Walsingham, and it was maintained as early as 1600 that he had invited Marlowe to Deptford. This is plausible, since they would have had good opportunity to meet at Scadbury—if indeed they had not met before.

Exactly what happened will never be known. The Coroner's inquisition (in Latin) on Marlowe stated that after the four had met at ten in the morning ' & there passed the time together & dined & after dinner were in quiet sort together there & walked in the garden belonging to the said house until the sixth hour after noon of the same day & then returned from the said garden to the room aforesaid & there together and in company supped; & after supper the said Ingram & Christopher Marley were in speech & uttered one to the other divers malicious words for the reason that they could not be at one nor agree about . . . *le recknynge*; & the said Christopher Marley then lying upon a bed in the room where they supped, & moved with anger against the said Ingram ffrysar upon the words aforesaid spoken between them . . . & there maliciously drew the dagger of the said Ingram which was at his back, and with the same dagger . . . then & there gave . . . Ingram two wounds on his head . . . whereupon the said Ingram, in fear of being slain, & sitting in the manner aforesaid between the said Nicholas Skeres & Robert Poley so that he could not in any wise get away, in his own defence . . . struggled with . . . Marley to get back from him his dagger . . . and . . . in defence of his life, with the dagger . . . to the value of 12d gave the said Christopher . . . a mortal wound over his right eye of the depth of two inches & of the width of one inch; of which . . . Marley then and there instantly died'.

Shakespeare, in an unmistakable reference, commented, through the mouth of the clown in *As You Like It:* '. . . when a mans good wit seconded with the forward childe, understanding: it strikes a man more dead than a great reckoning in a little roome. . . .'

The Coroner's inquest told an unlikely but plausible story. It is quite possible that their story was true.[1] It is just as possible that there was a real 'tavern brawl', that Marlowe got the worst of it, and that the others faked up the most convincing story they could. Or perhaps Marlowe was invited to Deptford—'set up'—and murdered by order of Thomas Walsingham, who may have felt himself in some way endangered; or by order of the Council. Perhaps he was the victim, not of his noted ill temper, but of a political plot. However, it would have pleased Marlowe's spirit if he could have known that his killer, Frizer, had ended his days a full thirty-four years later, respectable and—a churchwarden.

---

[1] It should be mentioned here that all theories of Marlowe's having survived, usually in order to write the plays of Shakespeare, are illiterate fantasies, and can only be treated with contempt.

GEORGE CHAPMAN: LIFE AND WORK

Little is known in detail about the life of George Chapman. He was born at Hitchin in Hertfordshire between 25 March 1559 and 24 March 1560—this period representing, by the Old Style then in use, the year 1559.[1] His father, like Marlowe's, was a freeholder. He had one elder brother and three sisters who married. His grandfather was George Nodes, master of the buckhounds to Henry VIII; through his grandmother Margaret Grimeston he was related to Edward Grimeston, translator of French and Spanish travel and history books. Chapman possibly went to Oxford, but there is no record of his taking a degree. He was in the service of Sir Ralph Sadler by 1583. He went abroad, and most probably served, like Ben Jonson, as a soldier in the Low Countries. His first poem, *The Shadow of Night*, was published in 1594. Another book of poems followed the next year. A third appeared in 1596, by which time he was already writing plays for the Admiral's Company. His translation of the first seven books of Homer's *Iliad*, and his play *The Blind Beggar of Alexandria*, were published in the same year as the continuation of *Hero and Leander*. Many other plays have been lost. *Bussy d'Ambois* was published in 1607. Two years before he had been in gaol with Jonson and John Marston, for making fun of the Scots in their play *Eastward Ho*.

Chapman had the usual Elizabethan poet-dramatist's rather difficult passage through life. When his *Conspiracy and Tragedy of Biron* was acted in 1608 it gave offence to the French ambassador, although he seems to have escaped imprisonment. But he had been in prison as early as February 1599/1600. In 1585, probably when he first came to London, he borrowed from a notorious moneylender, John Wolfull. Wolfull had him imprisoned in the Counter fifteen years later on account of this debt. As late as 1608 he was still defending himself from persecution from John Wolfull's son.

For a time after this his fortunes seem to have taken a turn for the

---

[1] Dates between 1 January and 24 March are usually given—as in this book—in such a manner as to combine Old and New Styles, e.g. 4 February 1568/69.

better, for he attracted the notice of Prince Henry. In 1609/10 the first twelve books of the *Iliad* appeared; the whole translation was published in 1611. But Prince Henry, who had probably commanded the Homer translations, died in 1611, and Chapman lost everything, doubtless through the characteristic callousness of Henry's treacherous father, James I. In 1616 the whole *Works* of Homer appeared. Chapman achieved a great reputation by it, but his arrogance and loftiness led his contemporaries to gibe at his reliance on Latin cribs. Sadly, he quarrelled with his old friend Jonson—perhaps because of the latter's criticism of his Homer. Nothing is known of his later years. He died 12 May 1634 and was buried, in a tomb designed by Inigo Jones, in St. Giles in the Fields.

HERO AND LEANDER: MARLOWE

Apart from a few odd fragments, the authorship of certain of which is disputed, the first two books of *Hero and Leander* are all that we possess of Marlowe's original non-dramatic poetry. It is unsafe (if not always acknowledged as such by critics) to be over-dogmatic in attributing to their authors opinions expressed by characters in plays. The same kind of caution must be applied, of course, to the opinions of the narrators of poems. But we are none the less a step closer to Marlowe himself in *Hero and Leander* than we are in the plays: here he has not only to manipulate his material but also to comment upon it, and in an appropriate narrator's voice. That voice is for most of the time sardonic, ironic, subtly outrageous. It reveals many aspects of Marlowe's mind and temperament: his learning, his scorn of conventionality, his sense of comedy, his realism.

Marlowe was probably a sceptic by temperament (rather than an atheist); but more evident and ascertainable than his 'religious thinking' is the fury of his attitude towards authority (and towards timid, 'bourgeois' acceptance of it), and the cleverness and self-critical subtlety of his modifications of this fury. Marlowe was a playwright primarily because drama was the only feasible strategy by which he could deal with the kind of explosive material that interested him: this may be summed up in the word 'subversive'; but intellectual curiosity—an interest in truth for its own sake—was quite as strong an element in Marlowe's subversion as rebelliousness.

There is no positive evidence as to when Marlowe wrote *Hero and Leander*. The general—almost unanimous—consensus is that it was written at Scadbury during the last months of Marlowe's life, when the Plague had closed the London theatres. The reasons for this supposition are: Blount dedicated his edition to Walsingham; the poem is unfinished; the style is generally more mature than that of the *Elegies*; there are technical differences from the *Elegies*—more use of *enjambement*, few colloquialisms. Against this impressive array of facts, however, must be set the Ovidian atmosphere of the poem. As Professor Boas has written, the poem 'is steeped in Ovidian memories of the *Amores* and *Heroides*'. My view—which is put forward as a speculation and which must not be given more weight than speculation can stand—is that Marlowe started a version of *Hero and Leander* while an undergraduate at Cambridge, and then extensively reworked it while he was at Scadbury in 1593. This at least has the negative virtues of being not unlikely, and of explaining the apparent contradictions.

The story of Hero and Leander is referred to in Ovid's *Amores*, II, xvi, *ll.* 31–2 (translated by Marlowe: 'The youth oft swimming to his *Hero* kinde,/Had then swum over, but the way was blinde'), and is fully recounted in his *Heroides*, XVIII and XIX. But Marlowe's main source was *The Divine Poem of Musaeus: Hero and Leander*, which George Chapman translated in 1616. This late fifth-century A.D. Greek narrative poem by Musaeus the Grammarian was thought by all the scholars of Marlowe's age to be by the legendary pupil of Orpheus, Musaeus, and was regarded by Chapman and others as in some respects poetically paradigmatic, as being by one of the original poets. The actual author was of the school of Nonnus, an Egyptian Greek whose epic in forty-eight books recounting Dionysus' journey to India is marked by linguistic exuberance; his disciple's miniature epic *Hero and Leander*, in hexameters, is more quaint and charming. It was popular in the sixteenth century, and

Marlowe may have known it in the original Greek, or, more likely, in one or two of the various Latin versions extant. The original had appeared in 1484, and since then had been translated into several languages, including Spanish, Italian and French.

Hero and Leander, on a popular and renowned subject, was one of the most successful poems of its day. In the forty years following its first known publication in 1598 it ran into ten editions. It was popular probably mostly because of the first two books, although I do not believe that Chapman's continuation evoked the scorn accorded to it in the nineteenth and twentieth centuries. But as well as the subject, readers delighted—some I suspect without being aware of it—in the way in which Marlowe, for much of the time, transformed his knowing cynicism into a triumph of style: subversive sophistication is brilliantly turned into skill and fun.

The first two Sestiads of *Hero and Leander* are until near the end mainly light in tone; but they reveal highly serious attitudes. Attempts to crystallize Marlowe's intentions into coherent philosophies or beliefs (e.g. that the Mercury story at I, *ll.* 386–484 was intended to show Marlowe's 'final acceptance of divine justice'[1]) should, however, be strenuously resisted. The poem as we have it, even if it may seem to some to be reaching out to genuine tragedy as well in its final lines, is essentially sceptical. With a delicate, clever preposterousness, it parades doubts about all accepted attitudes, and ironically exhibits curiosity about 'forbidden' subjects. But the cynicism and the sly comedy are aptly balanced by the undeniable freshness of the poem, which is in itself a form of beauty—and consequently, one may say, of hope. Furthermore, *Hero and Leander* is a protean poem, seeming somewhat to change upon each re-reading: a poem by an immensely gifted and skilful poet (he had effected a revolution in the London theatre within five years)—but not yet perhaps a wholly mature one within the terms of his own massive potentiality. Marlowe is brilliant, psychologically acute and superbly comic within this fragment; but he falls short

[1] Paul W. Miller, *A Function of Myth in Marlowe's 'Hero and Leander'*, Studies in Philology, April 1953, pp. 158–167.

of 'ripeness', of wisdom. However, this judgement must be qualified by the unfinished state of the poem, as well as by the nature of the last lines.

The critical attitude towards *Hero and Leander* prevalent until about twenty years ago is most aptly and intelligently illustrated by C. S. Lewis' essay on the poem (1952). (His important defence of Chapman's continuation is discussed below.) Lewis is not wrong in his estimation; but he simply does not see enough—or rather, his perversely anti-modernist, but never quite reactionary sensibility could not quite stomach what he calls Marlowe's 'shameless celebration of sensuality' as comic. Rather, he sees it as a curious form of 'innocence', presumably a sort of pre-Christian experience, and wants to know how Marlowe could write 'over eight hundred lines of almost unrelieved sensuality without ever becoming mawkish, ridiculous, or disgusting'. And his explanation is that Marlowe 'writes from within "the erotic frenzy"' : '. . . that . . . is his poetic salvation'. He discerns an absence of tenderness, but attributes this—one may infer—to unchristian 'heartlessness', to the hardness of pagan lust, rather than to any comic intention. He can recognize what he terms the insolence and the defiance—but not the sardonic humour. On the homosexual elements he remains silent. Lewis' appreciation is essentially of the poem's surface. He finds nothing very important beneath this, and celebrates it as a, so to say, 'poetic banquet'.

The view of the poem as humorous, whimsical or simply 'light' in tone, had in fact already been expressed by such critics as Paul H. Kocher; Una Ellis-Fermor had described it as 'written in a mood of dalliance' as early as 1927. But this opinion was slow to gain acceptance. Even slower was Miss M. C. Bradbrook's important essay in an early *Scrutiny*, which put the poem forward as being subtle as well as comic.

The current view, largely following from this, is in no way academically perverse, and has the advantage of understanding Marlowe's own intentions.

Marlowe was 'preposterous', and in this poem he was deliberately applying a hard-edged cynical scepticism to the fragrant theme of young love. His achievement is that he does manage to preserve a whiff of the fragrance. This resides in the delightful surface qualities of the poem as noted by Lewis and those before him. I think that—despite the jokes, particularly the Neptune incident—Marlowe was concerned to show (if only to show himself, perhaps) that male beauty was for female use, and not for that of other males. This may have reflected a personal problem; certainly it is interesting that Leander's initial sexual innocence is depicted as being so unutterably comic. One of my reasons for suggesting that Marlowe may have reworked *Hero and Leander* from a draft made at Cambridge is the existence in it of homosexual 'in' jokes—clearly the Neptune episode would have delighted members of a sophisticated homosexual fraternity. I have drawn attention to other examples in the commentary. But the fragment as it stands is not homosexually orientated, even though the account of Hero is. Leander's eventual heterosexual lust is not jokily presented as a mistake; the emphasis is rather upon the painful, ignorant and destructive aspects of young love. It is impossible to say how Marlowe would have ended the tale—but we may conjecture that he would have needed only one more book. The pace of his poem is much greater than that of Chapman's continuation; and his intention is less overtly serious—demanding more brevity.

Marlowe's poem then, needs to be read both as a delicately funny pricker of romantic bubbles and as a more seriously intended reminder of the true nature of young love. The lovers are not characterized: I cannot see them, as one or two critics have—as individual human beings at all. There is a significance even in this: for they only 'come to life' when seen or depicted in erotic terms. Their lust alone gives them any individuality in the terms of the ironic and detached narrator; otherwise they have no characteristics whatever—except those that the 'plot', the outlines of the story the poet is following, confer upon them; but these characteristics stem only from being 'in love'. Hero is represented as beautiful and desirable; but nothing is said of her personality. Leander is also

17

represented as beautiful. His sexual ignorance is not seen as a personal characteristic at all: it is, obviously, a comic device of the poet's.

These solely erotic characteristics may well be taken as symbolic of those of female and male in general. Woman is seen as the confused seducer, man as the ignorant. This view is not necessarily a homosexual one, although Marlowe had probably originally held it for some such reason. In *Hero and Leander*, though, there is little trace of real hostility towards Hero. Leander's innocence is not presented in the classic homosexual manner, as a fragrantly lovely thing threatened by hideous female lust; on the contrary, it is seen as comic. There is no particular feeling of sympathy for it. And the descriptions of Hero's strategems and confusions are not hostile, but rather touching. No homosexual horror is expressed in the charming account of her behaviour when she has allowed Leander to enter her bed:

> her silver body downeward went,
> With both her hands she made the bed a tent,
> And in her owne mind thought her selfe secure,
> O'recast with dim and darksome coverture.

This is so indulgent as to be positively sympathetic in feeling.

J. B. Steane interprets the poem as full of 'fierceness and destructiveness', and justifies this by pointing out how in it 'there is embarrassment, fear, conflict and farce. . . . Hero is a woman being . . . *exposed* . . .' This is true enough: one might almost say that Marlowe sounds in this ostensibly Ovidian epic a new and harsh note in English narrative poetry. But Mr Steane tends to put a little too much emphasis on the fierce and destructive elements in a fragment the subtlety of which he is always anxious to remind us. Apart from any other consideration, we can't be sure what Marlowe would have done with the rest of the story; and so we cannot be absolutely certain about his attitude. But certainly in his last fifty-four lines, where he deals with the consummation and its aftermath, Marlowe diminishes his comic tone—as though he already realized that the end of his story was going to have to be, after all, a tragedy, and that he had therefore better prepare for it.

Marlowe does in these lines become, among other things, fierce and destructive, especially in the lines,

> Love is not full of pittie (as men say)
> But deaffe and cruell, where he means to pray.
> Even as a bird, which in our hands we wring,
> Fourth plungeth, and oft flutters with her wing
> She trembling strove. . . .

But this is not the only feeling present. There is great tenderness and sympathy with Hero, who must now experience the pain involved in surrendering her body—the literal, physical pain, as well as the anxiety, doubt and sadness that, together with other sensations, are associated with this occasion. The feeling here, in fact, is exquisite. This strikes us, surely, more than the fierceness and destructiveness. Fate has doomed these lovers, and Marlowe and all his readers know it; but there is no gloating.

Hero wants, after the night of love, to be alone for a while. She tries to leave him, but

> as her naked feet were whipping out,
> He on the suddaine clingd her so about,
> That Meremaid-like unto the floor she slid,
> And halfe appear'd the other halfe was hid.
> Thus neere the bed she blushing stood upright,
> And from her countenance behold ye might,
> A kind of twilight breake, which through the heare,
> As from an orient cloud, glymse here and there.

Steane concedes that this 'contains the most beautiful and moving picture of Hero in the book', but suggests that 'in one sense' the passage 'represents . . . extreme, ultimate humiliation'. I do not see this at all. It shows the previously wilier Hero as Leander's, but not humiliatedly. True, the last few lines, in which Night (associated with love throughout the poem) is seen as 'ougly', full of 'anguish, shame and rage', and 'loathsome' do again assert the ruthlessness of fate. It seems as though Marlowe was preparing to confront love with lust (as destructive fate). For his characterization of the defeated Night hints at the element of repulsion after enjoyment— although nothing implies that love is not present.

Brian Morris goes further than Steane in seeing the whole fragment as comic, with Marlowe contrasting homosexual and heterosexual love and giving 'the persuasive poetry to the peripheral attitude'. Marlowe's 'bias', writes Morris, 'is increasingly towards the full burlesque, and away from the impending tragic end of the story'. This again seems to me to be a misreading, for it ignores the increasingly serious tone of the last section. I do not think that this part of the narrative is simply 'suave, brilliant and ruthlessly mannered'; and I do not take the comparison of Hero to a trembling bird in a fist to be simply 'a hyperbolic epic simile'. Morris' essay is, however, an excellent one; the reader of Marlowe's poem must finally decide for himself whether the poet maintains his comic hardness throughout, or whether—as I suggest—he approaches a genuinely tragic tone as he enters the decisive phase of his story. To read it as sheer burlesque, with a hard-minded, cynically homosexual bias, seems to me to be straining things too far.

HERO AND LEANDER: CHAPMAN

George Chapman was a 'dark' and involute poet. That he has not had anything like his due as an original poet is partly his own fault: he took up, from the beginning, a lofty attitude, and would make no concessions towards the 'common multitude'. He made a great thing of having been personally inspired by Homer in his justly famous translation, and while this was probably only a manner of speaking, his claims tended to make him something of a laughing stock. And although his poetry is full of passages of great magnificence, it cannot be said to be immediately rewarding. Probably it requires as much enodation as any English poetry.

Yet Chapman had a sense of humour and a subtle sense of irony. His early comedies are not at all bad; and frequently they rise above that. His tragedies, which are very readable, are splendid—their neglect is nothing short of scandalous. A good case could be made out for placing them alongside the plays of Jonson, Webster and the best of Middleton: amongst the best of a rich age.

Chapman's continuation of *Hero and Leander* is another of his more accessible works. A hundred years ago it was regarded as a sad anti-climax. Now more readers see it as remarkably successful. Of course Chapman does not have the panache, the 'attack', the brilliance of Marlowe. But he was a poet; and he understood both Marlowe's own poem and the impossibility of anyone's completing it in exactly his spirit. He applied his own gifts to the problem, and produced a solution that, surely, no English poet could have surpassed.

The worth of Chapman's continuation must finally be left to the individual reader. But he should not go to it with the old pre-conception that it is of little value. As C. S. Lewis wrote: 'At the very moment when the theme begins to demand a graver voice, a graver voice succeeds'. Chapman's concern was with the working out of the tragedy, with the fact that, as he says,

Joy graven in sence, like snow in water wasts.

He could have chosen simply to describe the tragedy, in a more or less conventional manner: young love in a vain struggle against a hostile fate. But he chose instead to make a moral poem out of it. He celebrates, not so much marriage itself—the formality—as what marriage represents or ought to represent. As C. S. Lewis wrote: '[Chapman's] part of *Hero and Leander* is to be taken as the product of serious thought'. I think Chapman himself understood Marlowe's mock-epic, comic intention; but this was not at all the kind of poem he could write, and he knew it. Besides, Lewis was right when he asserted that, with this story, a graver tone was now required. This is not of course at all how Marlowe would have finished the poem; but the way Chapman did it happens to work. There was something in Marlowe's beginning that impelled Chapman to finish. That the result is a success is not so surprising when we consider that Chapman, as well as Marlowe, was a poet of genius.

Lewis maintained that Chapman set out to 'make a distinction between lawless and wedded love'. But it is not quite as simple as that; or at any rate, this way of putting it is somewhat misleading. We must not think of Chapman as naïvely erecting an elaborate defence of wedding formalities, or even of the institution of marriage; 'lawless' misleads because it misses Chapman's point. There is no Puritanism whatever in Chapman's view. No disapproval. No harping on morals. Marlowe, in a kind of *tour de force* of which Chapman was not capable, showed how young love was simultaneously thrilling, touching, beautiful, absurd, dangerous —and terribly, tragically vulnerable to fate. Chapman, more earnestly if not more seriously, used the occasion to invent the key figures of Ceremony (Thesme) and Dissimulation (Eronusis), and to retell in his own manner and for his own purposes the story of Hymen and Eucharis—who, unlike Hero and Leander, observed the rites of Ceremony.

By the time Chapman came to write *Hero and Leander*, many translations of Ovid had appeared in English: the *Ars Amatoria* in 1513, Thurberville's *Heroides* in 1567, and, most famous of all, Golding's *Metamorphoses* in 1565 and 1567. Of course, the real Ovid —the erotic and pagan poet—would not have done at all for any medieval or even early Elizabethan circle of readers; no poet before the late 1580s could have got his work published who translated him exactly as he was. But the earlier Elizabethans inherited a system by which Ovid might be, so to speak, had and eaten: his poetry, whether or not its erotic and pagan qualities were enjoyed privately by some astute readers, could be read 'allegorically'. This system, which was well established on the continent by the eighth century, involved the application of complicated methods of interpretation. Arthur Golding's immensely influential and immediately successful *Metamorphoses* were conceived in this spirit, and presented as moral fables. The pagan gods represented people; the metamorphoses themselves stood for men's surrender to fleshly desires: the beasts they were turned into were symbols of their internal state. This way of getting round the difficulties presented by Ovid tended to be Christian and anti-feminine; stern moralists are frequently full of the viciousness and lustfulness of women.

However, some later Elizabethan poets of the generation of Marlowe reacted against the essential dullness of this approach, and sought to render some of Ovid's lusty delightfulness, his lightness of touch, even his (apparent) erotic irresponsibility, in English verse. Marlowe's approach is typical, both in his translations from Ovid and in *Hero and Leander*. In the latter one aspect of his whole tone is a mockery of the older, more solemn approach to Ovid. In the mid-nineties there was a spate of Ovidian erotic poetry. The most famous was Shakespeare's *Venus and Adonis*.

Chapman attacked this kind of use of Ovid; but his own deliberately 'dark', Neoplatonic approach to Ovid was not old-fashioned or reactionary. Chapman did not seek to return simply to the old methods of interpretation. His own procedures were, in fact, comparatively original—even if he did sacrifice many readers by his studied refusal to write for anyone except the simultaneously learned and intelligent (thus he said, in his dedication of *Ovids Banquet of Sence* to Matthew Roydon, 'that Poesie should be as perviall [intelligible] as Oratorie . . . were the plaine way to barbarisme . . . to take away strength from Lyons, and give Cammels hornes'). His Ovidian poetry, mainly *Ovids Banquet of Sence* (1595), is neither puritanical nor Christian. He makes no attempt to disguise or indeed to play down the erotic element. On the contrary, he asserted, in a key passage, that

> The sence is given us to excite the mind,
> And that can never be by sence excited
> But first the sence must her contentment finde,
> We therefore must procure the sence delighted,
>   That so the soule may use her faculty. . . .
>
> (*Ovids Banquet of Sence* 63, *ll.*1–5)

In other words, the flesh is the servant of the soul and a necessary aid to it in its search after beauty. It is right to banquet the senses, as Ovid does in the poem by watching his Corinna bathing, and thus inspiring each of his senses in turn. But it is wrong—Chapman reserves much of the most powerful invective in his poetry against this—to seek nothing but material pleasure. Such men are 'cripple-minded, Gowt-wit lamde . . . Stird up with nought, but hell-descending gaine. . . .' However, Chapman leaves his reader in no doubt of the culmination of Ovid's not merely sensual but also spiritually educative bout of voyeurism:

> *Ovid* well knew there was much more intended,
> With whose omition none must be offended. . . .
>
> *(Ovids Banquet of Sence,* 117, *ll.*8–9)

It is important to recognize that even if Chapman is involute and esoteric, sometimes to the point of tiresomeness, he is not morally pompous, didactic or humourless.

In *Ovids Banquet of Sence,* then, we may discover the key to Chapman's *Hero and Leander.* The same Neoplatonic philosophy lies behind it. But in *Hero and Leander* Chapman combined his allegorical treatment of Ovid with an epic treatment, as we see from his division of the book—on the analogy of Homer's *Iliad*—into *Sestiads.* The fullest account, from this point of view, is D. J. Gordon's *Chapman's 'Hero and Leander'.* Gordon shows that Chapman was deliberately 'imitating' classical antiquity—and that (if it matters) the charge against him of being 'unclassical' is false, because in fact, in his inventions, he was working in a recognizable tradition. I am deeply indebted to Gordon's essay in many of my notes.

It is likely that at this point many intelligent readers will ask some series of questions such as: 'What can Chapman's four books mean to us? We can well appreciate Marlowe's comic and subversive brilliance; but isn't Chapman dull in comparison—what can he say about our own contemporary experience? Honestly, has his part of the poem really lasted?'

Marlowe will always, of course, have a wider appeal than Chapman. But if the reader devoted to poetry gives him his full attention, his reward is a surprisingly substantial one. Chapman's work is not, after all, so impenetrably remote from ordinary experience—or dull. *Hero and Leander* contains many lines of astonishing beauty and startling aptness:

> *Leander* into *Hellespontus* throwes
> His *Hero*-handed bodie. . . .
>
> And to her singing like a shower he flew,
> Sprinkling the earth, that to their tombes tooke in
> Streames dead for love, to leave his ivorie skin,
> Which yet a snowie fome did leave above,
> As soule to the dead water that did love;
> And from thence did the first white Roses spring. . . .
> Feare fils the chamber, darknes decks the Bride. . . .

And there are many more such lines and whole passages. Nor are they isolated jewels sparkling in an arid greyness. They grace an essentially serious and by no means currently irrelevant theme.

If Eros dominated Marlowe's beginning, Chapman's key figure is Ceremony, Thesme—'Queen Elizabeth "moralized" in fact', as MaClure says in his book on Chapman. Gordon quotes a passage from Richard Hooker to explain what Chapman meant by her, and what most of his readers would have understood by her.

The end which is aimed at in setting down the outward form of all religious actions is the edification of the Church. Now men are edified, when either their understanding is taught somewhat whereof in such actions it behoveth all men to consider, or when their hearts are moved with any affection suitable thereunto; when their minds are in any sort stirred up into that reverence, devotion, attention, and due regard, which in those cases seemeth requisite. Because therefore unto this purpose not only speech but sundry sensible means besides have always been thought necessary, and especially those means which being object to the eye, the liveliest and the most apprehensive sense of all other, have in that respect seemed the fittest to make a deep and a strong impression: from hence have risen not only a number of prayers, readings, questionings, exhortations, but even of visible signs also; which being used in performance of holy actions, are undoubtedly most effectual to open such matter, as men when they know and remember carefully, must needs be a great deal the better informed to what effect such duties serve. We must not think but that there is some ground of reason even in nature, whereby it cometh to pass that no nation under heaven either doth or ever did suffer public actions which are of weight, whether they be civil and temporal or else spiritual and sacred, to pass without some visible solemnity: the very strangeness whereof and difference from that which is common, doth cause popular eyes to observe and to mark the same. Words, both because they are common, and do not so strongly move the fancy of man, are for the most part but slightly heard: and therefore with singular wisdom it hath been provided, that the deeds of men which are made in the presence of witnesses should pass not only with words, but also with certain sensible actions, the memory whereof is far more easy and durable than the memory of speech can be.

(Richard Hooker, *The Works*, ed. Keble, Church and Paget, Oxford, 1888, I, pp. 418-9)

This is an age when ritual, so important in Chapman's time, has appeared to some to be discredited. The rituals of war no longer appeal to everyone: their magnificence too evidently hides things much less than magnificent. The rhetoric of ritual—its powerful effect on the emotions and on the behaviour—seems to some to be sinister: a means of gaining obedience from exploited masses. And as belief in ritual has diminished, so perhaps has its standard, its quality, its effectuality in Hooker's sense. The Queen Elizabeth II who only nominally rules our democracy cannot, ritually, at all resemble the Elizabeth I who really ruled over her kingdom. Even as far back as 1952, the film of the former's coronation functioned more as a vulgar technicolour spectacle than as any kind of mystery.

But, however individual members of society may feel about it, the evidence provided by anthropology suggests that we should abolish all ritual at our peril. One of the troubles with 'civilization', it seems, is that the people in it are less happy—and do each other more harm—than do people in 'primitive' societies. The thoughtful amongst us do not need to be Christian or royalist in order to discover the value of trying to understand what Chapman and his contemporaries meant by law, order and ceremony. The violation of them, they believed, amounted to a violation of the laws of the universe. And whatever challenges these laws is on the side of confusion: chaos. When Ceremony appears to Leander and rebukes him, he is immediately abashed and tries to make amends by planning to marry Hero. But it is already too late. Hero's offence is even more serious and brazen—and is represented by Chapman as such. The priestess of love, she nevertheless decides to dissemble. Venus' reproof is cast in the form of her creation of Eronusis. Hypocrisy was always a serious crime in Chapman's eyes; and no doubt such misogynous feelings as he possessed at the time went into his picture of the deceiving Hero. But these never obtrude or affect the delicate balance that Chapman establishes between human frailty and the divine order.

Chapman's *Hero and Leander* would be worthy of attention if only because, beyond such poetic pleasures as it immediately offers, it gives a representative picture of a well-established Elizabethan way of looking at life and love. But it has a poetic value of its own. We may still read it as a subtle poem on the subject of sexual restraint; as an entirely unconventional and non-officious reminder that sexual union is social as well as private—and that love's highest joys may not be tasted by those who do not observe the laws of ceremony. Desire, the poem's message reads, should not be violent if it is to be fulfilled to its utmost, but composed. Every human being 'cares' in the exercise of his sexual function, however he may try to deny this; in order to appreciate Chapman's poem we only need to examine the nature and quality of our own concern. We then see that he is not solemn, puritanical or silly.

I have tried to make my commentary as full a guide as possible to Chapman's often complicated and highly allusive lines. Thus, more will be found about his mythological inventions—Thesme, Teras, and so on—in the notes. One further general remark is, however, necessary: this concerns Chapman's concept of 'form'. Chapman's Ceremony is related to human action in exactly the same way as form relates to matter in the familiar ontology that originates in Aristotle. As D. J. Gordon has written: 'There is an ambiguity in the word form: its meaning can shift—and does so almost imperceptibly—between "visible form" and "internal or organizing form". . . . By stressing the first meaning so that form means appearance or outward manner and behaviour in the simplest sense, Chapman extends the range of his subject so that he can introduce the problem of "appearance" and "reality". . . . It is on this nexus, this warp of ideas, that Chapman composes his version of what happened to Hero and Leander.' The idea underlying this is that nothing can be fully itself unless its appearance wholly reflects its reality. The true nature of anything is to seek out its own form, and thus attain perfection. Gordon shows that Chapman's ideas of form were dominated by Platonic and Ficinian ideas. Aristotelian ideas permeated the Christianity of Aquinas, of Hooker —and of Marsilio Ficino, whose philosophy exercised a strong influence on Chapman. For Ficino, matter achieves form—completeness, realization—through love. We can begin to see where, according to Chapman, Hero and Leander went wrong. Their lust is incomplete, because it lacks the delight of love; it has not been anticipated, it does not wait upon its time.

JOHN DONNE: LIFE AND WORK

John Donne is the subject of a volume, which contains a long biographical and critical introduction, in this series. I shall here confine myself to the briefest outline of his life. Born 1571/2, Donne was brought up as a recusant. He went to Hart Hall, Oxford, where he was not required, on account of being too young, to take the Oath of Supremacy. He left without a degree, and went on to Thavies' Inn, and then Lincoln's Inn (1592), to study law. He accompanied Essex on the Cadiz Expedition of 1596; and was with the Islands Voyage of the following year. He is known to have got through a comparatively large fortune before this—and there is some substance in the legend of 'Jack Donne', the rake and womanizer. He seems to have 'reformed' in about 1597, when he became secretary to Sir Thomas Egerton, the Lord Keeper. He must at this time have renounced his Roman Catholicism. In 1601 he secretly married Anne More, whose father insisted upon his imprisonment and dismissal. They were afterwards reconciled, but for many years Donne lived with great difficulty. His *Satires* and *Elegies* were early work; the *Songs and Sonets* are likely to have been written between the ages of twenty-four and about forty.

In 1615 Donne, unable to find secular preferment, was ordained. Some years previously he had refused to enter the Church. He became Dean of St. Paul's in 1621. He was the most successful and dramatic preacher of his day. His *Divine Poems* date from the later part of his life, when he was in orders. He died in 1631, a month after preaching his most famous sermon, *Death's Duel*.

Until the nineteenth century Donne was read but not much remarked upon. Pope 'versified' his satires, but without understanding them. He was much revived in the nineteenth century, through the admiration of Coleridge, Lamb, de Quincey and, later, Browning. In this century T. S. Eliot, acquainted with him through the pioneer two-volume edition of H. J. Grierson (1912), claimed him as a major poet, which is undoubtedly his standing today: in spite of renewed academic attention to Spenser and Milton, Donne is probably read and enjoyed more by the general reader.

THE PROGRESSE OF THE SOULE

Critical surveys of Donne's poetry tend to ignore, or at best treat very scantily indeed, *The Progresse of the Soule*. This is understandable: like Ralegh's *Cynthia*, although in an altogether different way, it is an enigmatic poem—and a fragment. But it deserves more attention than it has had. And while we cannot assert positively what Donne's exact intention was in writing it, we do have the poem itself to go on—and this is as delightful, witty and outrageous as we could wish. Unlike the Victorian critics, and indeed the more susceptible among us today, we have no need to be shocked by it. It contains some of his best lines—the famous 'For though through many streights, and lands I roame,/ I launch at paradise, and saile toward home' is only one example, as the attentive reader will discover for himself. Donne wrote it at a time of his life when he had come to no decisions; but he was never more bitter about the court, and about the active life in general, than at this period. *The Progresse of the Soule* is certainly, whatever it is not, a satire directed at public life. It is true that no one liked the poem until the beginning of the nineteenth century (when it was admired by Lamb, Coleridge and de Quincey) and that the late Victorians and Edwardians regarded it with considerable suspicion. Some modern critics, when they do not ignore it, dismiss it (like W. A. Murray) as 'neither very good nor of much literary importance'. But there are now a fair number of critics, I suspect, who would regard that last judgement as bizarre: the product, perhaps, of a mind stunned into weetless disapproval by Donne's apparent impropriety (in, for example, daring to adapt the epic form to a satire) and dangerous liveliness. We have arrived at a time where the poem can be enjoyed. And it is likely that in order to enjoy it to the full, we should desist from taking it too seriously, not to say solemnly.

The Progresse of the Soule is dated, by Donne himself, 16 August 1601, and was therefore written not long before he entered into the marriage that was to ruin his secular career. Its mood and meaning have been variously explained. What we know from Donne himself about his intentions amounts to very little. We cannot even be sure whether he ever seriously intended to complete the poem: his purpose, as he states it, is humorously grandiose. He will trace the progress of the soul that was in Eve's apple from its beginnings there until its habitation in an unspecified (but male) contemporary. The work is less important only than the scriptures, and should take thirty years uninterrupted concentration. In other words, whatever seriousnesses in the poet the poem may reflect, it was not itself wholly seriously conceived. We know from the poem itself that the theme is the progressive corruption of a soul by the various bodies it inhabits; but each episode is satirically treated. Donne was combining a (largely) mock 'high' (epic) style with a markedly 'low' (satirical) style. Thus this poem, which first appeared in the posthumous 1633 volume of Donne's poems, was of considerable originality.

Ben Jonson, Donne's friend, in the not always reliable *Conversations* recorded by Drummond of Hawthornden, said that 'The conceit of Dones transformation or μετεμψύχοσις [sic] was that he sought the soule of that Aple which Eva pulled, and thereafter made it the soule of a Bitch, then of a sheewolf [this is clearly a slip] & so of a woman. his generall purpose was to have brought in all the bodies of the Hereticks from the soule of Caine & at last left it in the body of Calvin. of this he never wrotte but one sheet'. Now this is certainly wrong in respect of Cain and Calvin: the soul cannot—in the theology Donne was exploiting—be in two places at once, and it cannot therefore be in Cain while it is in his wife, or in Calvin while it is in Luther (*l.*66).

Jonson must have got the idea that all the bodies inhabited by the soul were to be heretics from the fact that the satire is partially directed on innovators and on change (see *ll.*281–90 and notes). Donne must have officially and formally renounced Catholicism when he became Egerton's secretary: he would hardly write an ambitious poem satirizing Luther as a *heretic*. This is why Grierson's notion, put forward in his 1912 two-volume edition of the poems, that the poem is Roman Catholic in intention, is unlikely. Grierson also followed Gosse in his suggestion that the soul was to end up in Queen Elizabeth: there is not only no justification for this view, but also it is contradicted at the end of the epistle: '. . . to this time when shee [the soul] is *hee* [my italics], whose life you shall find at the end of this book'. This is not to say, of course, that Donne was anti-Roman Catholic, or approved of intolerance: he was a notable advocate of tolerance.

D. C. Allen in 'The Double Journey of John Donne' has traced some of the sources of the ideas in the poems, as has H. W. Janson in 'Apes and Ape Lore in the Middle Ages and the Renaissance'; neither has really cast light on Donne's state of mind. M. A. Mahood, in the chapter on Donne in her *Poetry and Humanism*, unfortunately follows Gosse and Grierson in their wrong view of the poem as an attack on Queen Elizabeth—but she is more convincing when she comes to suggest that the poem's mood owes something to the change of temper produced in England by the fall of Essex. She points out that he 'shared the time's discontent'; she might have said that he epitomized it. However, she does not, as W. A. Murray in 'What Was the Soul of the Apple?' charges her, quite say that the poem 'deals with the Essex revolt'. She acknowledges it as 'obscure', and believes that Donne resented the Queen's treatment of Essex; but goes no further.

For Murray, the poem is based on allegorical Judaism, particularly on the attempt of Philo Judaeus (20 B.C.—post A.D. 40) to allegorize *Genesis*. The soul represents the 'power of moral choice', and it is this which is progressively corrupted. W. Milgate convincingly refutes this view on the grounds that throughout the poem Donne insists 'over and over again that the soul is completely at the command of Destiny or Fate'. If Donne had wanted to emphasize the soul as the 'power of moral choice', he would have done so. Nevertheless, Murray's essay is worth reading for the incidental light it casts on the poem. Probably the least convincing interpretation is the wholly theological one advanced by Richard E. Hughes in *The Progress of the Soul: the Interior Career of John Donne* (1968): he believes it is based 'ultimately' on 'St. Augustine's account of the conflict between the two kingdoms [of Abel and Cain]'. However, Hughes is correct when he asserts that in the poem 'we see something very like "existential disappointment, a disappointment which penetrates into the very existence of man [Paul Tillich]" '.

The Progresse of the Soule is best read, I believe, as an ambivalent comic poem, by an undecided man. It was a largely unsuccessful (because ultimately so unwieldy) effort to resolve tension between intellectual curiosity and temperamental conservatism. The prevailing tone—but it is not wholly convincing, and was not in fact sustained—is one of cynical, baroque scepticism. I doubt if, as he initiated, rather casually, this project, Donne was himself at all certain what the 'soul' really did represent. And if I had to make a guess at the identity of the contemporary possessor of it, I should certainly say: Donne himself. The poem is ingeniously brilliant and irreverent, with much nervous sexual self-criticism: it served, in its gay way, as an exercise for relieving immediate and subjective tension. Donne's mind in it is explorative, and seldom if ever decided. But some of his personal predilections emerge: his impatience with those theological niceties that do not base themselves on psychological reality, and yet his fascination with them because of the human problems they embody; his desire for personal originality; his hatred of all intolerance; his belief in the spiritual viability of a soul's progress—which he was so triumphantly to express in *The Second Anniversarie*, not insignificantly also entitled *Of the Progresse of the Soule*. It is an important poem, although not one of Donne's best: it marks a necessary transitional phase in his thinking and feeling, and, as far as it goes, it is highly original. We can delight in it as he did.

SIR JOHN DAVIES: LIFE AND WORK

Sir John Davies was one of those Elizabethans, like Ralegh, for whom poetry was a recreation. He was as clever and nearly as enigmatic a man as Ralegh, but not so considerable a poet. A lawyer, whom only death prevented from taking the office of Lord Chief Justice, to which he had been appointed in 1626, he had offended as a young man both by wild behaviour and verses bawdy even by the standards of his not delicate times.

Davies was born, son of a Wiltshire gentleman, in 1569, five years after Shakespeare and Marlowe. He was educated at Winchester and Queen's College, Oxford. Like Donne and so many other gifted young men of the day he decided to become a lawyer, and was called to the Middle Temple in 1587. Eight years later he was called to the bar. Then, in 1597, there occurred the incident that led to his temporary disbarment—and to the composition of *Nosce Teipsum*, three sections from which are given here.

Richard Martin was a fellow member of the Middle Temple and

a friend of Davies'. He had been expelled for rioting at the officially prohibited festival of the Lord of Misrule in 1591, but readmitted. Davies had dedicated to Martin his poem *Orchestra, or, A Poeme of Dauncing* (his greatest achievement) in 1596, referring to him as 'Mine-owne-selves better halfe, my deerest frend'. Martin, a future M.P. and Recorder of London who was to die 'of a symposiaque excesse with his fellow-witts' (Aubrey) and/or 'from disorders produced by his devotion to the pleasures of the table' (Lord Stowell) was probably a sarcastic and provocative man, who would rather, as Grosart put it, 'lose his friend than his joke'. Certainly he annoyed Davies, for one evening as he was 'sitting quietly at dinner' in the Middle Temple, the poet entered the Hall 'with his hat on his head, attended by two persons armed with swords, and going up to the Barristers' table', pulled a cudgel from beneath his gown and struck Martin 'over the head repeatedly, with such violence that the bastinado was shivered into many pieces'.

For this gesture Davies was disbarred and 'deprived forever of all authority to speak or consult in law'. He retired to Oxford, pursued his studies, and rapidly wrote and published *Nosce Teipsum*: this was both a penance and an attempt to improve his difficult position. No Elizabethan would have regarded this as inconsistent. *Nosce Teipsum* ('Know Thyself') was dedicated to the Queen; Davies immediately followed it with a more fulsome flattery: *Hymes of Astraea, in Acrostic Verse* (1599). The initial letters of each line of every one of the twenty-six clever verses spell out 'Elizabeth Regina'. It was said that *Nosce Teipsum* did succeed in impressing the Queen, and that she promised him 'preferrment, and had him sworn her servant in ordinary'; but it is more likely that Davies owed his subsequent reinstatement in society and successful career to his highly placed older friends, such as Lord Ellesmere, Lord Keeper of the Great Seal, and Edward Coke, the Attorney-General. Ellesmere (previously Sir Thomas Egerton), whose chief secretary was John Donne, was a lover of books and a friend of poets; he procured a pardon for Davies, who, after he had been through the formalities of petitioning for reinstatement to the society of the

Middle Temple and publicly apologizing to Martin and the Benchers, found his way unimpeded. He published no new poetry, although his earlier poems were several times reprinted, and newly corrected versions of *Orchestra*, *Nosce Teipsum* and *Astraea* were collected together and published in 1622. The scurrilous *Epigrammes* that had appeared with Marlowe's translation of Ovid, and the gulling sonnets (trifles he had never published) parodying the conventional Elizabethan sonnet and therefore in 1622 totally unfashionable, were omitted.

Davies became M.P. for Corfe Castle in Dorset in 1601; when the Queen died and he went, with others, to congratulate the new King, James made it clear that he had read and admired *Nosce Teipsum*.

Indeed, it was as much to this philosophical poem, composed as an act of penance for a rash act, as to anything else that Davies owed his next appointment: Solicitor-General in Ireland. Later he became Attorney-General. Like Spenser before him, Davies performed his Irish duties conscientiously, but desired to return; he was finally allowed to do so in 1619, when he became an M.P. again and acted as King's Sergeant, which involved going on circuit as a judge.

In 1625 Charles came to the throne. In 1626 the then Chief Justice, Ranulphe Crew, courageously denied the legality of forced loans, and was dismissed (he lived on until 1646). Davies strenuously and possibly ambitiously and sycophantically supported the King— he had already written a treatise, dedicated to James, defending the royal practice in respect of impositions, tunnage and poundage, etc. —and was appointed Crew's successor. But he did not live to take office: on the morning after a supper-party, in December 1626, he was found dead in bed. He was fifty-seven.

Davies married Eleonor Touchet, daughter of Lord Audley, in 1608 or 1609. She was a markedly eccentric woman, a sister of the Earl of Castlehaven who was executed for sodomizing his unwilling wife in 1631. Davies' marriage to her seems to have been unhappy, probably owing to her eccentricities. They had two children: one, an idiot son, was drowned in Ireland; the other Lucy, became Countess of Huntingdon and wrote some exceptional letters.

Davies was a versatile poet, all of whose work was written before he reached the age of thirty. *Orchestra*, a *tour de force* of 131 seven-line stanzas in which dancing is joyously used as a metaphor for the rhythm of the universe and the resolution of chaos, is his greatest achievement. But *Nosce Teipsum* was even more popular—over a much longer period—and it provides the supreme example of an Elizabethan 'philosophical poem'.

NOSCE TEIPSUM

Nosce Teipsum is not original; but it is none the less an interesting, highly gifted and most attractive poem. 'It is extraordinary how Davies,' the American critic Marius Bewly has written, 'has managed to sustain page after page of this kind of verse at a level which consistently illuminates his argument without ever obtruding itself as nonfunctional ornament or decoration.'

The dedication to the Queen is followed by a series of introductory stanzas, *Of Humane Knowledge*, which is reprinted here; the main body of the poem, *Of the Soule of Man and the Immortalitie Thereof*, is divided into the following sections (those asterisked appear here):

What the soule is
That the soule is a thing subsisting by itself without the body
That the soule is more than a perfection or reflection of the sense
That the soule is more than the temperature of the humors of the body
That the soule is a spirit
That it cannot be a body
That the soule is created immediately by God
Erroneous opinions of the creation of soules
Objection: that the soule is ex traduce
The answer to the objection
Reasons drawne from nature
Reasons drawne from divinity
Why the soule is united to the body

In what manner the soule is united to the body
How the soule doth exercise her powers in the body★
The vegetative or quickening power★
The power of sense★
Sight★
Hearing★
Taste★
Smelling★
Feeling★
The imagination or common sense★
The fantasie★
The sensitive memorie★
The passions of sense★
The motion of life
The locall motion
The intellectual powers of the soule
The wit or understanding
Reason, understanding
Opinion, judgement
The power of will
The relations betwixt wit and will
The intellectual memorie
An acclamation
That the soule is immortal, and cannot die:
Reason I: Drawne from the desire of knowledge
Reason II: Drawne from the motion of the soule; the soul compared to
    a river
Reason III: From contempt of death in the better sort of spirits
Reason IV: From the feare of death in the wicked soules
Reason V: From the general desire of immortalitie
Reason VI: From the very doubt and disputation of immortalitie
That the soule cannot be destroyed
Her cause ceaseth not
She hath no contrary
She cannot die for want of food
Violence cannot destroy her
Time cannot destroy her
Objections to the immortalitie of the soule:

Objection I: Answere
Objection II: Answere
Objection III: Answere
Objection IV: Answere
Objection V: Answere
The general consent of all
Three kinds of life answerable to the three powers of the soule
An acclamation★

Out of a total of 1774 lines, this selection gives 526.

I have set out the list of titles of the sections because it conveys, better than any description, a sense of the kind of poem *Nosce Teipsum* is, and of its structure.

Actually, Davies' poem is by no means as tedious as the list implies. It is highly ingenious, often breathtakingly skilful—and by far the finest example of argumentation in verse in English poetry both before and since Dryden's *Religio Laici* (1682). Doubtless poetry is not, ultimately, to be considered as the most suitable vehicle for argument, especially for theological and philosophical argument; but Davies' attempt is something of an exception. Furthermore, the poetry (like the cheerfulness of Oliver Edwards in Boswell's *Johnson*[1]) is always breaking in. There is a force of personal feeling behind such lines as

> What can we know? or what can we discerne?
> When *Error* chokes the windowes of the minde,
> The divers formes of things, how can we learne
> That have been ever from our birth-day, blind?

as well as polemic. In the allusion to Io, Davies obviously displays as much interest in the subject-matter as in the argument which he is illustrating:

> As in the fable of the Lady faire,
> Which for her lust was turnd into a cow;
> When thirstie to a streame she did repaire,
> And saw her selfe transform'd she wist not how:

---

[1] Edwards is quoted by Boswell as having said: 'I have tried too in my time to be a philosopher; but, I don't know how, the cheerfulness was always breaking in'.

> At first she startles, then she stands amaz'd,
>   At last with terror she from thence doth flye;
>   And loathes the watry glasse wherein she gaz'd,
>   And shunnes it still, though she for thirst doe die.

The poem has passages, too, of enormous charm:

> These wickets of the *Soule* are plac't on hie
>   Because all sounds doe lightly mount aloft;
>   And that they may not pierce too violently,
>   They are delaied with turnes, and windings off. . . .

The 'philosophy' of *Nosce Teipsum* is not, as Davies' indefatigable nineteenth-century editor Alexander Grosart believed, in the least original. Davies was, as his most recent editor Clare Howard remarks, 'heir to the whole volume of the Renaissance': nearly all his ideas, which may confidently be described as Neoplatonic, are to be found in Plato, Aristotle, Nemesius, Aquinas, Calvin, Ficino. He was most particularly indebted, however, to another unoriginal thinker, the French Huguenot Pierre de Primaudaye, author of *Academie François, en laquelle il est traité de l'institution des mœurs et de ce qui concerne le bien et heureusement vivre*, which had been translated by 'T.B.' in 1586 as *The French Academie: Wherein is Discoursed the Institution of Manners*. L. I. Bredvold devoted an interesting article to tracing what he believed to be Davies' exact indebtedness to Primaudaye. I have given, in my notes, a number of the parallels Bredvold adduces; the reader may then decide for himself whether Davies consciously borrowed from—or 'used'—Primaudaye; or whether *Nosce Teipsum*, like Primaudaye's book, represents what Clare Howard calls 'the average Christian philosophy at the end of the Renaissance'. Most will feel that the evidence provided by Bredvold precludes doubt. Certain other passages have been thought to derive from Philip Sidney's translation of Philip Mornay's poem *Truness of the Christian Religion* (Sidney died before finishing this task, which was completed by Arthur Golding in 1587).

This 'average Christian philosophy' was very largely Platonic or, more specifically, Neoplatonic. In Davies' poem we see it operating in a much simpler, less esoteric form than in Chapman's *Hero and Leander*. For several centuries the main problem for Christians had been (as it still is) to reconcile Christian faith with rational thought. Aquinas, writing in the thirteenth century, had constructed a persuasive amalgam of Christian faith and Aristotelian logic. But Davies, in accordance with sixteenth-century doctrine, rejected the Aristotelian theory of the soul as *form* (this excluded personal survival after death), and accepted the more comforting view of the soul as *substance*.

> *The soule a substance*, and a *spirit* is,
>   Which *God* Himselfe doth in the body make;
>   Which makes the *Man*: for every man from this,
>   The *nature* of a *Man*, and name doth take.
>
> And though this spirit be to the body knit,
>   As an apt meane her powers to exercise;
>   Which are *life*, *motion*, *sense*, and *will*, and *wit*,
>   Yet she *survives*, although the body *dies*.

Nosce Teipsum is essentially in the tradition of one of the earliest of Neoplatonists, Saint Augustine, rather than in that of Aquinas. His purpose is to refute materialism; his means—like Augustine's—are essentially Platonic and transcendental. As Bredvold points out, when he does recognize an Aristotelian doctrine, it is only to employ it as a metaphor.

Davies propounds the theory that: (i) the five senses are separate from the soul, merely faculties by which it knows the world; (ii) the soul is not of the same substance as the body; (iii) each individual soul was directly created by God and breathed by him into its body (thus, the soul is not pre-existent and it is not migratory); (iv) the soul, thus propagated, is polluted, because Adam sinned; (v) the sinful soul may, however, be redeemed by the grace of Christ, if Christ is believed in; (vi) God allowed the Fall because he created man with freedom of choice—his greatest glory.

The soul is immortal because: it desires knowledge; it is restless; virtuous men are contemptuous of death; the wicked fear it; all men desire immortality; even sceptics can understand and desire immortality.

This was a highly orthodox type of educated, thoughtful Christian position. What distinguishes Davies' poem is its mastery of the plain form—the quatrain—and its simplicity, which is in marked contrast to most of the poetry of the time. *Nosce Teipsum* is by no means a difficult poem, and it remained extremely popular for over one hundred years as a polemic against the increasing scepticism of the later seventeenth century. Thomas Jenner, who opposed both the disbelief and the sceptical temper of his age, published a curtailed version in 1653; in 1658 he published a straightforward prose version. He added virtually nothing of his own, feeling that Davies had already done the job sufficiently well. Modern readers, whatever their opinion of the theology Davies was expounding, will probably agree that no poem in the English language—even *Religio Laici*—so gracefully, skilfully and attractively puts forward an argument.

SIR WALTER RALEGH: LIFE AND WORK

The facts of Sir Walter Ralegh's life are so well known to students of even elementary history that I shall give only the baldest summary of them, preferring to concentrate upon the circumstances surrounding the composition of his most substantial poem.

Ralegh was born about 1552 at Hayes Barton in Devon. His father was a country gentleman of somewhat similar status to John Davies'. Ralegh went up to Oriel, Oxford; there is no record of his taking a degree. It is not known how, by the age of thirty, he had sufficiently distinguished himself to become one of Queen Elizabeth's foremost favourites. The famous story about the cloak spread out over the mud for the Queen to walk on is possibly true; but it is not well authenticated—and in any case this typically Elizabethan gesture could not alone have accounted for the high esteem in which the Queen was to hold him for over a decade. He had fought in the French Wars of Religion, and in Ireland under Lord Grey, and had attracted some attention by his dash and daring. The editor of his poetry, Miss Agnes M. C. Latham, believes it likely that, 'pushed forward in someone else's game of preferment', he seized 'the opportunity for his own'. Ralegh was certainly, from at least 1582—or earlier, since in 1592 in *Cynthia* he speaks of his 'twelve years' war—in one sense a reigning favourite. But it is as well to remember that he himself was never actually allowed to be an architect of policy—however attentively the Queen may have listened to his opinions. Nor was he ever a member of the Privy Council. Already handsome, this obscure son of a Devonshire gentleman became proud and rich. He was well hated for his airs— but only until Queen Elizabeth's successor, the pederastic James I, framed him on a treason charge. Then his speech in his own defence gained him the sympathy of the people. Of him in his period of favour, Agnes Latham writes: 'He was at home with magnificence, that renaissance virtue. . . . Everything he did was done with an air. There was to be no possibility of mistaking him for an ordinary man'.

In 1592 Ralegh fell into disgrace and was sent to the Tower— where, almost certainly, he wrote *The Ocean to Cynthia*. The circumstances are obscure. Ralegh either 'wronged' one of the Queen's maids of honour, Elizabeth Throckmorton, and was forced to marry her by the Queen; or, more likely, he married her secretly. He was in the Tower for some months, and only managed to reinstate himself at court—but on a lower rung of the ladder than before—after five years. What is most puzzling about the affair is the unusual extent of the Queen's wrath.

By the end of Elizabeth's life Ralegh was back in favour. But her successor, who loathed courage, had him brought to trial on a false charge of treason within a few months of his accession; and after his death-sentence had been commuted to one of life imprisonment, he spent fifteen years in the Tower. Here he wrote the first volume of his *History of the World*. Everyone knows the story of Ralegh's end. Allowed by the King to go on an expedition to the gold mines of Guinea, provided he kept peace with Spain—an impossible condition—he failed. His men were involved in a fight with the Spaniards in which Ralegh's son was killed, and when he returned James I, to placate the Spaniards, had him beheaded on the old charge of 1603. It was one of the most disgraceful episodes of a disgraceful reign. As James's own son Henry had said, before his untimely death in 1612, 'Only my father would keep such a bird in a cage'.

Ralegh was a part-time poet, who never published his poetry—and was probably casual about it for most of the time. It was not, of course, the habit of gentlemen to publish. But Ralegh's is an important poetry—*The Ocean to Cynthia*, at least, anticipates the 'metaphysical' poetry that was to follow it, in some remarkable ways—and it represents the most interesting side of its author. Much of it is most rewardingly read, not as the paradoxically contemplative and unworldly expression of a wordly activist—although it has this aspect—but as the quietist comments of a poet on his ambitious actions. Ralegh's poetry was unusual for its age because it permeated the familiar ingredient of beauty with personal passion. Agnes Latham has put it most aptly, when she says that Ralegh 'wrestled to express the thoughts that actually stirred him, the emotions he was actually feeling'. He was, to use what is in some of today's criticism a dirty word, sincere. There is a certain tone in *The Ocean to Cynthia*, puzzling though it is, that is not unlike Shakespeare's in his sonnets: a nakedly personal tone, of no compromise. Ralegh borrowed rather less from other languages than most of his minor contemporaries: his work almost always carries a personal (and usually melancholy) burden. *The Ocean to Cynthia* is in many ways a confused poem, and it is certainly incomplete, unfinished. But it is the summit of Ralegh's literary achievement, and in certain respects surpasses anything of its century. No one will fully explain its meaning—to Ralegh or to ourselves—but the enigma it presents is one of the most fascinating ones in English literature.

THE 11th: AND LAST BOOK OF THE OCEAN TO CYNTHIA

This long fragment, together with twenty-one and a half lines of a successor, and two short poems, exists in what is without doubt Ralegh's own handwriting, in the Cecil Papers at Hatfield House in Hertfordshire, the home of the Cecils. The two short poems are as follows:

If Synthia be a Queene, a princes, and supreame

If Synthia be a Queene, a princess, and supreame,
Keipe thes amonge the rest, or say it was a dreame;
For thos that like, expound, and those that louth, express,
Meanings accordinge as their minds, are moved more or less;
For writinge what thow art, or shewinge what thow weare;
Adds to the one dysdayne, to th'other butt dyspaire;
  Thy minde of neather needs, in both seinge it exceeds.

My boddy in the walls captived

My boddy in the walls captived
Feels not the wounds of spightfull envy,
Butt my thralde mind, of liberty deprived,
Fast fettered in her auntient memory,
Douth nought beholde butt sorrowes diinge face;
Such prison earst was so delightfull
As it desirde no other dwellinge place,
Butt tymes effects, and destinies dispightfull
Have changed both my keeper and my fare,
Loves fire, and bewties light I then had store,
Butt now close keipt, as captives wounted are,
That food, that heat, that light I finde no more,
  Dyspaire bolts up my dores, and I alone
  Speake to dead walls, butt thos heare not my mone.

Now Edmund Spenser, who was friendly with Ralegh in Ireland—the first three books of *The Faerie Queene* are prefaced by a letter to him—had spoken of a poem by Ralegh called *Cynthia*, both in his *Colin Clouts Come Home Again* and in the first instalment

44

of *The Faerie Queene*. It is reasonable to suppose that the allusions in *Colin Clout* pre-date Ralegh's imprisonment in the Tower in 1592; *The Faerie Queene* was published in 1590. In *Colin Clout* Spenser speaks of Ralegh as 'the Shepherd of the Ocean', whose song is 'all a lamentable lay/Of great unkindness and of usage hard/ Of Cynthia, the Lady of the sea,/Which from her presence faultless him debard', and who desires to break Cynthia's 'sore displeasure/ And move to take him to her grace again'. In the third book of *The Faerie Queene* Ralegh is again spoken of, in an invocation to Elizabeth, as a 'gracious servant' who pictured 'Cynthia' in 'sweet verse'. So Ralegh had been writing a poem suing for the Queen's favour before 1592. There was another reference, made by Spenser's friend Gabriel Harvey—also before 1592. What relationship, if any, does this have with the *11th Book* as we have it?

If this was written in the Tower in 1592, left there on Ralegh's release and delivered to Cecil—who stored it amongst his own papers—then it could, of course, be a continuation of an epic poem, ten books of which had already been completed. These ten books, if ever they existed, could easily have been cast in the form of a 'lamentable lay', which sought to regain entrance to Cynthia's 'presence faultless'. Every one of Elizabeth's favourites fell into disfavour at one time or another, and it was actually rumoured that Ralegh, when he came to Ireland to his estate in 1599, had left the Court in some kind of disgrace—if not so serious a disgrace as that of 1592. What does seem unlikely is that the *Cynthia* we have was written at any time other than 1592. But the ambitious Spenser would not have felt it safe to recommend so equivocal a poem, one so easily interpretable as a criticism of the Queen. And again, the poem we have complains of something much more serious than a mere enforced retirement to an Irish estate. The two poems I have quoted, which also come from the Hatfield House papers, do appear to refer to an actual imprisonment; and they fit in well with their companion.

Further conjecture is fruitless. (It should be noted that some scholars believe 11th to be a misreading of 21st, and 12th, of 22nd.)

What is important is: What does this poem, clearly written at a time when Ralegh was in grave disfavour, mean? We can assume, with every confidence, that it was written in the Tower in 1592. This will not affect our reading, because the evidence that the author of the poem is in disfavour comes, essentially, from its text—not from any undue biographical inference. There is a very full and interesting study of the text of the poem, and of Ralegh's relationship with the Queen, in Walter Oakeshott's *The Queen and the Poet* (1960). But this is predominantly biographical. Less dispensable to students of the poem itself are two other studies: those in Philip Edwards' *Sir Walter Ralegh* (1953), and Donald Davie's brilliant 'A Reading of *The Ocean's Love to Cynthia*' contained in *Stratford-upon-Avon Studies, 2: Elizabethan Poetry* (1960). Edwards' detailed commentary is most valuable, and I have made use of it in my own. Davie's article defines the only fruitful critical approach to this enigmatic poem.

Elizabeth's favourites all treated her as though they were in love with her in all ways, including physically. It was a courtly game, played with great skill, to amusing rules that were well understood by all the players to be both amusing and dangerously ambiguous. Elizabeth may (possibly) have loved Leicester sexually and wanted him (and even, though this is unlikely, had him); there is no question of such a relationship with Ralegh. The discrepancy in age was far too great. To say that Ralegh's behaviour towards the Queen was sexually nauseating is to misunderstand the nature of the courtly game. Nor is there anything in *Cynthia* to suggest that he loves the Queen *as a lover*. To treat it as an insincerely ardent love poem (since the Queen was years older than Ralegh, and in one sense a painted old hag) constitutes a serious misreading. No one has put it more succinctly than Davie: '. . . the literal sense of the poem is now clear: Ralegh, a favourite out of favour with his sovereign, pretends for the purpose of the poem to be a lover out of favour with his mistress, who writes a poem of expostulation, complaint, flattery, and emotional blackmail, in order to be restored to his former privileges'. Thus, the love-theme is merely the convention, combined with that of the pastoral, in which Ralegh chose to write.

The real meaning of the poem, however, as Davie rightly insists, is not to be sought just in Ralegh's personal disappointment, but in what, in it, is 'relevant and interesting . . . to all men at all times, and in particular to ourselves, in the twentieth century in England'.

Davie's interpretation, briefly summarized, is as follows: Cynthia 'stands for the whole culture of which she was the focus'. Ralegh has been deprived of the opportunity to serve the civilization of which she was the centre, and 'asks himself what difference this makes to him'. (We must not, I think, imagine Ralegh as having consciously asked himself this question: Davie is talking about the question he believes the poem itself to be asking—about Ralegh's total, unconscious as well as conscious, intentions.) Ralegh sees that 'even in his years of power his reason had condemned him' (*ll*.120–31). But reason was and is ineffective; and in 'what are perhaps the five finest stanzas' (*ll*.173–192) 'his attitude changes and . . . he exults in the constancy of his will that can overbear all reasonable injunctions'. Here Davie makes one of his most important points: that in this passage—as throughout the poem— Ralegh's use of the word 'love' is ambiguous: he means by it not only 'energy directed towards the object of love' but also 'the object of love' (Cynthia). And as Davie points out, this is why the word 'ripeth' in the line 'A springe of bewties which time ripeth not' (*l*.185) is so appropriate: if Elizabeth were spoken of, then the proper word would be 'withereth'. 'The word "ripeth" provides a sardonic surprise and commands immediate assent because it fits Ralegh's situation so well'. We have to be on the look out for this ambiguity, with here more emphasis on the 'object', and there more on the 'energy', meaning, throughout the poem. This constitutes its metaphysical element; in this respect Ralegh—and particularly here—anticipated a later manner. Ironically, however, *Cynthia* was not discovered until just over a century ago.

Davie goes on to describe the poem, surely correctly, as 'a turbulent flux and reflux of feeling': a painfully vivid record of a series of moods. (Possibly if Ralegh had ever corrected the poem to his satisfaction—for it is clear from his manuscript that he was making a fair copy with the intention of providing himself with a draft upon which to work—it would have lost the urgency and intensity, the sincerity, the almost disturbing 'privacy', that are so peculiar to it.) Davie ends the first part of his examination of the poem by describing it as, after *l*.306, 'a celebration of . . . his constancy . . . at the end. . . . the mind that began by being so divided against itself is at one, resolved and even calm'. Davie ends by putting Ralegh forward as an unexpectedly 'modern' poet: his sentences *are* (claims Davie) what they say; *Cynthia* in certain passages 'describes its own creation, as does Valéry's *Cimitière Marin*. And as an example of 'exceptionally subtle and masterful use of syntax' Davie cites the passage *ll*.73–103. It would be difficult to deny this particular passage the status of great poetry; I quote Davie's explication and appreciation of it in full.

Three-quarters of the way through this sentence, there is a patch of very loose construction, the phrase beginning 'the soul even then departing'. But this apart, the control is imperious and magnificent. First, three images, of the slain but stirring body, of the wintry earth, and of the waterwheel, are presented as it were in parallel, each paralleling both the others but parallel also to an image from the previous sentence, of the lamb weaned but still sucking the dug:

> Mich like the gentell Lamm, though lately waynde,
> Playes with the dug though find no cumfort ther.

So far the syntax is austerely logical, and this is made conspicuous by assigning a quatrain to each image. But the stiffness of the logical parallelism is saved from tedium by the very various affective colouring of the images; the lamb is 'innocent', where the image of the slain body is brutal; the lamb has life before it, the corpse has life behind it; and the images are ranged on a scale from the tender vitality of the lamb through the monstrous life of the murdered body and the exiguous life of wintry nature to the material lifelessness, the mere illusion of life, in the wooden wheel. Moreover, the symmetry is saved from seeming a constraint by the very fact that one of the series of images, the lamb, is carried in a different metrical and grammatical unit from the others. Only now, after twelve lines have already unwound themselves, does the subject of the sentence emerge; and this ('my forsaken hart') has then to wait through no less than nine delays of various kinds (phrases in apposition, an ablative absolute construction, three epithets and three adjectival phrases) before it is allowed to find its verb, 'writes'. Even then, before we learn what is to be written, we are sucked back once again into yet further qualification of this subject so much qualified already:

> as one that could no more,
> Whom love, and time, and fortune had defaced; . . .

Surely this impetus which so slowly and uncertainly gets the sentence into motion, which, having moved it at last, still rocks back hopelessly upon its starting-point, positively enacts in the reader's mind just what it says, the 'waterwheel inertly turning round/Under a stream that would not fill a jug'. And the crowning triumph remains, when the sentence, having struggled up through its interminable preliminaries to the high point of its verb, rocked back there uncertainly, and at last tumbled over, prolongs itself in a seven-line image of the evening twilight. For this image is parallel once again to the three images, now so distant, from which the sentence started. The day lives on borrowed time after sunset, as the twitching body lived on borrowed time after being slain, and the waterwheel moved on borrowed time after the millstream had been diverted. But what I call the affective colouring is now poignantly different again. Above all (with 'every toil and labour wholly ended') it is wretchedly weary; the day longs for death in nightfall whereas the slain body still struggled for life. And so the speaker longs for release from the faint but nagging compulsion to struggle through how many more sentences as laborious as this one. For the attempt is in any case foredoomed; the weary activity is in any case futile.

On its own evidence, and not at all on our assessment of Ralegh, *Cynthia* is a passionate, turbulent and profound meditation on the collapse, the disappointment, of a truly loving ambition. We encounter the thoughts and emotions of a poet even as they are being created. *Cynthia* is itself Ralegh's reaction to his unhappy predicament; it is not an afterthought. Asked, he would not have said that poetry was particularly important to him: it would probably not have occurred to him that it was. . . . But at the moments of greatest stress in his life he does seem to have turned to it—and never more so than in 1592. It tells us much about the nature of Elizabeth's subjects' devotion to her; and, perhaps more important, much about the dynamics of grief, for Ralegh's grief in this poem *is* the poem. Instead of lamenting its unfinished state, we should be grateful that we have it as it is: unaltered, indiscreet, raw, the spontaneous outpourings of a subtle sensibility and a highly developed intellect under irresistible emotional pressure.

EDMUND SPENSER: LIFE AND WORK

Edmund Spenser was born in London in or about 1552, of middle class parents. He went to Merchant Taylors' School. In 1569 he went up to Pembroke College, Cambridge. In 1578 he became secretary to John Young, the ex-master of Pembroke, from whose service he passed, in the following year, to that of the Earl of Leicester. He remained loyal to the memory of Leicester for the rest of his life—hence the tribute in *Prothalamion*. While with him he met and became friendly with Sir Philip Sidney and the poets Edward Dyer and Fulke Greville. He brought out his brilliant and charming *Shepheardes Calendar* in 1579. This was an auspicious beginning for a man who had high hopes of patronage. But for some reason he left Leicester's service in 1580 and became secretary to Lord Grey, the Lord Deputy in Ireland. He remained in Ireland, except for short visits, for the rest of his life. He had married Machabyas Chyld in 1579; she died twelve years later, and in 1594 he married Elizabeth Boyle—for whom he wrote the sonnet sequence *Amoretti* and the wedding song *Epithalamion* (1595).

It seems that Spenser enjoyed some aspects of his life in Ireland, where he owned an estate in Cork from 1589 and was a neighbour of Sir Walter Ralegh. He was busy at official tasks until 1593. But he always hoped for a triumphant return to England as the author of the epic-in-progress, *The Faerie Queene*. These hopes of pre-

50

ferment were never fulfilled, as the intrusive bitterness of certain lines in *Prothalamion*, written only three years before his death, reminds us. Spenser travelled, with Ralegh, to England for the publication of the first three books of *The Faerie Queene* (1590); this was dedicated to the Queen, but brought him no honour. The second three books appeared in the same year as the *Prothalamion*. Spenser arrived in England late in 1598 with despatches, from an Ireland stirred up by Tyrone's rebellion; his own estate, Kilcolman, had been despoiled. In January 1599 he died.

PROTHALAMION

Spenser's *Epithalamion*, which he wrote for his own second marriage, has been called 'surely the most beautiful love poem in the language'; and even those who cannot agree will see immediately why the claim is made. The manner in which the poem combines personal occasion, Irish reality and Renaissance decorum is the very epitome of elegance and sensibility. Furthermore, as Professor Douglas Bush has written, 'there are sinister hints of the perils that encompass frail humanity': the poem is by no means coldly symbolic or, in psychological terms, artificial.

Its companion piece, *Prothalamion*—written, as the title page says, for the double wedding of the Earl of Worcester's two daughters Elizabeth and Katherine to Henry Gilford and William Peters respectively—is on a slighter scale. It is less personal, and, as Bush says, more dream-like. And yet even it must surely be classed as one of the most beautiful set pieces ever written. It was an incidental result of Spenser's visit to London to see the second instalment of his *Faerie Queene* through the press. It is obvious that the Earl of Worcester, impressed like everyone else by the *Epithalamion* of the previous year, and seeing the author at court, had the happy thought of commissioning him to do a poem for the forthcoming double wedding of his own daughters—an event which such a poem would crown, and would represent something of a social '*coup*' for the happy father.

Prothalamion does not express personal feeling about the event it celebrates; one of the reasons for its success is that it does not try to. Spenser does not pretend to have, for two young couples whom he has never met, the emotion that he had for his own marriage. He is decorously polite, but no more. Within a mere five lines of the opening he is exercising an old personal grievance (what poetic self-confidence this showed!); and he uses the poem to do tribute to Leicester and Essex, and to his own birthplace of London. *Prothalamion* is an effective poem, in fact, because it expresses such personal feelings as Spenser had on his English visit of 1596, in particular his love of London, without violating the official occasion. This occasion is treated with grace and graciousness—but no false familiarity.

Prothalamion is not a 'very great poem', as Tucker Brooke once called it; but it is a minor poem of great exquisiteness, demonstrating how perfectly the poets of the Elizabethan age could accomplish the smallest things.

SELECT BIBLIOGRAPHY

Abbreviations of titles referred to in the notes are given in square brackets.

GENERAL

Elizabethan Poetry, H. D. Smith. 1953.

Silver Poets of the Sixteenth Century, ed. G. Bullet. [Bullett]. Contains uncritical, modernized texts of *Cynthia* and *Nosce Teipsum*, as well as selections from Ralegh, Davies, Sidney, Surrey and Wyatt.

The Sixteenth Century Excluding Drama, C. S. Lewis. (Vol. III of *The Oxford History of English Literature*.) This contains a full bibliography.

MARLOWE

Hero and Leander, ed. S. W. Singer. 1821 [Singer].

Works, ed. C. F. Tucker Brooke. 1910. [CFTB].

Works and Life, ed. R. M. Case and Others. 1930–3.

Vol. VI of above, *Poems*, ed. L. C. Martin. 1933. [LCM]. Annotated modernized text of the whole of *Hero and Leander*. The basis of all subsequent editions.

Poems, ed. M. Maclure. 1960. [MM]. Annotated modernized text of the whole of *Hero and Leander*, incorporating many new notes. A valuable edition.

Christopher Marlowe: A Biographical and Critical Study, F. S. Boas. 1940.

Christopher Marlowe: His Thought, Learning and Character, P. M. Kocher. 1946. [Kocher].

The Overreacher: A Study of Christopher Marlowe, H. Levin. 1954.

Marlowe, J. B. Steane. 1964.

Critics on Marlowe, ed. J. O'Neill. 1969.

Christopher Marlowe, ed. B. Morris. 1968. Contains the editor's 'Comic Method in *Hero and Leander*' (113–132). [BM].

CHAPMAN

Plays, ed. T. M. Parrott. 2 vols. 1910–14.

Poems, ed. P. B. Bartlett. 1941. [PPB].

George Chapman: Sa Vie, Sa Poésie, J. Jacquot. 1951. The best study, unfortunately not translated.

George Chapman, M. Maclure. 1966. The best English-language study, with an excellent section on *Hero and Leander*.

The Tragedies of Chapman, E. Rees. 1954.

'Hero and Leander' in *Selected Literary Essays*, C. S. Lewis, pp. 58–73. 1967. [CSL]. Deals with *Hero and Leander* as a whole, but is most notable for its defence of Chapman's continuation.

'Chapman's *Hero and Leander*', D. J. Gordon. *English Miscellany* (Rome), V (1954), pp. 41–94. [DJG].

DONNE

Poems, ed. H. Grierson. 2 vols. 1912. [Grierson].

The Satires, Epigrams and Verse Letters, ed. W. Milgate. 1967. [WM]. The best edition of *The Progresse of the Soule*.

Selected Poems, ed. J. Reeves. 1954. Contains a long biographical and critical introduction.

John Donne: A Life, R. C. Bald. 1970. The standard life.

'The Double Journey of John Donne': D. C. Allen. In *A Tribute to George Coffin Taylor*, ed. A. Williams. 1952.

On *The Progresse of the Soule*.

'What Was the Soul of the Apple?', W. A. Murray in *Review of English Studies*, 1959. [Murray].

The Progress of the Soul, R. E. Hughes. 1969. Contains a short section on the poem.

'Apes and Ape lore in the Middle Ages and Renaissance', H. W. Janson in *Studies of the Warburg Institute*, XX, 1952.

JOHN DAVIES

Complete Works, ed. A. B. Grosart. 4 vols. 1869.

Complete Poems, ed. A. B. Grosart. 2 vols. 1876. [Grosart]. Grosart prints the 1622 text.

Poems, ed. C. Howard. 1941. Prints a facsimile of the 1599 text.

Orchestra, ed. E. M. W. Tillyard. 1947.

'John Donne', T. S. Eliot in *On Poets and Poetry*, 1957.

'The Source used by Davies in *Nosce Teipsum*', L. I. Bredvold in *Publications of the Modern Language Association of America*, XXXVIII, 1923, pp. 745–69.

RALEGH

Poems, ed. A. M. C. Latham. 1929 rev. 1951. [Latham]. The standard edition of the poems: all previous editions are of dubious value.

The Life of Walter Ralegh, together with his Letters, ed. E. Edwards. 2 vols. 1868. Still invaluable.

Walter Ralegh: A Study in Elizabethan Scepticism, E. A. Strathmann. 1951. An excellent and learned study.

Walter Ralegh, P. Edwards. 1953. Contains a section on *Cynthia*.

The Queen and the Poet, W. Oakeshott. 1960. More conjecturally biographical than critical; but useful. Contains the author's detailed commentary on *Cynthia* [WO].

'A Reading of The Ocean's Love to Cynthia', D. Davie in *Elizabethan Poetry*, ed. Brown and Harris, 1960. [Davie].

Walter Ralegh, A. M. C. Latham. 1964.

SPENSER

Edmund Spenser: Works, eds. J. C. Smith, Eide Selincourt, 9 vols., 1932–49.

Poetical Works, eds. E. Greenlaw, C. O. Osgood, F. M. Padelford, 1912 (the best single volume edition).

A Spenser Handbook, A. S. V. Jones. 1930.

The Allegory of Love, C. S. Lewis. 1936.

All references to Ovid's *Metamorphoses* are taken from the excellent prose translation in Penguin Classics: *The Metamorphoses by Ovid* translated by Mary M. Innes with introduction and notes, 1955.

Hero and Leander

To the Right Worshipfull,
Sir Thomas Walsingham, Knight

Sir, wee thinke not our selves discharged of the dutie wee owe to our friend, when wee have brought the breathlesse bodie to the earth: for albeit the eye there taketh his ever farwell of that beloved object, yet the impression of the man, that hath beene deare unto us, living an after life in our memory, there putteth us in mind of farther obsequies due unto the deceased. And namely of the performance of whatsoever 5 *we may judge shal make to his living credit, and to the effecting of his determinations prevented by the stroke of death. By these meditations (as by an intellectuall will) I suppose my selfe executor to the unhappily deceased author of this Poem, upon whom knowing that in his life time you bestowed many kind favors, entertaining the parts of reckoning and woorth which you found in him, with good countenance and* 10 *liberall affection: I cannot but see so far into the will of him dead, that whatsoever issue of his brain should chance to come abroad, that the first breath it should take might be the gentle aire of your liking: for since his selfe had ben accustomed therunto, it would proove more agreeable and thriving to his right children, than any other foster countenance whatsoever. At this time seeing that this unfinished* 15 *Tragedy happens under my hands to be imprinted; of a double duty, the one to your selfe, the other to the deceased, I present the same to your most*
favourable allowance, offring my utmost selfe
now and ever to bee readie, At your
Worships disposing:

Edward Blunt

Hero and Leander

THE ARGUMENT OF THE FIRST SESTYAD

[Heros *description and her Loves,*
The Phane of Venus; *where he moves*
His worthie Love-suite, and attaines;
Whose blisse the wrath of Fates restraines,
For Cupids *grace to* Mercurie,
Which tale the Author doth implie.]

On *Hellespont* guiltie of True-loves blood,
In view and opposit two citties stood,
Seaborderers, disjoin'd by *Neptunes* might:
The one *Abydos*, the other *Sestos* hight.
At *Sestos*, *Hero* dwelt; *Hero* the faire,   5
Whom young *Apollo* courted for her haire,
And offred as a dower his burning throne,
Where she should sit for men to gaze upon.
The outside of her garments were of lawne,
The lining purple silke, with guilt starres drawne,   10
Her wide sleeves greene, and bordered with a grove,
Where *Venus* in her naked glory strove,
To please the carelesse and disdainfull eies
Of proud *Adonis* that before her lies.
Her kirtle blew, whereon was many a staine,   15
Made with the blood of wretched Lovers slaine.
Upon her head she ware a myrtle wreath,
From whence her vaile reacht to the ground beneath.
Her vaile was artificiall flowers and leaves,
Whose workmanship both man and beast deceaves.   20
Many would praise the sweet smell as she past,

When t'was the odour which her breath foorth cast,
And there for honie bees have sought in vaine,
And beat from thence, have lighted there againe.
About her necke hung chaines of peble stone, 25
Which lightned by her necke, like Diamonds shone.
She ware no gloves, for neither sunne nor wind
Would burne or parch her hands, but to her mind,
Or warme or coole them, for they tooke delite
To play upon those hands, they were so white. 30
Buskins of shels all silvered used she,
And brancht with blushing corall to the knee;
Where sparrowes pearcht, of hollow pearle and gold,
Such as the world would woonder to behold:
Those with sweet water oft her handmaid fils, 35
Which as shee went would cherupe through the bils.
Some say, for her the fairest *Cupid* pyn'd,
And looking in her face, was strooken blind.
But this is true, so like was one the other,
As he imagyn'd *Hero* was his mother. 40
And oftentimes into her bosome flew,
About her naked necke his bare armes threw,
And laid his childish head upon her brest,
And with still panting rockt, there tooke his rest.
So lovely faire was *Hero*, *Venus* Nun, 45
As nature wept, thinking she was undone;
Because she tooke more from her than she left,
And of such wondrous beautie her bereft:
Therefore in signe her treasure suffred wracke,
Since *Heroes* time, hath halfe the world beene blacke. 50
Amorous *Leander*, beautifull and yoong,
(Whose tragedie divine *Musæus* soong)
Dwelt at *Abidus*: since him dwelt there none,
For whom succeeding times make greater mone.
His dangling tresses that were never shorne, 55
Had they beene cut, and unto *Colchos* borne.

60

Would have allur'd the vent'rous youth of *Greece*
To hazard more than for the golden Fleece.
Faire *Cinthia* wisht his armes might be her spheare,
Greefe makes her pale, because she mooves not there.   60
His bodie was as straight as *Circes* wand,
Jove might have sipt out *Nectar* from his hand.
Even as delicious meat is to the tast,
So was his necke in touching, and surpast
The white of *Pelops* shoulder. I could tell ye,   65
How smooth his brest was, & how white his bellie,
And whose immortall fingars did imprint
That heavenly path, with many a curious dint,
That runs along his backe, but my rude pen
Can hardly blazon foorth the loves of men,   70
Much lesse of powerfull gods: let it suffise,
That my slacke muse sings of *Leanders* eies,
Those orient cheekes and lippes, exceeding his
That leapt into the water for a kis
Of his owne shadow, and despising many,   75
Died ere he could enjoy the love of any.
Had wilde *Hippolitus Leander* seene,
Enamoured of his beautie had he beene,
His presence made the rudest paisant melt,
That in the vast uplandish countrie dwelt,   80
The barbarous *Thratian* soldier moov'd with nought,
Was moov'd with him, and for his favour sought.
Some swore he was a maid in mans attire,
For in his lookes were all that men desire,
A pleasant smiling cheeke, a speaking eye,   85
A brow for love to banquet roiallye,
And such as knew he was a man would say,
Leander, thou art made for amorous play:
Why art thou not in love, and lov'd of all?
Though thou be faire, yet be not thine owne thrall.   90
  The men of wealthie *Sestos*, everie yeare,

(For his sake whom their goddesse held so deare,
Rose-cheekt *Adonis*) kept a solemne feast.
Thither resorted many a wandring guest,
To meet their loves; such as had none at all,   95
Came lovers home from this great festivall.
For everie street like to a Firmament
Glistered with breathing stars, who where they went,
Frighted the melancholie earth, which deem'd
Eternall heaven to burne, for so it seem'd,   100
As if another *Phaeton* had got
The guidance of the sunnes rich chariot.
But far above the loveliest *Hero* shin'd,
And stole away th'inchaunted gazers mind,
For like Sea-nimphs inveigling harmony,   105
So was her beautie to the standers by.
Nor that night-wandring pale and watrie starre
(When yawning dragons draw her thirling carre
From *Latmus* mount up to the glomie skie,
Where crown'd with blazing light and majestie,   110
She proudly sits) more over-rules the flood,
Than she the hearts of those that neere her stood.
Even as, when gawdie Nymphs pursue the chace,
Wretched *Ixions* shaggie footed race,
Incenst with savage heat, gallop amaine   115
From steepe Pine-bearing mountains to the plaine:
So ran the people foorth to gaze upon her,
And all that view'd her, were enamour'd on her.
And as in furie of a dreadfull fight,
Their fellowes being slaine or put to flight,   120
Poore, soldiers stand with fear of death dead strooken,
So at her presence all surpris'd and tooken,
Await the sentence of her scornefull eies:
He whom she favours lives, the other dies.
There might you see one sigh, another rage,   125
And some (their violent passions to asswage)

62

Compile sharpe satyrs, but alas too late,
For faithful love will never turne to hate.
And many seeing great princes were denied,
Pyn'd as they went, and thinking on her died.   130
On this feast day, O cursed day and hower,
Went *Hero* thorow *Sestos*, from her tower
To *Venus* temple, w(h)ere unhappilye,
As after chaunc'd, they did each other spye.
So faire a church as this, had *Venus* none,   135
The wals were of discoloured *Jasper* stone,
Wherein was *Proteus* carved, and o'rehead,
A livelie vine of greene sea agget spread;
Where by one hand, light headed *Bacchus* hoong,
And with the other, wine from grapes out wroong.   140
Of Christall shining faire the pavement was,
The towne of *Sestos* cal'd it *Venus* glasse.
There might you see the gods in sundrie shapes,
Committing headdie ryots, incest, rapes:
For know, that underneath this radiant floure   145
Was *Danaes* statue in a brazen tower,
Jove slylie stealing from his sisters bed,
To dallie with *Idalian Ganimed*,
And for his love *Europa* bellowing loud,
And tumbling with the Rainbow in a cloud: 150
Blood-quaffing *Mars* heaving the yron net,
Which limping *Vulcan* and his *Cyclops* set:
Love kindling fire, to burne such townes as *Troy*,
Sylvanus weeping for the lovely boy
That now is turn'd into a *Cypres* tree,   155
Under whose shade the Wood-gods love to bee.
And in the midst a silver altar stood;
There *Hero* sacrificing turtles blood,
Vaild to the ground, vailing her eie-lids close,
And modestly they opened as she rose: 160
Thence flew Loves arrow with the golden head,

And thus *Leander* was enamoured.
Stone still he stood, and evermore he gazed,
Till with the fire that from his count'nance blazed,
Relenting *Heroes* gentle heart was strooke,   165
Such force and vertue hath an amorous looke.
   It lies not in our power to love, or hate,
For will in us is over-rul'd by fate.
When two are stript long ere the course begin,
We wish that one should loose, the other win;   170
And one especiallie doe we affect
Of two gold Ingots like in each respect.
The reason no man knowes, let it suffise,
What we behold is censur'd by our eies.
Where both deliberat, the love is slight,   175
Who ever lov'd, that lov'd not at first sight?
   He kneel'd, but unto her devoutly praid;
Chast *Hero* to her selfe thus softly said:
Were I the saint hee worships, I would heare him,
And as shee spake those words, came somewhat nere
    him.   180
He started up, she blusht as one asham'd;
Wherewith *Leander* much more was inflam'd.
He toucht her hand, in touching it she trembled,
Love deepely grounded, hardly is dissembled.
These lovers parled by the touch of hands,   185
True love is mute, and oft amazèd stands.
Thus while dum signs their yeelding harts entangled,
The aire with sparkes of living fire was spangled,
And night deepe drencht in mystie *Acheron*
Heav'd up her head, and halfe the world upon   *A periphrasis*
Breath'd darkenesse forth (darke night is *Cupids* day). *of night*
And now begins *Leander* to display
Loves holy fire, with words, with sighs and teares,
Which like sweet musicke entred *Heroes* eares,
And yet at everie word shee turn'd aside,   195

And alwaies cut him off as he replide.
At last, like to a bold sharpe Sophister,
With chearefull hope thus he accosted her.
  Faire creature, let me speake without offence,
I would my rude words had the influence,   200
To lead thy thoughts as thy faire lookes doe mine,
Then shouldst thou bee his prisoner who is thine.
Be not unkind and faire, mishapen stuffe
Are of behaviour boisterous and ruffe.
O shun me not, but heare me ere you goe,   205
God knowes I cannot force love, as you doe.
My words shall be as spotlesse as my youth,
Full of simplicitie and naked truth.
This sacrifice (whose sweet perfume descending,
From *Venus* altar to your footsteps bending)   210
Doth testifie that you exceed her farre,
To whom you offer, and whose Nunne you are.
Why should you worship her? her you surpasse,
As much as sparkling Diamonds flaring glasse.
A Diamond set in lead his worth retaines,   215
A heavenly Nimph, belov'd of humane swaines,
Receives no blemish, but oft-times more grace,
Which makes me hope, although I am but base,
Base in respect of thee, divine and pure,
Dutifull service may thy love procure,   220
And I in dutie will excell all other,
As thou in beautie doest exceed loves mother.
Nor heaven, nor thou, were made to gaze upon,
As heaven preserves all things, so save thou one.
A stately builded ship, well rig'd and tall,   225
The Ocean maketh more majesticall:
Why vowest thou then to live in *Sestos* here,
Who on Loves seas more glorious wouldst appeare?
Like untun'd golden strings all women are,
Which long time lie untoucht, will harshly jarre.   230

Vessels of Brasse oft handled, brightly shine,
What difference betwixt the richest mine
And basest mold, but use? for both, not us'de,
Are of like worth. Then treasure is abus'de,
When misers keepe it; being put to lone,   235
In time it will returne us two for one.
Rich robes themselves and others do adorne,
Neither themselves nor others, if not worne.
Who builds a pallace and rams up the gate,
Shall see it ruinous and desolate.   240
Ah simple *Hero*, learne thy selfe to cherish,
Lone women like to emptie houses perish.
Lesse sinnes the poore rich man that starves himselfe,
In heaping up a masse of drossie pelfe,
Than such as you: his golden earth remains,   245
Which after his disceasse, some other gains.
But this faire jem, sweet in the losse alone,
When you fleet hence, can be bequeath'd to none.
Or if it could, downe from th'enameld skie
All heaven would come to claime this legacie,   250
And with intestine broiles the world destroy,
And quite confound natures sweet harmony.
Well therefore by the gods decreed it is,
We humane creatures should enjoy that blisse
One is no number, mayds are nothing then,   255
Without the sweet societie of men.
Wilt thou live single still? one shalt thou bee,
Though never-singling *Hymen* couple thee.
Wild savages, that drinke of running springs,
Thinke water farre excels all earthly things: 260
But they that dayly tast neat wine, despise it.
Virginitie, albeit some highly prise it,
Compar'd with marriage, had you tried them both,
Differs as much as wine and water doth.
Base boullion for the stampes sake we allow,   265

Even so for mens impression do we you,
By which alone, our reverend fathers say,
Women receave perfection everie way.
This idoll which you terme *Virginitie*,
Is neither essence subject to the eie,   270
No, nor to any one exterior sence,
Nor hath it any place of residence,
Nor is't of earth or mold celestiall,
Or capable of any forme at all.
Of that which hath no being doe not boast,   275
Things that are not at all are never lost.
Men foolishly doe call it vertuous,
What vertue is it that is borne with us?
Much lesse can honour bee ascrib'd thereto,
Honour is purchac'd by the deedes wee do.   280
Beleeve me *Hero*, honour is not wone,
Untill some honourable deed be done.
Seeke you for chastitie, immortall fame,
And know that some have wrong'd *Dianas* name?
Whose name is it, if she be false or not,   285
So she be faire, but some vile toongs will blot?
But you are faire (aye me) so wondrous faire,
So yoong, so gentle, and so debonaire,
As *Greece* will thinke, if thus you live alone,
Some one or other keepes you as his owne.   290
Then *Hero* hate me not, nor from me flie,
To follow swiftly blasting infamie.
Perhaps, thy sacred Priesthood makes thee loath,
Tell me, to whom mad'st thou that heedlesse oath?
    To *Venus*, answered shee, and as shee spake,   295
Foorth from those two tralucent cesternes brake
A streame of liquid pearle, which downe her face
Made milk-white paths, whereon the gods might trace
To *Joves* high court. Hee thus replide: The rites
In which Loves beauteous Empresse most delites,   300

L.E.P.—3*   67

Are banquets, Dorick musicke, midnight-revell,
Plaies, maskes, and all that stern age counteth evill.
Thee as a holy Idiot doth she scorne,
For thou in vowing chastitie hast sworne
To rob her name and honour, and thereby   305
Commit'st a sinne far worse than perjurie,
Even sacrilege against her Deitie,
Through regular and formall puritie.
To expiat which sinne, kisse and shake hands,
Such sacrifice as this *Venus* demands.   310
   Thereat she smild, and did denie him so,
As put thereby, yet might he hope for mo.
Which makes him quickly re-enforce his speech,
And her in humble manner thus beseech.
   Though neither gods nor men may thee deserve,   315
Yet for her sake whom you have vow'd to serve,
Abandon fruitlesse cold Virginitie,
The gentle queene of Loves sole enemie.
Then shall you most resemble *Venus* Nun,
   When *Venus* sweet rites are perform'd and done   320
Flint-brested *Pallas* joies in single life,
But *Pallas* and your mistresse are at strife.
Love *Hero* then, and be not tirannous,
But heale the heart, that thou hast wounded thus,
Nor staine thy youthfull years with avarice,   325
Faire fooles delight to be accounted nice.
The richest corne dies, if it be not reapt,
Beautie alone is lost, too warily kept.
These arguments he us'de, and many more,
Wherewith she yeelded, that was woon before   330
Heroes lookes yeelded, but her words made warre,
Women are woon when they begin to jarre.
Thus having swallow'd *Cupids* golden hooke,
The more she striv'd, the deeper was she strooke.
Yet evilly faining anger, strove she still,   335

And would be thought to graunt against her will.
So having paus'd a while, at last shee said:
Who taught thee Rhethoricke to deceive a maid?
Aye me, such words as these should I abhor,
And yet I like them for the Orator.   340
   With that *Leander* stoopt, to have imbrac'd her,
But from his spreading armes away she cast her,
And thus bespake him: Gentle youth forbeare
To touch the sacred garments which I weare.
Upon a rocke, and underneath a hill,   345
Far from the towne (where all is whist and still,
Save that the sea playing on yellow sand,
Sends foorth a ratling murmure to the land,
Whose sound allures the golden *Morpheus*
In silence of the night to visite us.)   350
My turret stands, and there God knowes I play
With *Venus* swannes and sparrowes all the day.
A dwarfish beldame beares me companie,
That hops about the chamber where I lie,
And spends the night (that might be better spent)   355
In vaine discourse, and apish merriment.
Come thither. As she spake this, her toong tript,
For unawares (*Come thither*) from her slipt,
And sodainly her former colour chang'd,
And here and there her eies through anger rang'd.   360
And like a planet, mooving severall waies,
At one selfe instant, she poore soule assaies,
Loving, not to love at all, and everie part
Strove to resist the motions of her hart.
And hands so pure, so innocent, nay such,   365
As might have made heaven stoope to have a touch,
Did she uphold to *Venus*, and againe
Vow'd spotlesse chastitie, but all in vaine.
Cupid beats downe her praiers with his wings,
Her vowes above the emptie aire he flings: 370

All deepe enrag'd, his sinowie bow he bent,
And shot a shaft that burning from him went,
Wherewith she strooken look'd so dolefully,
As made Love sigh, to see his tirannie.
And as she wept, her teares to pearle he turn'd, 375
And wound them on his arme, and for her mourn'd.
Then towards the pallace of the destinies,
Laden with languishment and griefe he flies,
And to those sterne nymphs humblie made request,
Both might enjoy ech other, and be blest. 380
But with a ghastly dreadful countenaunce,
Threatning a thousand deaths at everie glaunce,
They answered Love, nor would vouchsafe so much
As one poore word, their hate to him was such.
Harken a while, and I will tell you why: 385
Heavens winged herrald, *Jove-borne Mercury*,
The selfe-same day that he asleepe had layd
Inchaunted Argus, spied a countrie mayd,
Whose carelesse haire, in stead of pearle t'adorne it,
Glist'red with deaw, as one that seem'd to skorne it: 390
Her breath as fragrant as the morning rose,
Her mind pure, and her toong untaught to glose.
Yet prowd she was, (for loftie pride that dwels
In tow'red courts is oft in sheapheards cels.)
And too too well the faire vermilion knew, 395
And silver tincture of her cheekes, that drew
The love of everie swaine: On her, this god
Enamoured was, and with his snakie rod,
Did charme her nimble feet, and made her stay,
The while upon a hillocke downe he lay, 400
And sweetly on his pipe began to play,
And with smooth speech her fancie to assay,
Till in his twining armes he lockt her fast,
And then he woo'd with kisses, and at last,
As sheap-heards do, her on the ground hee layd, 405

And tumbling in the grasse, he often strayd
Beyond the bounds of shame, in being bold
To eie those parts, which no eie should behold.
And like an insolent commaunding lover,
Boasting his parentage, would needs discover   410
The way to new *Elisium*: but she,
Whose only dower was her chastitie,
Having striv'ne in vaine, was now about to crie,
And crave the helpe of sheap-heards that were nie.
Herewith he stayd his furie, and began   415
To give her leave to rise: away she ran,
After went *Mercurie*, who us'd such cunning,
As she to heare his tale, left off her running.
Maids are not woon by brutish force and might,
But speeches full of pleasure and delight.   420
And knowing *Hermes* courted her, was glad
That she such lovelinesse and beautie had
As could provoke his liking, yet was mute,
And neither would denie, nor graunt his sute.
Still vowd he love, she wanting no excuse   425
To feed him with delaies, as women use,
Or thirsting after immortalitie,—
All women are ambitious naturallie,—
Impos'd upon her lover such a taske,
As he ought not performe, nor yet she aske.   430
A draught of flowing *Nectar* she requested,
Wherewith the king of Gods and men is feasted.
He readie to accomplish what she wil'd,
Stole some from *Hebe* (*Hebe Joves* cup fil'd,)
And gave it to his simple rustike love,   435
Which being knowne (as what is hid from *Jove*?)
He inly storm'd, and waxt more furious
Than for the fire filcht by *Prometheus*,
And thrusts him down from heaven: he wandring here,
In mournfull tearmes, with sad and heavie cheare   440

71

Complaind to *Cupid*. *Cupid* for his sake,
To be reveng'd on Jove did undertake,
And those on whom heaven, earth, and hell relies,
I mean the Adamantine Destinies,
He wounds with love, and forst them equallie 445
To dote upon deceitfull *Mercurie*.
They offred him the deadly fatall knife,
That sheares the slender threads of humane life,
At his faire feathered feet the engins layd,
Which th'earth from ougly *Chaos* den up-wayd: 450
These he regarded not, but did intreat,
That Jove, usurper of his fathers seat,
Might presently be banisht into hell,
And aged *Saturne* in *Olympus* dwell.
They granted what he crav'd, and once againe 455
Saturne and *Ops* began their golden raigne.
Murder, rape, warre, lust and trecherie,
Were with *Jove* clos'd in *Stigian* Emprie.
But long this blessed time continued not:
As soone as he his wished purpose got, 460
He recklesse of his promise did despise
The love of th'everlasting Destinies.
They seeing it, both Love and him abhor'd,
And *Jupiter* unto his place restor'd.
And but that Learning, in despight of Fate, 465
Will mount aloft, and enter heaven gate,
And to the seat of *Jove* it selfe advaunce,
Hermes had slept in hell with ignoraunce,
Yet as a punishment they added this,
That he and *Povertie* should alwaies kis. 470
And to this day is everie scholler poore,
Grosse gold from them runs headlong to the boore.
Likewise the angrie sisters thus deluded,
To venge themselves on *Hermes*, have concluded
That *Midas* brood shall sit in Honors chaire, 475

To which the *Muses* sonnes are only heire:
And fruitfull wits that in aspiring are,
Shall discontent run into regions farre;
And few great lords in vertuous deeds shall joy,
But be surpris'd with every garish toy;   480
And still inrich the loftie servile clowne,
Who with incroching guile keepes learning downe
Then muse not *Cupids* sute no better sped,
Seeing in their loves the Fates were injured.

The end of the first Sestyad.

THE ARGUMENT OF THE SECOND SESTYAD

[Hero *of love takes deeper sence,*
And doth her love more recompence.
Their first nights meeting, where sweet kisses
Are th' only crownes of both their blisses.
He swims t' Abydus, *and returnes;*
Cold Neptune *with his beautie burnes,*
Whose suite he shuns, and doth aspire
Heros *faire towre, and his desire.*]

By this, sad *Hero*, with love unacquainted,
Viewing *Leanders* face, fell downe and fainted.
He kist her, and breath'd life into her lips,
Wherewith as one displeas'd, away she trips.
Yet as she went, full often look'd behind,   5
And many poore excuses did she find
To linger by the way, and once she stayd,
And would have turn'd againe, but was afrayd,
In offring parlie, to be counted light.
So on she goes, and in her idle flight,   10
Her painted fanne of curled plumes let fall,
Thinking to traine *Leander* therewithall.
He being a novice, knew not what she meant,

But stayd, and after her a letter sent,
Which joyfull *Hero* answerd in such sort, 15
As he had hope to scale the beauteous fort,
Wherein the liberall graces lock'd their wealth,
And therefore to her tower he got by stealth.
Wide open stood the doore, hee need not clime,
And she her selfe before the pointed time 20
Had spread the boord, with roses strowed the roome,
And oft look't out, and mus'd he did not come.
At last he came, O who can tell the greeting
These greedie lovers had at their first meeting.
He askt, she gave, and nothing was denied, 25
Both to each other quickly were affied.
Looke how their hands, so were their hearts united,
And what he did she willingly requited.
(Sweet are the kisses, the imbracements sweet,
When like desires and affections meet, 30
For from the earth to heaven is *Cupid* raid'd,
Where fancie is in equall ballance pais'd)
Yet she this rashnesse sodainly repented,
And turn'd aside, and to her selfe lamented,
As if her name and honour had beene wrong'd, 35
By being possest of him for whom she long'd:
I, and shee wisht, albeit not from her hart,
That he would leave her turret and depart.
The mirthfull God of amorous pleasure smil'd,
To see how he this captive Nymph beguil'd. 40
For hitherto hee did but fan the fire,
And kept it downe that it might mount the hier.
Now waxt she jealous, least his love abated,
Fearing her owne thoughts made her to be hated.
Therefore unto him hastily she goes, 45
And like *Salmacis* her body throes
Upon his bosome, where with yeelding eyes
She offers up her selfe a sacrifice,

To slake his anger if he were displeas'd.
O what god would not therewith be appeas'd? 50
Like *Æsops* cocke, this jewell he enjoyed,
And as a brother with his sister toyed,
Supposing nothing else was to be done,
Now he her favour and good will had wone.
But know you not that creatures wanting sence 55
By nature have a mutuall appetence,
And wanting organs to advaunce a step,
Mov'd by Loves force, unto ech other lep?
Much more in subjects having intellect,
Some hidden influence breeds like effect. 60
Albeit *Leander* rude in love, and raw,
Long dallying with *Hero*, nothing saw
That might delight him more, yet he suspected
Some amorous rites or other were neglected.
Therefore unto his bodies hirs he clung, 65
She, fearing on the rushes to be flung,
Striv'd with redoubled strength: the more she strived,
The more a gentle pleasing heat revived,
Which taught him all that elder lovers know,
And now the same gan so to scorch and glow, 70
As in plaine termes (yet cunningly) he crav'd it,
Love alwaies makes those eloquent that have it.
Shee, with a kind of graunting, put him by it,
And ever as he thought himselfe most nigh it,
Like to the tree of *Tantalus* she fled, 75
And seeming lavish, sav'de her maydenhead.
Ne're king more sought to keepe his diademe,
Than Hero this inestimable gemme.
Above our life we love a stedfast friend,
Yet when a token of great worth we send, 80
We often kisse it, often looke thereon,
And stay the messenger that would be gon:
No marvell then, though *Hero* would not yeeld

So soone to part from that she deerely held.
Jewels being lost are found againe, this never, 85
T'is lost but once, and once lost, lost for ever.
   Now had the morne espy'de her lovers steeds,
Whereat she starts, puts on her purple weeds,
And red for anger that he stayd so long,
All headlong throwes her selfe the clouds among, 90
And now *Leander* fearing to be mist,
Imbrast her sodainly, tooke leave, and kist.
Long was he taking leave, and loath to go,
And kist againe, as lovers use to do.
Sad *Hero* wroong him by the hand, and wept, 95
Saying, let your vowes and promises be kept.
Then standing at the doore, she turnd about,
As loath to see *Leander* going out.
And now the sunne that through th'orizon peepes,
As pittying these lovers, downewarde creepes, 100
So that in silence of the cloudie night,
Though it was morning, did he take his flight.
But what the secret trustie night conceal'd
Leanders amorous habit soone reveal'd,
With *Cupids* myrtle was his bonet crownd, 105
About his armes the purple riband wound,
Wherewith she wreath'd her largely spreading heare,
Nor could the youth abstaine, but he must weare
The sacred ring wherewith she was endow'd,
When first religious chastitie she vow'd: 110
Which made his love through *Sestos* to bee knowne,
And thence unto *Abydus* sooner blowne
Than he could saile, for incorporeal Fame,
Whose waight consists in nothing but her name,
Is swifter than the wind, whose tardie plumes 115
Are reeking water and dull earthlie fumes.
Home when he came, he seem'd not to be there,
But like exiled aire thrust from his sphere,

Set in a forren place, and straight from thence,
Alcides like, by mightie violence   120
He would have chac'd away the swelling maine,
That him from her unjustly did detaine.
Like as the sunne in a Dyameter,
Fires and inflames objects remooved farre,
And heateth kindly, shining lat'rally;   125
So beautie, sweetly quickens when t'is ny,
But being separated and remooved,
Burnes where it cherisht, murders where it loved.
Therefore even as an Index to a booke,
So to his mind was yoong *Leanders* looke.   130
O none but gods have power their love to hide,
Affection by the count'nance is descride.
The light of hidden fire itselfe discovers,
And love that is conceal'd, betraies poore lovers.
His secret flame apparantly was seene,   135
Leanders Father knew where hee had beene,
And for the same mildly rebuk't his sonne,
Thinking to quench the sparckles new begonne.
But love resisted once, growes passionate,
And nothing more than counsaile lovers hate.   140
For as a hote prowd horse highly disdaines
To have his head control'd, but breakes the raines,
Spits foorth the ringled bit, and with his hoves
Checkes the submissive ground: so hee that loves,
The more he is restrain'd, the woorse he fares.   145
What is it now, but mad *Leander* dares?
O *Hero, Hero*, thus he cry'de full oft,
And then he got him to a rocke aloft,
Where having spy'de her tower, long star'd he on't,
And pray'd the narrow toyling *Hellespont*   150
To part in twaine, that hee might come and go,
But still the rising billowes answered no.
With that hee stript him to the yu'rie skin,

And crying, Love I come, leapt lively in.
Whereat the saphir visag'd god grew prowd, 155
And made his capring *Triton* sound alowd,
Imagining that *Ganimed* displeas'd,
Had left the heavens; therefore on him hee seaz'd.
Leander striv'd, the waves about him wound,
And puld him to the bottome, where the ground 160
Was strewd with pearle, and in low corrall groves
Sweet singing Meremaids, sported with their loves
On heapes of heavie gold, and tooke great pleasure
To spurne in carelesse sort the shipwracke treasure.
For here the stately azure pallace stood, 165
Where kingly *Neptune* and his traine abode.
The lustie god imbrast him, cald him love,
And swore he never should returne to Jove.
But when he knew it was not *Ganimed*,
For under water he was almost dead, 170
He heav'd him up, and looking on his face,
Beat downe the bold waves with his triple mace,
Which mounted up, intending to have kist him,
And fell in drops like teares, because they mist him.
Leander being up, began to swim, 175
And looking backe, saw *Neptune* follow him,
Whereat agast, the poore soule gan to crie,
O let mee visite *Hero* ere I die.
The god put *Helles* bracelet on his arme,
And swore the sea should never doe him harme. 180
He clapt his plumpe cheekes, with his tresses playd,
And smiling wantonly, his love bewrayd.
He watcht his armes, and as they opend wide,
At every stroke, betwixt them would he slide,
And steale a kisse, and then run out and daunce, 185
And as he turnd, cast many a lustfull glaunce,—
And threw him gawdie toies to please his eie,—
And dive into the water, and there prie

Upon his brest, his thighs, and everie lim,
And up againe, and close beside him swim, 190
And talke of love: *Leander* made replie,
You are deceav'd, I am no woman I.
Thereat smilde *Neptune*, and then told a tale,
How that a sheapheard sitting in a vale
Playd with a boy so faire and kind, 195
As for his love both earth and heaven pyn'd;
That of the cooling river durst not drinke,
Least water-nymphs should pull him from the brinke.
And when hee sported in the fragrant lawnes,
Gote-footed Satyrs and up-staring Fawnes 200
Would steale him thence. Ere halfe this tale was done,
Aye me, *Leander* cryde, th'enamoured sunne,
That now should shine on *Thetis* glassie bower,
Descends upon my radiant *Heroes* tower.
O that these tardie armes of mine were wings! 205
And as he spake, upon the waves he springs
Neptune was angrie that hee gave no eare,
And in his heart revenging malice bare:
He flung at him his mace, but as it went,
He cald it in, for love made him repent. 210
The mace returning backe his owne hand hit,
As meaning to be veng'd for darting it.
When this fresh bleeding wound *Leander* viewd,
His colour went and came, as if he rewd
The greefe which *Neptune* felt. In gentle brests, 215
Relenting thoughts, remorse and pittie rests.
And who have hard hearts, and obdurat minds,
But vicious, harebraind, and illit'rat hinds?
The god seeing him with pittie to be moved,
Thereon concluded that he was beloved. 220
(Love is too full of faith, too credulous,
With follie and false hope deluding us.)
Wherefore *Leanders* fancie to surprize.

To the rich *Ocean* for gifts he flies.
'Tis wisedome to give much, a gift prevailes,   225
When deepe perswading Oratorie failes.
By this *Leander* being nere the land,
Cast downe his wearie feet, and felt the sand.
Breathlesse albeit he were, he rested not,
Till to the solitarie tower he got,   230
And knockt and cald, at which celestiall noise
The longing heart of *Hero* much more joies
Then nymphs & sheapheards, when the timbrell rings,
Or crooked Dolphin when the sailer sings;
She stayd not for her robes, but straight arose,   235
And drunke with gladnesse, to the dore she goes,
Where seeing a naked man, she scriecht for feare,
Such sights as this to tender maids are rare,
And ran into the darke herselfe to hide.
Rich jewels in the darke are soonest spide.   240
Unto her was he led, or rather drawne,
By those white limmes, which sparckled through the lawne.
The neerer that he came, the more she fled,
And seeking refuge, slipt into her bed.
Whereon *Leander* sitting, thus began,   245
Though numming cold all feeble, faint and wan:
    If not for love, yet, love, for pittie sake,
Me in thy bed and maiden bosome take,
At least vouchsafe these armes some little roome,
Who hoping to imbrace thee, cherely swome.   250
This head was beat with manie a churlish billow,
And therefore let it rest upon thy pillow.
Herewith afrighted *Hero* shrunke away,
And in her luke-warme place *Leander* lay,
Whose lively heat like fire from heaven fet,   255
Would animate grosse clay, and higher set
The drooping thoughts of base declining soules,
Then drerie *Mars* carowsing *Nectar* boules.

80

His hands he cast upon her like a snare,
She overcome with shame and sallow feare, 260
Like chast *Diana*, when *Acteon* spyde her,
Being sodainly betraide, dyv'd downe to hide her.
And as her silver body downeward went,
With both her hands she made the bed a tent,
And in her owne mind thought her selfe secure, 265
O'recast with dim and darksome coverture.
And now she lets him whisper in her eare,
Flatter, intreat, promise, protest and sweare,
Yet ever as he greedily assayd
To touch those dainties, she the *Harpey* playd, 270
And every lim did as a soldier stout,
Defend the fort, and keep the foe-man out.
For though the rising yu'rie mount he scal'd,
Which is with azure circling lines empal'd,
Much like a globe, (a globe may I tearme this, 275
By which love sailes to regions full of blis,)
Yet there with *Sysiphus* he toyld in vaine,
Till gentle parlie did the truce obtaine.
Wherein *Leander* on her quivering brest,
Breathlesse spoke some thing, and sigh'd out the rest; 280
Which so prevail'd, as he with small ado
Inclos'd her in his armes and kist her to.
And eve'rie kisse to her was as a charme,
And to *Leander* as a fresh alarme,
So that the truce was broke, and she alas, 285
(Poore sillie maiden) at his mercie was.
Love is not ful of pittie (as men say)
But deaffe and cruell, where he meanes to pray.
Even as a bird, which in our hands we wring,
Foorth plungeth, and oft flutters with her wing, 290
She trembling strove, this strife of hers (like that
Which made the world) another world begat
Of unknowne joy. Treason was in her thought,

And cunningly to yeeld her selfe she sought.
Seeming not woon, yet woon she was at length, 295
In such warres women use but halfe their strength.
Leander now like Theban *Hercules*,
Entred the orchard of *Th'esperides*,
Whose fruit none rightly can describe but hee
That puls or shakes it from the golden tree: 300
And now she wisht this night were never done,
And sigh'd to thinke upon th'approching sunne,
For much it greev'd her that the bright day-light
Should know the pleasure of this blessed night,
And them like *Mars* and *Ericine* display, 305
Both in each others armes chaind as they lay.
Againe she knew not how to frame her looke,
Or speake to him who in a moment tooke
That which so long so charily she kept,
And faine by stealth away she would have crept, 310
And to some corner secretly have gone,
Leaving *Leander* in the bed alone.
But as her naked feet were whipping out,
He on the suddaine cling'd her so about,
That Meremaid-like unto the floore she slid, 315
One half appear'd, the other halfe was hid.
Thus neere the bed she blushing stood upright,
And from her countenance behold ye might
A kind of twilight breake, which through the heare,
As from an orient cloud, glymse here and there. 320
And round about the chamber this false morne
Brought foorth the day before the day was borne.
So *Heroes* ruddie cheeke *Hero* betrayd,
And her all naked to his sight displayed,
Whence his admiring eyes more pleasure tooke 325
Than *Dis*, on heapes of gold fixing his looke.
By this *Apollos* golden harpe began
To sound foorth musicke to the *Ocean*,

82

Which watchfull *Hesperus* no sooner heard,
But he the day bright-bearing Car prepar'd,   330
And ran before, as Harbenger of light,
And with his flaring beames mockt ougly night,
Till she o'recome with anguish, shame, and rage,
Dang'd downe to hell her loathsome carriage.

Desunt nonnulla

To my Best Esteemed and Worthely Honored Lady, The Lady Walsingham,

*one of the Ladies of her Majesties
Bed-chamber*

I present your Ladiship with the last affections of the first two Lovers that ever Muse shrinde in the Temple of Memorie; being drawne by strange instigation to employ some of my serious time in so trifeling a subject, which yet made the first Author, divine Musæus, eternall. And were it not that wee must subject our accounts of these common received conceits to servile custome; it goes much against my hand to signe that for a trifling subject, on which more worthines of soule hath been shewed, and weight of divine wit, than can vouchsafe residence in the leaden gravitie of any Mony-Monger; in whose profession all serious subjects are concluded. But he that shuns trifles must shun the world; out of whose reverend heapes of substance and austeritie, I can, and will, ere long, single, or tumble out as brainles and passionate fooleries, as ever panted in the bosome of the most ridiculous Lover. Accept it therefore (good Madam) though as a trifle, yet as a serious argument of my affection: for to bee thought thankefull for all free and honourable favours, is a great summe of that riches my whole thrift intendeth.

Such uncourtly and sillie dispositions as mine, whose contentment hath other objects than profit or glorie; are as glad, simply for the naked merit of vertue, to honour such as advance her, as others that are hired to commend with deepeliest politique bountie.

It hath therefore adjoynde much contentment to my desire of your true honour to heare men of desert in Court adde to mine owne knowledge of your noble disposition, how gladly you doe your best to preferre their desires; and have as absolute respect to their meere good parts, as if they came perfumed and charmed with golden incitements. And this most sweet inclination, that flowes from the truth and eternitie of Nobles, assure your Ladiship doth more suite your other Ornaments, and makes more to the advancement of your Name, and happines of your proceedings, then if (like others) you displaied Ensignes of state and sowrenes in your forehead, made smooth with nothing but sensualitie and presents.

This poore Dedication (in figure of the other unitie betwixt Sir Thomas and

your selfe) hath rejoynd you with him, my honoured best friend, whose continuance
of ancient kindnes to my still-obscured estate, though it cannot encrease my love to 30
him, which hath ever entirely circulare; yet shall it encourage my deserts to their
utmost requitall, and make my hartie gratitude
speake; to which the unhappines of my life
hath hetherto been uncomfortable and
painfull dumbnes. 35

By your Ladiships vowd in
most wished service:
George Chapman.

THE ARGUMENT OF THE THIRD SESTYAD

> [Leander *to the envious light*
> *Resignes his night-sports with the night,*
> *And swims the* Hellespont *againe;*
> Thesme *the Deitie soveraigne*
> *Of Customes and religious rites*
> *Appeares, improving his delites*
> *Since Nuptiall honors he neglected;*
> *Which straight he vowes shall be effected.*
> *Faire* Hero *left Devirginate*
> *Waies, and with furie wailes her state:*
> *But with her love and womans wit*
> *She argues, and approveth it.*]

New light gives new directions, Fortunes new
To fashion our indevours that ensue,
More harsh (at lest more hard) more grave and hie
Our subject runs, and our sterne *Muse* must flie.
Loves edge is taken off, and that light flame, 5
Those thoughts, joyes, longings, that before became
High unexperienst blood, and maids sharpe plights
Must now grow staid, and censure the delights,
That being enjoyed aske judgement; now we praise,
As having parted; Evenings crowne the daies. 10
   And now ye wanton loves, and yong desires,

Pied vanitie, the mint of strange Attires;
Ye lisping Flatteries, and obsequious Glances,
Relentfull Musicks, and attractive Dances,
And you detested Charmes constraining love,   15
Shun loves stolne sports by that these Lovers prove.
  By this the Soveraigne of Heavens golden fires,
And yong *Leander*, Lord of his desires,
Together from their lovers armes arose:
Leander into *Hellespontus* throwes   20
His *Hero*-handled bodie, whose delight
Made him disdaine each other Epethite.
And as amidst the enamourd waves he swims,
The God of gold of purpose guilt his lims,   *He cals Phœbus The*
That this word guilt, including double sence,   *God of Gold, since the*
The double guilt of his *Incontinence*,   *vertue of his beams*
Might be exprest, that had no stay t'employ   *creates it*
The treasure which the Love-god let him joy
In his deare *Hero*, with such sacred thrift,
As had beseemed so sanctified a gift: 30
But like a greedie vulgar Prodigall
Would on the stock dispend, and rudely fall
Before his time, to that unblessed blessing,
Which for lusts plague doth perish with possessing.
  Joy graven in sence, like snow in water wasts;   35
    Without preserve of vertue nothing lasts.
What man is he that with a welthie eie
Enjoyes a beautie richer than the skie,
Through whose white skin, softer then soundest sleep,
With damaske eyes, the rubie blood doth peep,   40
And runs in branches through her azure vaines,
Whose mixture and first fire, his love attaines;
Whose both hands limit both Loves deities,
And sweeten humane thoughts like Paradise;
Whose disposition silken is and kinde,   45
Directed with an earth-exempted minde;

Who thinks not heaven with such a love is given?
And who like earth would spend that dower of heaven,
With ranke desire to joy it all at first?
What simply kils our hunger, quencheth thirst, 50
Clothes but our nakednes, and makes us live,
Praise doth not any of her favours give:
But what doth plentifully minister
Beautious apparell and delicious cheere,
So ordered that it still excites desire, 55
And still gives pleasure freenes to aspire
The palme of *Bountie*, ever moyst preserving:
To loves sweet life this is the courtly carving.
Thus *Time*, and all-states-ordering *Ceremonie*
Had banisht all offence: *Times* golden Thie 60
Upholds the flowrie bodie of the earth
In sacred harmonie, and every birth
Of men, and actions makes legitimate,
Being usde aright; *The use of time is Fate.*
    Yet did the gentle flood transfer once more 65
This prize of Love home to his fathers shore;
Where he unlades himselfe of that false welth
That makes few rich, treasures composde by stelth;
And to his sister kinde *Hermione*,
(Who on the shore kneeld, praying to the sea 70
For his returne) he all Loves goods did show
In *Hero* seasde for him, in him for *Hero*.
    His most kinde sister all his secrets knew,
And to her singing like a shower he flew,
Sprinkling the earth, that to their tombs tooke in 75
Streames dead for love to leave his ivorie skin,
Which yet a snowie fome did leave above,
As soule to the dead water that did love;
And from thence did the first white Roses spring,
(For love is sweet and faire in every thing) 80
And all the sweetned shore as he did goe,

87

Was crowned with odrous roses white as snow.
Love-blest *Leander* was with love so filled,
That love to all that toucht him he instilled.
And as the colours of all things we see,   85
To our sights powers communicated bee:
So to all objects that in compasse came
Of any sence he had, his sences flame
Flowd from his parts with force so virtuall,
It fir'd with sence things weere insensuall.   90
    Now (with warme baths and odours comforted)
When he lay downe he kindly kist his bed,
As consecrating it to *Heros* right,
And vowd thereafter that what ever sight
Put him in minde of *Hero*, or her blisse,   95
Should be her Altar to prefer a kisse.
    Then laid he forth his late inriched armes,
In whose white circle Love writ all his charmes,
And made his characters sweet *Heros* lims,
When on his breasts warme sea she sideling swims.   100
And as those armes (held up in circle) met,
He said: See sister *Heros* Carquenet,
Which she had rather weare about her neck,
Then all the jewels that doth *Juno* deck.
    But as he shooke with passionate desire,   105
To put in flame his other secret fire,
A musick so divine did pierce his eare,
As never yet his ravisht sence did heare:
When suddenly a light of twentie hews
Brake through the roofe, and like the Rainbow views   110
Amazd *Leander*; in whose beames came downe
The Goddesse *Ceremonie*, with a Crowne
Of all the stars, and heaven with her descended.
Her flaming haire to her bright feete extended,
By which hung all the bench of Deities;   115
And in a chaine, compact of eares and eies,

She led Religion; all her bodie was
Cleere and transparent as the purest glasse:
For she was all presented to the sence;
Devotion, Order, State, and Reverence   120
Her shadowes were; Societie, Memorie;
All which her sight made live, her absence die.
A rich disparent Pentackle she weares,
Drawne full of circles and strange characters:
Her face was changeable to everie eie;   125
One way lookt ill, another graciouslie;
Which while men viewd, they cheerfull were & holy:
But looking off, vicious and melancholy:
The snakie paths to each observed law
Did *Policie* in her broad bosome draw: 130
One hand a Mathematique Christall swayes,
Which gathering in one line a thousand rayes
From her bright eyes, *Confusion* burnes to death,
And all estates of men distinguisheth.
By it *Morallitie* and *Comelinesse*   135
Themselves in all their sightly figures dresse.
Her other hand a lawrell rod applies,
To beate back *Barbarisme*, and *Avarice*,
That followd eating earth, and excrement
And humane lims; and would make proud ascent   140
To seates of Gods, were *Ceremonie* slaine;
The *Howrs* and *Graces* bore her glorious traine,
And all the sweetes of our societie
Were Spherde, and treasurde in her bountious eie.
Thus she appeard, and sharply did reprove   145
Leanders bluntnes in his violent love;
Tolde him how poore was substance without rites,
Like bils unsignd, desires without delites;
Like meates unseasoned; like ranke corne that growes
On Cottages, that none or reapes or sowes: 150
Not being with civill forms confirm'd and bounded,

For humane dignities and comforts founded:
But loose and secret all their glories hide,
Feare fils the chamber, darknes decks the Bride.
 She vanisht, leaving pierst *Leanders* hart   155
With sence of his unceremonious part,
In which with plaine neglect of Nuptiall rites,
He close and flatly fell to his delites:
And instantly he vowd to celebrate
All rites pertaining to his maried state.   160
So up he gets and to his father goes,
To whose glad eares he doth his vowes disclose:
The Nuptials are resolv'd with utmost powre,
And he at night would swim to *Heros* towre.
From whence he ment to *Sestus* forked Bay   165
To bring her covertly, where ships must stay,
Sent by her father throughly rigd and mand,
To wait her safely to *Abydus* Strand.
There leave we him, and with fresh wing pursue
Astonisht *Hero*, whose most wished view   170
I thus long have forborne, because I left her
So out of countnance, and her spirits bereft her.
To looke of one abasht is impudence,
When of sleight faults he hath too deepe a sence.
Her blushing het her chamber: she lookt out,   175
And all the ayre she purpled round about,
And after it a foule black day befell,
Which ever since a red morne doth foretell,
And still renewes, our woes for *Heros* wo,
And foule it prov'd, because it figur'd so   180
The next nights horror, which prepare to heare;
I faile if it prophane your daintiest eare.
 Then thou most strangely-intellectuall fire,
That proper to my soule hast power t'inspire
Her burning faculties, and with the wings   185
Of thy unspheared flame visitst the springs

Of spirits immortall; Now (as swift as Time
Doth follow Motion) finde th'eternall Clime
Of his free soule, whose living subject stood
Up to the chin in the Pyerean flood,   190
And drunke to me halfe this Musean storie,
Inscribing it to deathles Memorie:
Confer with it, and make my pledge as deepe,
That neithers draught be consecrate to sleepe.
Tell it how much his late desires I tender,   195
(If yet it know not) and to light surrender
My soules darke ofspring, willing it should die
To loves, to passions, and societie.
    Sweet *Hero* left upon her bed alone,
Her maidenhead, her vowes, *Leander* gone,   200
And nothing with her but a violent crew
Of new come thoughts that yet she never knew,
Even to her selfe a stranger; was much like
Th' *Iberian* citie that wars hand did strike
By English force in princely *Essex* guide,   205
When peace assur'd her towres had fortifide;
And golden-fingered *India* had bestowd
Such wealth on her, that strength and Empire flowd
Into her Turrets; and her virgin waste
The wealthie girdle of the Sea embraste: 210
Till our *Leander* that made *Mars* his *Cupid*,
For soft love-sutes, with iron thunders chid:
Swum to her Towers, dissolv'd her virgin zone;
Lead in his power, and made Confusion
Run through her streets amazd, that she supposde   215
She had not been in her owne walls inclosde,
But rapt by wonder to some forraine state,
Seeing all her issue so disconsolate:
And all her peaceful mansions possest
With wars just spoyle, and many a forraine guest   220
From every corner driving an enjoyer,

Supplying it with power of a destroyer.
So far'd fayre *Hero* in th'expugned fort
Of her chast bosome, and of every sort
Strange thoughts possest her, ransacking her brest   225
For that that was not there, her wonted rest.
She was a mother straight and bore with paine
Thoughts that spake straight and wisht their mother slaine;
She hates their lives, & they their own & hers:
Such strife still growes where sin the race prefers.   230
Love is a golden bubble full of dreames,
That waking breakes, and fils us with extreames.
She mus'd how she could looke upon her Sire,
And not shew that without, that was intire.
For as a glasse is an inanimate eie,   235
And outward formes imbraceth inwardlie:
So is the eye an animate glasse that showes
In-formes without us. And as *Phœbus* throwes
His beames abroad, though he in clowdes be closde,
Still glancing by them till he finde opposde   240
A loose and rorid vapour that is fit
T'event his searching beames, and useth it
To forme a tender twentie-coloured eie,
Cast in a circle round about the skie.
So when our firie soule, our bodies starre,   245
(That ever is in motion circulare)
Conceives a forme; in seeking to display it
Through all our clowdie parts, it doth convey it
Forth at the eye, as the most pregnant place,
And that reflects it round about the face.   250
And this event uncourtly *Hero* thought
Her inward guilt would in her lookes have wrought:
For yet the worlds stale cunning she resisted
To beare foule thoughts, yet forge what lookes she listed,
And held it for a very sillie sleight,   255
To make a perfect mettall counterfeit,

Glad to disclaime her selfe, proud of an **Art**,
That makes the face a Pandar to the hart.
Those be the painted Moones, whose lights prophane
Beauties true Heaven, at full still in their wane. 260
Those be the Lapwing faces that still crie,
Here tis, when that they vow is nothing nie.
Base fooles, when every moorish fowle can teach
That which men thinke the height of humane reach.
But custome that the Apoplexie is 265
Of beddred nature and lives led amis,
And takes away all feeling of offence:
Yet brazde not *Heros* brow with impudence;
And this she thought most hard to bring to pas,
To seeme in countnance other then she was, 270
As if she had two soules; one for the face,
One for the hart; and that they shifted place
As either list to utter, or conceale
What they conceiv'd: or as one soule did deale
With both affayres at once, keeps and ejects 275
Both at an instant contrarie effects:
Retention and ejection in her powrs
Being acts alike: for this one vice of ours,
That forms the thought, and swaies the countenance,
Rules both our motion and our utterance. 280
    These and more grave conceits toyld *Heros* spirits:
For though the light of her discoursive wits
Perhaps might finde some little hole to pas
Through all these worldly cinctures; yet (alas)
There was a heavenly flame incompast her; 285
Her Goddesse, in whose Phane she did prefer
Her virgin vowes; from whose impulsive sight
She knew the black shield of the darkest night
Could not defend her, nor wits subtilst art:
This was the point pierst *Hero* to the hart. 290
Who heavie to the death, with a deep sigh

93

And hand that languisht, tooke a robe was nigh,
Exceeding large, and of black Cypres made,
In which she sate, hid from the day in shade,
Even over head and face downe to her feete; 295
Her left hand made it at her bosome meete;
Her right hand leand on her hart-bowing knee,
Wrapt in unshapefull foulds twas death to see:
Her knee stayd that, and that her falling face
Each limme helpt other to put on disgrace. 300
No forme was seene, where forme held all her sight:
But like an Embrion that saw never light:
Or like a scorched statue made a cole
With three-wingd lightning: or a wretched soule
Muffled with endles darknes, she did sit: 305
The night had never such a heavie spirit.
Yet might an imitating eye well see,
How fast her cleere teares melted on her knee
Through her black vaile, and turnd as black as it,
Mourning to be her teares: then wrought her wit 310
With her broke vow, her Goddesse wrath, her fame,
All tooles that enginous despayre could frame:
Which made her strow the floore with her torne haire,
And spread her mantle peece-meale in the aire.
Like *Joves* sons club, strong passion strook her downe, 315
And with a piteous shrieke inforst her swoune:
Her shrieke made with another shrieke ascend
The frighted Matron that on her did tend:
And as with her owne crie her sence was slaine,
So with the other it was calde againe. 320
She rose and to her bed made forced way,
And layd her downe even where *Leander* lay:
And all this while the red sea of her blood
Ebd with *Leander*: but now turnd the flood,
And all her fleete of sprites came swelling in 325
With childe of saile, and did hot fight begin

With those severe conceits, she too much markt,
And here *Leanders* beauties were imbarkt.
He came in swimming painted all with joyes,
Such as might sweeten hell: his thought destroyes   330
All her destroying thoughts: she thought she felt
His heart in hers with her contentions melt,
And chid her soule that it could so much erre,
To check the true joyes he deserv'd in her.
Her fresh heat blood cast figures in her eyes,   335
And she supposde she saw in *Neptunes* skyes
How her star wandred, washt in smarting brine
For her loves sake, that with immortall wine
Should be embath'd, and swim in more hearts ease,
Than there was water in the Sestian seas.   340
Then said her *Cupid* prompted spirit: Shall I
Sing mones to such delightsome harmony?
Shall slick-tongde fame patcht up with voyces rude,
The drunken bastard of the multitude,
(Begot when father Judgement is away,   345
And gossip-like, sayes because others say,
Takes newes as if it were too hot to eate,
And spits it slavering forth for dog-fees meate)
Make me for forging a phantastique vow,
Presume to beare what makes grave matrons bow?   350
Good vowes are never broken with good deedes,
For then good deedes were bad: vowes are but seedes,
And good deeds fruits; even those good deedes that grow
From other stocks than from th'observed vow.
That is a good deede that prevents a bad: 355
Had I not yeelded, slaine my selfe I had.
Hero Leander is, Leander Hero:
Such vertue love hath to make one of two.
If then *Leander* did my maydenhead git,
Leander being my selfe I still retaine it.   360
We breake chast vowes when we live loosely ever:

95

But bound as we are, we live loosely never.
Two constant lovers being joynd in one,
Yeelding to one another, yeeld to none.
We know not how to vow, till love unblinde us, 365
And vowes made ignorantly never binde us.
Too true it is that when t'is gone men hate
The joyes as vaine they tooke in loves estate:
But that's since they have lost the heavenly light
Should shew them way to judge of all things right. 370
When life is gone death must implant his terror,
As death is foe to life, so love to error.
Before we love how range we through this sphere,
Searching the sundrie fancies hunted here:
Now with desire of wealth transported quite 375
Beyond our free humanities delight:
Now with ambition climing falling towrs,
Whose hope to scale our feare to fall devours:
Now rapt with pastimes, pomp, all joyes impure;
In things without us no delight is sure. 380
But love with all joyes crownd, within doth sit;
O Goddesse pitie Jove and pardon it.
This spake she weeping: but her Goddesse eare
Burnd with too sterne a heat, and would not heare.
Aie me, hath heavens straight fingers no more graces 385
For such as *Hero*, then for homeliest faces?
Yet she hopte well, and in her sweet conceit
Waying her arguments, she thought them weight:
And that the logick of *Leanders* beautie,
And them together would bring proofes of dutie. 390
And if her soule, that was a skilfull glance
Of Heavens great essence, found such imperance
In her loves beauties; she had confidence
Jove lov'd him too, and pardond her offence.
  Beautie in heaven and earth this grace doth win, 395
  It supples rigor, and it lessens sin.

96

Thus, her sharpe wit, her love, her secrecie,
(Trouping together, made her wonder why
She should not leave her bed, and to the Temple?
Her health said she must live; her sex, dissemble.   400
She viewed *Leanders* place, and wisht he were
Turnd to his place, so his place were *Leander*.
Aye me (said she) that loves sweet life and sence
Should doe it harme! my love had not gone hence,
Had he been like his place. O blessed place,   405
Image of Constancie. Thus my loves grace
Parts no where but it leaves some thing behinde
Worth observation: he renownes his kinde.
His motion is like heavens Orbiculer:
For where he once is, he is ever there.   410
This place was mine: *Leander* now t'is thine;
Thou being my selfe, then it is double mine:
Mine, and *Leanders* mine, *Leanders* mine.
O see what wealth it yeelds me, nay yeelds him:
For I am in it, he for me doth swim.   415
Rich, fruitfull love, that doubling selfe estates
Elixer-like contracts, though separates.
Deare place, I kisse thee, and doe welcome thee,
As from *Leander* ever sent to mee.

The end of the Third Sestyad.

THE ARGUMENT OF THE FOURTH SESTYAD

> [Hero, *in sacred habit deckt*,
> *Doth private sacrifice effect.*
> *Her Skarfs description wrought by fate,*
> *Ostents that threaten her estate.*
> *The strange, yet Phisicall events,*   5
> Leanders *counterfeit presents.*
> *In thunder* Ciprides *descends.*

Presaging both the lovers ends.
Ecte the Goddesse of remorce,
With vocall and articulate force 10
Inspires Leucote, Venus swan,
T' excuse the beautious Sestian.
Venus, to wreake her rites abuses,
Creates the monster Eronusis;   *Eronusis,*
Enflaming Heros Sacrifice,   *Dissi(mu)lation.*
With lightning darted from her eyes:
And thereof springs the painted beast,
That ever since taints every breast.]

Now from *Leanders* place she rose, and found
Her haire and rent robe scattred on the ground:
Which taking up, she every peece did lay
Upon an Altar; where in youth of day
She usde t'exhibite private Sacrifice: 5
Those would she offer to the Deities
Of her faire Goddesse, and her powerful son,
As relicks of her late-felt passion:
And in that holy sort she vowd to end them,
In hope her violent fancies that did rend them, 10
Would as quite fade in her loves holy fire,
As they should in the flames she ment t'inspire.
Then put she on all her religious weedes,
That deckt her in her secret sacred deedes:
A crowne of Isickles, that sunne nor fire 15
Could ever melt, and figur'd chast desire.
A golden star shinde in her naked breast,
In honour of the Queene-light of the East.
In her right hand she held a silver wand,
On whose bright top *Peristera* did stand, 20
Who was a Nymph, but now transformed a Dove,
And in her life was deare in *Venus* love:
And for her sake she ever since that time,
Chusde Doves to draw her Coach through heavens blew clime.

Her plentious haire in curled billowes swims 25
On her bright shoulder: her harmonious lims
Sustainde no more but a most subtile vaile
That hung on them, as it durst not assaile
Their different concord: for the weakest ayre
Could raise it swelling from her bewties fayre 30
Nor did it cover, but adumbrate onelie
Her most heart-piercing parts, that a blest eie
Might see (as it did shadow) fearfullie
All that all-love-deserving Paradise:
It was as blew as the most freezing skies, 35
Neere the Seas hew, for thence her Goddesse came:
On it a skarfe she wore of wondrous frame;
In midst whereof she wrought a virgins face,
From whose each cheeke a firie blush did chace
Two crimson flames, that did two waies extend, 40
Spreading the ample skarfe to either end,
Which figur'd the division of her minde,
Whiles yet she rested bashfully inclinde,
And stood not resolute to wed *Leander*.
This serv'd her white neck for a purple sphere, 45
And cast it selfe at full breadth downe her back.
There (since the first breath that begun the wrack
Of her free quiet from *Leanders* lips)
She wrought a Sea in one flame full of ships:
But that one ship where all her wealth did passe 50
(Like simple marchants goods) *Leander* was:
For in that Sea she naked figured him;
Her diving needle taught him how to swim,
And to each thred did such resemblance give,
For joy to be so like him, it did live. 55
  Things senceles live by art, and rationall die,
  By rude contempt of art and industrie.
Scarce could she work but in her strength of thought,
She feard she prickt *Leander* as she wrought:

L.E.P.—4*   99

And oft would shrieke so, that her Guardian frighted,   60
Would staring haste, as with some mischiefe cited.
   They double life that dead things griefs sustayne:
   They kill that feele not their friends living payne.
Sometimes she feard he sought her infamie,
And then as she was working of his eie,   55
She thought to pricke it out to quench her ill:
But as she prickt, it grew more perfect still.
   Trifling attempts no serious acts advance;
   The fire of love is blowne by dalliance.
In working his fayre neck she did so grace it,   70
She still was working her owne armes t'imbrace it:
That, and his shoulders, and his hands were seene
Above the streame, and with a pure Sea greene
She did so quiently shadow every lim,
All might be seene beneath the waves to swim.   75
  In this conceited skarfe she wrought beside
A Moone in change, and shooting stars did glide
In number after her with bloodie beames,
Which figur'd her affects in their extreames,
Pursuing Nature in her Cynthian bodie,   80
And did her thoughts running on change implie:
For maids take more delights when they prepare
And thinke of wives states, than when wives they are.
Beneath all these she wrought a Fisherman,
Drawing his nets from forth that Ocean;   85
Who drew so hard ye might discover well,
The toughned sinewes in his neck did swell:
His inward straines draue out his blood-shot eyes,
And springs of sweat did in his forehead rise:
Yet was of nought but of a Serpent sped,   90
That in his bosome flew and stung him dead.
And this by fate into her minde was sent,
Not wrought by meere instinct of her intent.
At the skarfs other end her hand did frame,

100

Neere the forkt point of the devided flame, 95
A countrie virgin keeping of a Vine,
Who did of hollow bulrushes combine
Snares for the stubble-loving Grashopper,
And by her lay her skrip that nourisht her.
Within a myrtle shade she sate and sung, 100
And tufts of waving reedes about her sprung:
Where lurkt two Foxes, that while she applide
Her trifling snares, their theeveries did devide:
One to the vine, another to her skrip,
That she did negligently overslip: 105
By which her fruitfull vine and holesome fare
She suffred spoyld to make a childish snare.
These omenous fancies did her soule expresse,
And every finger made a Prophetesse,
To shew what death was hid in loves disguise, 110
And make her judgement conquer destinies.
O what sweet formes fayre Ladies soules doe shrowd,
Were they made seene & forced through their blood,
If through their beauties like rich work through lawn,
They would set forth their minds with virtues drawn, 115
In letting graces from their fingers flie,
To still their yasty thoughts with industrie:
That their plied wits in numbred silks might sing
Passions huge conquest, and their needels leading
Affection prisoner through their own-built citties, 120
Pinniond with stories and Arachnean ditties.
    Proceed we now with *Heros* sacrifice;
She odours burnd, and from their smoke did rise
Unsavorie fumes, that ayre with plagues inspired,
And then the consecrated sticks she fired, 125
On whose pale flame an angrie spirit flew,
And beate it downe still as it upward grew.
The virgin Tapers that on th'altar stood,
When she inflam'd them burnd as red as blood:

All sad ostents of that too neere successe, 130
That made such moving beauties motionlesse.
Then *Hero* wept; but her affrighted eyes
(She quickly wrested from the sacrifice:
Shut them, and inwards for *Leander* lookt,
Searcht her soft bosome, and from thence she pluckt 135
His lovely picture: which when she had viewd,
Her beauties were with all loves joyes renewd.
The odors sweetned, and the fires burnd cleere,
Leanders forme left no ill object there.
Such was his beautie that the force of light, 140
Whose knowledge teacheth wonders infinite,
The strength of number and proportion,
Nature had plaste in it to make it knowne
Art was her daughter, and what humane wits
For studie lost, intombd in drossie spirits. 145
After this accident (which for her glorie
Hero could not but make a historie)
Th' inhabitants of *Sestus*, and *Abydus*
Did everie yeare with feasts propitious
To faire *Leanders* picture sacrifice, 150
And they were persons of especiall prize
That were allowd it, as an ornament
T' inrich their houses; for the continent
Of the strange vertues all approv'd it held:
For even the very looke of it repeld 155
All blastings, witchcrafts, and the strifes of nature
In those diseases that no hearbs could cure.
The woolfie sting of Avarice it would pull,)
And make the rankest miser bountifull.
It kild the feare of thunder and of death; 160
The discords that conceits ingendereth
Twixt man and wife if for the time would cease:
The flames of love it quencht, and would increase:
Held in a princes hand it would put out

102

The dreadfulst Comet: it would ease all doubt 165
Of threatned mischiefes: it would bring asleepe
Such as were mad: it would enforce to weepe
Most barbarous eyes: and many more effects
This picture wrought, and sprung *Leandrian* sects,
Of which was *Hero* first: For he whose forme 170
(Held in her hand) cleerd such a fatall storme,
From hell she thought his person would defend her,
Which night and *Hellespont* would quickly send her.
With this confirmed, she vowd to banish quite
All thought of any check to her delite: 175
And in contempt of sillie bashfulnes,
She would the faith of her desires professe:
Where her Religion should be Policie,
To follow love with zeale her pietie:
Her chamber her Cathedrall Church should be, 180
And her *Leander* her chiefe Deitie.
For in her love these did the gods forego;
And though her knowledge did not teach her so,
Yet did it teach her this, that what her hart
Did greatest hold in her selfe greatest part, 185
That she did make her god; and t'was lesse nought
To leave gods in profession and in thought,
Than in her love and life: for therein lies
Most of her duties, and their dignities;
And raile the brain-bald world at what it will, 190
Thats the grand Atheisme that raignes in it still.
Yet singularitie she would use no more,
For she was singular too much before:
But she would please the world with fayre pretext;
Love would not leave her conscience perplext. 195
Great men that will have lesse doe for them still,
Must beare them out though th'acts be nere so ill.
Meannes must Pandar be to Excellencie,
Pleasure attones Falshood and Conscience:

103

Dissembling was the worst (thought *Hero* then) 200
And that was best now she must live with men.
O vertuous love that taught her to doe best,
When she did worst, and when she thought it lest.
Thus would she still proceed in works divine,
And in her sacred state of priesthood shine, 205
Handling the holy rites with hands as bold,
As if therein she did *Joves* thunder hold;
And need not feare those menaces of error,
Which she at others threw with greatest terror.
O lovely *Hero*, nothing is thy sin, 210
Wayd with those foule faults other Priests are in;
That having neither faiths, nor works, nor bewties,
T'engender any scuse for slubberd duties,
With as much countnance fill their holie chayres,
And sweat denouncements gainst prophane affayres, 215
As if their lives were cut out by their places,
And they the only fathers of the Graces.
   Now as with setled minde she did repaire
Her thoughts to sacrifice her ravisht haire
And her torne robe which on the altar lay, 220
And only for Religions fire did stay;
She heard a thunder by the Cyclops beaten,
In such a volley as the world did threaten,
Given *Venus* as she parted th'ayrie Sphere,
Discending now to chide with *Hero* here: 225
When suddenly the Goddesse waggoners,
The Swans and Turtles that in coupled pheres
Through all worlds bosoms draw her influence,
Lighted in *Heros* window, and from thence
To her fayre shoulders flew the gentle Doves, 230
Graceful *Ædone* that sweet pleasure loves,
And ruffoot *Chreste* with the tufted crowne,
Both which did kisse her, though their Goddes frownd.
The Swans did in the solid flood, her glasse,

104

Proyne their fayre plumes; of which the fairest was 235
Jove-lov'd *Leucote*, that pure brightnes is;
The other bountie-loving *Dapsilis*.
All were in heaven, now they with *Hero* were:
But *Venus* lookes brought wrath, and urged feare.
Her robe was skarlet, black her heads attire, 240
And through her naked breast shinde streames of fire,
As when the rarefied ayre is driven
In flashing streames, and opes the darkned heaven.
In her white hand a wreath of yew she bore,
And breaking th'icie wreath sweet *Hero* wore, 245
She forst about her browes her wreath of yew,
And sayd: Now minion to thy fate be trew,
Though not to me, indure what this portends;
Begin where lightnes will, in shame it ends.
Love makes thee cunning; thou art currant now 250
By being counterfeit: thy broken vow
Deceit with her pide garters must rejoyne,
And with her stampe thou countnances must coyne:
Coynes and pure deceits for purities,
And still a mayd wilt seeme in cosoned eies, 255
And have an antike face to laugh within,
While thy smooth lookes make men digest thy sin.
But since thy lips (lest thought forsworne) forswore,
Be never virgins vow worth trusting more.
    When Beauties dearest did her Goddesse heare 260
Breathe such rebukes gainst that she could not cleare,
Dumbe sorrow spake alowd in teares and blood
That from her griefe-burst vaines in piteous flood,
From the sweet conduits of her savor fell:
The gentle Turtles did with moanes make swell 265
Their shining gorges: the white black-eyde Swans
Did sing as wofull Epicedians,
As they would straightwaies dye: when pities Queene
The Goddesse *Ecte*, that had ever beene

Hid in a watrie clowde neere *Heros* cries, 270
Since the first instant of her broken eies,
Gaue bright *Leucote* voyce, and made her speake,
To ease her anguish, whose swolne breast did breake
With anger at her Goddesse, that did touch
Hero so neere for that she usde so much. 275
And thrusting her white neck at *Venus*, sayd:
Why may not amorous *Hero* seeme a mayd,
Though she be none, as well as you suppresse
In modest cheekes your inward wantonnesse?
How often have wee drawne you from above, 280
T'exchange with mortals rites for rites in love?
Why in your preist then call you that offence
That shines in you, and is your influence?
With this the furies stopt *Leucotes* lips,
Enjoynd by *Venus*, who with Rosie whips 285
Beate the kind Bird. Fierce lightning from her eyes
Did set on fire faire *Heros* sacrifice,
Which was her torne robe, and inforced hayre;
And the bright flame became a mayd most faire
For her aspect: her tresses were of wire, *Description and*
Knit like a net, where harts all set on fire *creation of Dissimula-*
Strugled in pants and could not get release: *tion.*
Her armes were all with golden pincers drest,
And twentie fashioned knots, pullies, and brakes,
And all her bodie girdled with painted Snakes. 295
Her doune parts in a Scorpions taile combinde,
Freckled with twentie colours; pyed wings shinde
Out of her shoulders; Cloth had never die,
Nor sweeter colours never viewed eie,
In scorching *Turkie, Cares, Tartarie,* 300
Than shinde about this spirit notorious;
Nor was *Arachnes* web so glorious.
Of lightning and of shreds she was begot;
More hold in base dissemblers is there not.

106

Her name was *Eronusis*. *Venus* flew 305
From *Heros* sight, and at her Chariot drew
This wondrous creature to so steepe a height,
That all the world she might command with sleight
Of her gay wings: and then she bad her hast,
Since *Hero* had dissembled, and disgrast 310
Her rites so much, and every breast infect
With her deceits; she made her Architect
Of all dissimulation, and since then
Never was any trust in maides nor men.
               O it spighted 315
Fayre *Venus* hart to see her most delighted,
And one she chusde for temper of her minde,
To be the only ruler of her kinde,
So soone to let her virgin race be ended;
Not simply for the fault a whit offended, 320
But that in strife for chastnes with the Moone,
Spiteful *Diana* bad her shew but one,
That was her servant vowd, and liv'd a mayd,
And now she thought to answer that upbrayd,
Hero had lost her answer; who knowes not 325
Venus would seeme as farre from any spot
Of light demeanour, as the very skin
Twixt *Cynthias* browes? Sin is asham'd of Sin.
Up *Venus* flew, and scarce durst up for feare
Of *Phœbes* laughter, when she past her Sphere: 330
And so most ugly clowded was the light,
That day was hid in day; night came ere night,
And *Venus* could not through the thick ayre pierce,
Till the daies king, god of undanted verse,
Because she was so plentifull a theame 335
To such as wore his Lawrell *Anademe*,
Like to a firie bullet made descent,
And from her passage those fat vapours rent,
That being not thoroughly rarefide to raine,

107

Melted like pitch as blew as any vaine, 340
And scalding tempests made the earth to shrinke
Under their fervor, and the world did thinke
In every drop a torturing Spirit flew,
It pierst so deeply, and it burnd so blew.
    Betwixt all this and *Hero*, *Hero* held 345
Leanders picture as a Persian shield:
And she was free from feare of worst successe;
The more ill threats us, we suspect the lesse:
As we grow haples, violence subtle growes,
Dumb, deafe, & blind, & comes when no man knowes. 350

The end of the fourth Sestyad.

THE ARGUMENT OF THE FIFT SESTYAD

> [*Day doubles her accustomd date,*
> *As loth the night, incenst by fate,*
> *Should wrack our lovers;* Heros *plight,*
> *Longs for* Leander, *and the night:*
> *Which ere her thirstie wish recovers,* 5
> *She sends for two betrothed lovers,*
> *And marries them, that (with their crew,*
> *Their sports and ceremonies due)*
> *She covertly might celebrate*
> *With secret joy her owne estate.* 10
> *She makes a feast, at which appeares*
> *The wilde Nymph* Teras, *that still beares*
> *An Ivory Lute, tels Omenous tales,*
> *And sings at solemne festivales.*]

Now was bright *Hero* weary of the day,
Thought an Olympiad in *Leanders* stay.
Sol, and the soft-foote *Howrs* hung on his armes,
And would not let him swim, foreseeing his harmes:
That day *Aurora* double grace obtainde 5

108

Of her love *Phœbus*; she his Horses rainde,
Set on his golden knee, and as she list
She puld him back; and as she puld, she kist
To have him turne to bed; he lov'd her more,
To see the love *Leander Hero* bore.   10
Examples profit much; ten times in one,
In persons full of note, good deedes are done.
  Day was so long, men walking fell asleepe,
The heavie humors that their eyes did steepe,
Made them feare mischiefs. The hard streets were beds   15
For covetous churles, and for ambitious heads,
That spight of Nature would their busines plie.
All thought they had the falling *Epilepsie*,
Men groveld so upon the smotherd ground,
And pittie did the hart of heaven confound.   20
The Gods, the Graces, and the Muses came
Downe to the Destinies, to stay the frame
Of the true lovers deaths, and all worlds teares:
But death before had stopt their cruell eares.
All the Celestials parted mourning then,   25
Pierst with our humane miseries more then men.
Ah, nothing doth the world with mischiefe fill,
But want of feeling one anothers ill.
  With their descent the day grew something fayre,
And cast a brighter robe upon the ayre.   30
Hero to shorten time with merriment,
For yong *Alcmane*, and bright *Mya* sent,
Two lovers that had long crav'd mariage dues
At *Heros* hands: but she did still refuse,
For lovely *Mya* was her consort vowd   35
In her maids state, and therefore not allowd
To amorous Nuptials: yet faire *Hero* now
Intended to dispence with her cold vow,
Since hers was broken, and to marrie her:
The rites would pleasing matter minister   40

To her conceits, and shorten tedious day.
They came; sweet Musick usherd th'odorous way,
And wanton Ayre in twentie sweet forms danst
After her fingers; Beautie and Love advanst
Their ensignes in the downles rosie faces 45
Of youths and maids, led after by the Graces.
For all these *Hero* made a friendly feast,
Welcomd them kindly, did much love protest,
Winning their harts with all the meanes she might,
That when her fault should chance t'abide the light, 50
Their loves might cover or extenuate it,
And high in her worst fate make pittie sit.
　She married them, and in the banquet came
Borne by the virgins: *Hero* striv'd to frame
Her thoughts to mirth. Aye me, but hard it is 55
To imitate a false and forced blis.
Ill may a sad minde forge a merrie face,
Nor hath constrained laughter any grace.
Then layd she wine on cares to make them sinke;
Who feares the threats of fortune, let him drinke. 60
　To these quick Nuptials entred suddenly
Admired *Teras* with the Ebon Thye,
A Nymph that haunted the greene *Sestyan* groves,
And would consort soft virgins in their loves,
At gaysome Triumphs, and on solemne dayes, 65
Singing prophetike Elegies and Layes:
And fingring of a silver Lute she tide
With black and purple skarfs by her left side.
Apollo gave it, and her skill withall,
And she was term'd his Dwarfe she was so small. 70
Yet great in vertue, for his beames enclosde
His vertues in her: never was proposde
Riddle to her, or Augurie, strange or new,
But she resolv'd it: never sleight tale flew
From her charmd lips without important sence, 75

Shewne in some grave succeeding consequence.
  This little Silvane with her songs and tales
Gave such estate to feasts and Nuptiales,
That though oft times she forewent Tragedies,
Yet for her strangenes still she pleasde their eyes,   80
And for her smalnes they admir'd her so,
They thought her perfect borne and could not grow.
  All eyes were on her: *Hero* did command
An Altar deckt with sacred state should stand,
At the Feasts upper end close by the Bride,   85
On which the pretie Nymph might sit espide.
Then all were silent; every one so heares,
As all their sences climbd into their eares:
And first this amorous tale that fitted well
Fayre *Hero* and the Nuptials she did tell: 90

The tale of Teras

Hymen that now is god of Nuptiall rites,
And crownes with honor love and his delights,
Of *Athens* was a youth so sweet of face,
That many thought him of the femall race:
Such quickning brightnes did his cleere eyes dart,   95
Warme went their beames to his beholders hart.
In such pure leagues his beauties were combinde,
That there your Nuptiall contracts first were signde.
For as proportion, white and crimsine, meet
In Beauties mixture, all right cleere, and sweet;   100
The eye responsible, the golden haire,
And none is held without the other faire:
All spring together, all together fade;
Such intermixt affections should invade
Two perfect lovers: which being yet unseene,   105
Their vertues and their comforts copied beene,
In Beauties concord, subject to the eie;

III

And that, in *Hymen*, pleasde so matchleslie,
That lovers were esteemde in their full grace,
Like forme and colour mixt in *Hymens* face; 110
And such sweete concord was thought worthie then
Of torches, musick, feasts, and greatest men:
So *Hymen* lookt, that even the chastest minde
He mov'd to joyne in joyes of sacred kinde:
For onely now his chins first doune consorted 115
His heads rich fleece, in golden curles contorted;
And as he was so lov'd, he lov'd so too,
So should best bewties, bound by Nuptialls doo.
  Bright *Eucharis*, who was by all men saide
The noblest, fayrest, and the richest maide 120
Of all th' *Athenian* damzels, *Hymen* lov'd
With such transmission, that his heart remov'd
From his white brest to hers, but her estate
In passing his was so interminate
For wealth and honor, that his love durst feede 125
On nought but sight and hearing, nor could breede
Hope of requitall, the grand prise of love;
Nor could he heare or see but he must prove
How his rare bewties musick would agree
With maids in consort: therefore robbed he 130
His chin of those same few first fruits it bore,
And clad in such attire as Virgins wore,
He kept them companie, and might right well,
For he did all but *Eucharis* excell
In all the fayre of Beautie: yet he wanted 135
Vertue to make his owne desires implanted
In his deare *Eucharis*; for women never
Love beautie in their sex, but envie ever.
His judgement yet (that durst not suite addresse,
Nor past due meanes presume of due successe) 140
Reason gat fortune in the end to speede
To his best prayes: but strange it seemd indeede,

That fortune should a chast affection blesse,
Preferment seldome graceth bashfulnesse.
Nor grast it *Hymen* yet; but many a dart   145
And many an amorous thought enthrald his hart,
Ere he obtain her; and he sick became,
Forst to abstaine her sight, and then the flame
Rag'd in his bosome. O what griefe did fill him:
Sight made him sick, and want of sight did kill him.   150
The virgins wondred where *Diætia* stayd,
For so did *Hymen* terme himselfe a mayd.
At length with sickly lookes he greeted them:
Tis strange to see gainst what an extreame streame
A lover strives; poore *Hymen* lookt so ill,   155
That as in merit he increased still,
By suffring much, so he in grace decreast.
Women are most wonne when men merit least:
If merit looke not well, love bids stand by,
Loves speciall lesson is to please the eye.   160
And *Hymen* soone recovering all he lost,
Deceiving still these maids, but himselfe most.
His love and he with many virgin dames,
Noble by birth, noble by beauties flames,
Leaving the towne with songs and hallowed lights,   165
To doe great *Ceres Eleusina* rites
Of zealous Sacrifice, were made a pray
To barbarous Rovers that in ambush lay,
And with rude hands enforst their shining spoyle,
Farre from the darkned Citie, tir'd with toyle.   170
And when the yellow issue of the skie
Came trouping forth, jelous of crueltie
To their bright fellowes of this under heaven,
Into a double night they saw them driven,
A horride Cave, the theeves black mansion,   175
Where wearie of the journey they had gon,
Their last nights watch, and drunke with their sweete gains,

Dull *Morpheus* entred, laden with silken chains,
Stronger then iron, and bound the swelling vaines
And tyred sences of these lawles Swaines.　　　　　180
But when the virgin lights thus dimly burnd;
O what a hell was heaven in! how they mournd
And wrung their hands, and wound their gentle forms
Into the shapes of sorrow! Golden storms
Fell from their eyes: As when the Sunne appeares,　185
And yet it raines, so shewd their eyes their teares.
And as when funerall dames watch a dead corse,
Weeping about it, telling with remorse
What paines he felt, how long in paine he lay,
How little food he eate, what he would say;　　　190
And then mixe mournfull tales of others deaths,
Smothering themselves in clowds of their owne breaths;
At length, one cheering other, call for wine,
The golden boale drinks teares out of their eine,
As they drinke wine from it; and round it goes,　195
Each helping other to relieve their woes:
So cast these virgins beauties mutuall raies,
One lights another, face the face displaies;
Lips by reflexion kist, and hands hands shooke,
Even by the whitenes each of other tooke.　　　200
　　But *Hymen* now usde friendly *Morpheus* aide,
Slew every theefe, and rescude every maide.
And now did his enamourd passion take
Hart from his hartie deede, whose worth did make
His hope of bounteous *Eucharis* more strong;　　205
And now came *Love* with *Proteus*, who had long
Inggl'd the little god with prayers and gifts,
Ran through all shapes, and varied all his shifts,
To win *Loves* stay with him, and make him love him:
And when he saw no strength of sleight could move him　210
To make him love, or stay, he nimbly turnd
Into *Loves* selfe, he so extreamely burnd.

114

And thus came *Love* with *Proteus* and his powre,
T'encounter *Eucharis*: first like the flowre
That *Junos* milke did spring, the silver Lillie,   215
He fell on *Hymens* hand, who straight did spie
The bounteous Godhead, and with wondrous joy
Offred it *Eucharis*. She wondrous coy
Drew back her hand: the subtle flowre did woo it,
And drawing it neere, mixt so you could not know it.   220
As two cleere Tapers mixe in one their light,
So did the Lillie and the hand their white:
She viewd it, and her view the forme bestowes
Amongst her spirits: for as colour flowes
From superficies of each thing we see,   225
Even so with colours formes emitted bee:
And where Loves forme is, love is, love is forme;
He entred at the eye, his sacred storme
Rose from the hand, loves sweetest instrument:
It stird her bloods sea so, that high it went,   230
And beate in bashfull waves gainst the white shore
Of her divided cheekes; it rag'd the more,
Because the tide went gainst the haughtie winde
Of her estate and birth: And as we finde
In fainting ebs, the flowrie Zephire hurles   235
The greene-hayrd *Hellespont*, broke in silver curles,
Gainst *Heros* towre: but in his blasts retreate,
The waves obeying him, they after beate,
Leaving the chalkie shore a great way pale,
Then moyst it freshly with another gale: 240
So ebd and flowde the blood in *Eucharis* face,
Coynesse and Love striv'd which had greatest grace.
Virginitie did fight on Coynesse side;
Feare of her parents frownes, and femall pride,
Lothing the lower place more then it loves   245
The high contents desert and vertue moves.
With love fought *Hymens* beautie and his valure,

Which scarce could so much favour yet allure
To come to strike, but fameles idle stood,
Action is firie valours soveraigne good.   250
But Love once entred, wisht no greater ayde
Then he could find within; thought thought betrayd,
The bribde, but incorrupted Garrison
Sung *Io Hymen*; there those songs begun,
And Love was growne so rich with such a gaine,   255
And wanton with the ease of his free raigne,
That he would turne into her roughest frownes
To turne them out; and thus he *Hymen* crownes
King of his thoughts, mans greatest Emperie:
This was his first brave step to deitie.   260
 Home to the morning cittie they repayre,
With newes as holesome as the morning ayre
To the sad parents of each saved maid:
But *Hymen* and his *Eucharis* had laid
This plat, to make the flame of their delight   265
Round as the Moone at full, and full as bright.
 Because the parents of chast *Eucharis*
Exceeding *Hymens* so, might crosse their blis;
And as the world rewards deserts, that law
Cannot assist with force: so when they saw   270
Their daughter safe, take vantage of their owne,
Praise *Hymens* valour much, nothing bestowne:
Hymen must leave the virgins in a Grove
Farre off from *Athens*, and go first to prove
If to restore them all with fame and life,   275
He should enjoy his dearest as his wife.
This told to all the maids, the most agree:
The riper sort knowing what t'is to bee
The first mouth of a newes so farre deriv'd,
And that to heare and beare newes brave folks liv'd,   280
As being a carriage speciall hard to beare
Occurrents, these occurrents being so deare,

116

They did with grace protest, they were content
T'accost their friends with all their complement
For *Hymens* good: but to incurre their harme,   285
There he must pardon them. This wit went warme
To *Adoleshes* braine, a Nymph borne hie,
Made all of voyce and fire, that upwards flie:
Her hart and all her forces neither traine
Climbd to her tongue, and thither fell her braine,   290
Since it could goe no higher, and it must go:
All powers she had, even her tongue, did so.
In spirit and quicknes she much joy did take,
And lov'd her tongue, only for quicknes sake,
And she would hast and tell. The rest all stay,   295
Hymen goes on(e), the Nymph another way:
And what became of her Ile tell at last:
Yet take her visage now: moyst lipt, long fa'st,
Thin like an iron wedge, so sharpe and tart,
As twere of purpose made to cleave *Loves* hart.   300
Well were this lovely Beautie rid of her,
And *Hymen* did at *Athens* now prefer
His welcome suite, which he with joy aspirde:
A hundred princely youths with him retirde
To fetch the Nymphs: Chariots and Musick went,   305
And home they came: heaven with applauses rent.
The Nuptials straight proceed, whiles all the towne
Fresh in their joyes might doe them most renowne.
First gold-lockt *Hymen* did to Church repaire,
Like a quick offring burnd in flames of haire.   310
And after, with a virgin firmament,
The Godhead-proving Bride attended went
Before them all; she lookt in her command,
As if forme-giving *Cyprias* silver hand
Gripte all their beauties, and crusht out one flame,   315
She blusht to see how beautie overcame
The thoughts of all men. Next before her went

Five lovely children deckt with ornament
Of her sweet colours, bearing Torches by,
For light was held a happie Augurie   320
Of generation, whose efficient right
Is nothing else but to produce to light.
The od disparent number they did chuse,
To shew the union married loves should use,
Since in two equall parts it will not sever,   325
But the midst holds one to rejoyne it ever,
As common to both parts: men therefore deeme,
That equall number Gods doe not esteeme,
Being authors of sweet peace and unitie,
But pleasing to th'infernall Emperie,   330
Under whose ensignes Wars and Discords fight,
Since an even number you may disunite
In two parts equall, nought in middle left,
To reunite each part from other reft:
And five they hold in most especiall prise,   335
Since t'is the first od number that doth rise
From the two formost numbers unitie
That od and even are; which are two, and three,
For one no number is: but thence doth flow
The powerfull race of number. Next did go   340
A noble Matron that did spinning beare
A huswifes rock and spindle, and did weare
A Weathers skin, with all the snowy fleece,
To intimate that even the daintiest peece,
And noblest borne dame should industrious bee: 345
That which does good disgraceth no degree.
    And now to *Junos* Temple they are come,
Where her grave Priest stood in the mariage rome.
On his right arme did hang a skarlet vaile,
And from his shoulders to the ground did traile,   350
On either side, Ribands of white and blew;
With the red vaile he hid the bashfull hew

Of the chast Bride, to shew the modest shame,
In coupling with a man should grace a dame.
Then tooke he the disparent Silks, and tide   355
The Lovers by the wasts, and side to side,
In token that thereafter they must binde
In one selfe sacred knot each others minde.
Before them on an Altar he presented
Both fire and water: which was first invented,   360
Since to ingenerate every humane creature,
And every other birth produ'st by Nature,
Moysture and heate must mixe: so man and wife
For humane race must joyne in Nuptiall life.
Then one of *Junos* Birds, the painted Jay,   365
He sacrifisde, and tooke the gall away.
All which he did behinde the Altar throw,
In signe no bitternes of hate should grow
Twixt maried loves, nor any least disdaine.
Nothing they spake, for twas esteemd too plaine   370
For the most silken mildnes of a maid,
To let a publique audience heare it said
She boldly tooke the man: and so respected
Was bashfulnes in *Athens*: it erected
To chast *Agneia*, which is Shamefastnesse,   375
A sacred Temple, holding her a Goddesse.
And now to Feasts, Masks, and triumphant showes,
The shining troupes returnd, even till earths throwes
Brought forth with joy the thickest part of night,
When the sweet Nuptiall song that usde to cite   380
All to their rest, was by *Phemonoe* sung,
First *Delphian* Prophetesse, whose graces sprung
Out of the *Muses* well: she sung before
The Bride into her chamber: at which dore
A Matron and a Torch-bearer did stand;   385
A painted box of Confits in her hand
The Matron held, and so did other some

119

That compast round the honourd Nuptiall rome.
The custome was that every maid did weare,
During her maidenhead, a silken Sphere 390
About her waste, above her inmost weede,
Knit with *Minervas* knot, and that was freede
By the faire Bridegrome on the mariage night,
With many ceremonies of delight:
And yet eternisde *Hymens* tender Bride, 395
To suffer it dissolv'd so sweetly cride.
The maids that heard so lov'd, and did adore her,
They wisht with all their hearts to suffer for her.
So had the Matrons, that with Confits stood
About the chamber, such affectionate blood, 400
And so true feeling of her harmeles paines,
That every one a showre of Confits raines.
For which the Brideyouths scrambling on the ground,
In noyse of that sweet haile her cryes were drownd.
And thus blest *Hymen* joyde his gracious Bride, 405
And for his joy was after deifide.
  The Saffron mirror by which *Phœbus* love,
Greene *Tellus* decks her, now he held above
The clowdy mountaines: and the noble maide,
Sharp-visag'd *Adolesche*, that was straide 410
Out of her way, in hasting with her newes,
Not till this houre th' *Athenian* turrets viewes,
And now brought home by guides, she heard by all
That her long kept occurrents would be stale,
And how faire *Hymens* honors did excell 415
For those rare newes, which she came short to tell.
To heare her deare tongue robd of such a joy
Made the well-spoken Nymph take such a toy,
That downe she sunke: when lightning from above
Shrunk her leane body, and for meere free love, 420
Turnd her into the pied-plum'd *Psittacus*,
That now the Parrat is surnam'd by us,

Who still with counterfeit confusion prates
Nought but newes common to the commonst mates.
This tolde, strange *Teras* toucht her Lute and sung   425
This dittie, that the Torchie evening sprung.

Epithalamion Teratos

Come, come deare night, Loves Mart of kisses,
Sweet close of his ambitious line,
The fruitfull summer of his blisses,
Loves glorie doth in darknes shine.   430
O come soft rest of Cares, come night,
Come naked vertues only tire,
The reaped harvest of the light,
Bound up in sheaves of sacred fire.
   Love cals to warre,   435
   Sighs his Alarmes,
   Lips his swords are,
   The field his Armes.
Come Night and lay thy velvet hand
On glorious Dayes outfacing face;   440
And all thy crouned flames command
For Torches to our Nuptiall grace.
   Love cals to warre,
   Sighs his Alarmes,
   Lips his swords are,   445
   The field his Armes.
No neede have we of factious Day,
To cast in envie of thy peace
Her bals of Discord in thy way:
Here beauties day doth never cease,   450
Day is abstracted here,
And varied in a triple sphere.
Hero, Alcmane, Mya so outshine thee,
Ere thou come here let *Thetis* thrice refine thee.

Love cals to warre, 455
Sighs his Alarmes,
Lips his swords are,
The field his Armes.
The Evening starre I see:
Rise youths, the Evening starre 460
Helps Love to summon warre,
Both now imbracing bee.
Rise youths, loves right claims more then banquets, rise.
Now the bright Marygolds that deck the skies,
Phœbus celestiall flowrs, that (contrarie 465
To his flowers here) ope when he shuts his eie,
And shuts when he doth open, crowne your sports:
Now love in night, and night in love exhorts
Courtship and Dances: All your parts employ,
And suite nights rich expansure with your joy, 470
Love paints his longings in sweet virgins eyes:
Rise youths, loves right claims more then banquets, rise.
Rise virgins, let fayre Nuptiall loves enfolde
Your fruitles breasts: the maidenheads ye holde
Are not your owne alone, but parted are; 475
Part in disposing them your Parents share,
And that a third part is: so must ye save
Your loves a third, and you your thirds must have.
Love paints his longings in sweet virgins eyes:
Rise youths, loves right claims more then banquets, rise. 480

Herewith the amorous spirit that was so kinde
To *Teras* haire, and combd it downe with winde,
Still as it Comet-like brake from her braine,
Would needes have *Teras* gone, and did refraine
To blow it downe: which staring up, dismaid 485
The timorous feast, and she no longer staid:
But bowing to the Bridegrome and the Bride,
Did like a shooting exhalation glide

Out of their sights: the turning of her back
Made them all shrieke, it lookt so ghastly black.   490
O haples *Hero*, that most haples clowde
Thy soone-succeeding Tragedie foreshowde.
Thus all the Nuptiall crew to joyes depart,
But much-wrongd *Hero* stood Hels blackest dart:
Whose wound because I grieve so to display,   495
I use digressions thus t'encrease the day.

The end of the fift Sestyad.

THE ARGUMENT OF THE SIXT SESTYAD

> [*Leucote flyes to all the windes,*
> *And from the fates their outrage bindes,*
> *That* Hero *and her love may meete.*
> *Leander (with* Loves *compleate Fleete*
> *Mand in himselfe) puts forth to Seas,*   5
> *When straight the ruthles Destinies*
> *With* Ate *stirre the windes to warre*
> *Upon the* Hellespont: *Their jarre*
> *Drownes poore* Leander. Heros *eyes,*
> *Wet witnesses of his surprise,*   10
> *Her Torch blowne out, Griefe casts her downe*
> *Upon her love, and both doth drowne.*
> *In whose just ruth the God of Seas*
> *Transformes them to th' Acanthides.*]

No longer could the day nor Destinies
Delay the night, who now did frowning rise
Into her Throne; and at her humorous brests
Visions and Dreames lay sucking: all mens rests
Fell like the mists of death upon their eyes,   5
Dayes too long darts so kild their faculties.
The windes yet, like the flowrs to cease began:
For bright *Leucote*, *Venus* whitest Swan,

That held sweet *Hero* deare, spread her fayre wings,
Like to a field of snow, and message brings 10
From *Venus* to the Fates, t'entreate them lay
Their charge upon the windes their rage to stay,
That the sterne battaile of the Seas might cease,
And guard *Leander* to his love in peace.
The Fates consent, (aye me dissembling Fates) 15
They shewd their favours to conceale their hates,
And draw *Leander* on, least Seas too hie
Should stay his too obsequious destinie:
Who like a fleering slavish Parasite,
In warping profit or a traiterous sleight, 20
Hoopes round his rotten bodie with devotes,
And pricks his decant face full of false notes,
Praysing with open throte (and othes as fowle
As his false heart) the beautie of an Owle,
Kissing his skipping hand with charmed skips, 25
That cannot leave, but leapes upon his lips
Like a cock-sparrow, or a shameles queane
Sharpe at a red-lipt youth, and nought doth meane
Of all his antick shewes, but doth repayre
More tender fawnes, and takes a scattred hayre 30
From his tame subjects shoulder; whips, and cals
For every thing he lacks; creepes gainst the wals
With backward humblesse, to give needles way:
Thus his false fate did with *Leander* play.

First to black *Eurus* flies the white *Leucote*, 35
Borne mongst the *Negros* in the *Levant* Sea,
On whose curld head the glowing Sun doth rise, ⎫
And shewes the soveraigne will of Destinies, ⎬
To have him cease his blasts, and downe he lies. ⎭
Next, to the fennie *Notus* course she holds, 40
And found him leaning with his armes in folds
Upon a rock, his white hayre full of showres,
And him she chargeth by the fatall powres,

124

To hold in his wet cheekes his clowdie voyce.
To *Zephire* then that doth in flowres rejoyce. 45
To snake-foote *Boreas* next she did remove,
And found him tossing of his ravisht love,
To heate his frostie bosome hid in snow,
Who with *Leucotes* sight did cease to blow.
Thus all were still to *Heros* harts desire, 50
Who with all speede did consecrate a fire
Of flaming Gummes, and comfortable Spice,
To light her Torch, which in such curious price
She held, being object to *Leanders* sight,
That nought but fires perfum'd must give it light. 55
She lov'd it so, she griev'd to see it burne,
Since it would waste and soone to ashes turne:
Yet if it burnd not, twere not worth her eyes,
What made it nothing, gave it all the prize.
Sweet Torch, true Glasse of our societie; 60
What man does good, but he consumes thereby?
But thou wert lov'd for good, held high, given show:
Poore vertue loth'd for good, obscur'd, held low.
Doe good, be pinde; be deedles good, disgrast:
Unles we feede on men, we let them fast. 65
Yet *Hero* with these thoughts her Torch did spend.
When Bees makes waxe, Nature doth not intend
It shall be made a Torch: but we that know
The proper vertue of it make it so,
And when t'is made we light it: nor did Nature 70
Propose one life to maids, but each such creature
Makes by her soule the best of her free state,
Which without love is rude, disconsolate,
And wants loves fire to make it milde and bright,
Till when, maids are but Torches wanting light. 75
Thus gainst our griefe, not cause of griefe we fight,
The right of nought is gleande, but the delight.
Up went she, but to tell how she descended,

Would God she were not dead, or my verse ended.
She was the rule of wishes, summe and end   80
For all the parts that did on love depend:
Yet cast the Torch his brightnes further forth;
But what shines neerest best, holds truest worth.
Leander did not through such tempests swim
To kisse the Torch, although it lighted him: 85
But all his powres in her desires awaked,
Her love and vertues cloth'd him richly naked.
Men kisse but fire that only shewes pursue,
Her Torch and *Hero*, figure shew and vertue.
    Now at opposde *Abydus* nought was heard,   90
But bleating flocks, and many a bellowing herd,
Slaine for the Nuptials, cracks of falling woods,
Blowes of broad axes, powrings out of floods.
The guiltie *Hellespont* was mixt and stainde
With bloodie Torrents, that the shambles raind;   95
Not arguments of feast, but shewes that bled,
Foretelling that red night that followed.
More blood was spilt, more honors were addrest,
Then could have graced any happie feast.
Rich banquets, triumphs, every pomp employes   100
His sumptuous hand: no misers nuptiall joyes.
Ayre felt continuall thunder with the noyse,
Made in the generall mariage violence:
And no man knew the cause of this expence,
But the two haples Lords, *Leanders* Sire,   105
And poore *Leander*, poorest where the fire
Of credulous love made him most rich surmisde.
As short was he of that himselfe he prisde,
As is an emptie Gallant full of forme,
That thinks each looke an act, each drop a storme, 110
That fals from his brave breathings; most brought up
In our *Metropolis*, and hath his cup
Brought after him to feasts; and much Palme beares,

For his rare judgement in th'attire he weares,
Hath seene the hot Low Countries, not their heat, 115
Observes their rampires and their buildings yet.
And for your sweet discourse with mouthes is heard,
Giving instructions with his very beard.
Hath gone with an Ambassadour, and been
A great mans mate in travailing, even to *Rhene*, 120
And then puts all his worth in such a face,
As he saw brave men make, and strives for grace
To get his newes forth; as when you descrie
A ship with all her sayle contends to flie
Out of the narrow Thames with windes unapt, 125
Now crosseth here, then there, then this way rapt,
And then hath one point reacht; then alters all,
And to another crooked reach doth fall
Of halfe a burdbolts shoote; keeping more coyle,
Then if she danst upon the Oceans toyle: 130
So serious is his trifling companie,
In all his swelling ship of vacantrie.
And so short of himselfe in his high thought.
Was our *Leander* in his fortunes brought
And in his fort of love that he thought won, 135
But otherwise he skornes comparison.
   O sweet *Leander*, thy large worth I hide
In a short grave; ill favourd stormes must chide
Thy sacred favour; I in floods of inck
Must drowne they graces, which white papers drink, 140
Even as thy beauties did the foule black Seas:
I must describe the hell of thy disease,
That heaven did merit: yet I needes must see
Our painted fooles and cockhorse Pessantrie
Still still usurp, with long lives, loves, and lust, 145
The seates of vertue, cutting short as dust
Her deare bought issue; ill to worse converts,
And tramples in the blood of all deserts.

Night close and silent now goes fast before
The Captaines and their souldiers to the shore,   150
On whom attended the appointed Fleete
At *Sestus* Bay, that should *Leander* meete,
Who fainde he in another ship would passe:
Which must not be, for no one meane there was
To get his love home, but the course he tooke.   155
Forth did his beautie for his beautie looke,
And saw her through her Torch, as you beholde
Sometimes within the Sunne a face of golde,
Form'd in strong thoughts, by that traditions force,
That saies a God sits there and guides his course.   160
His sister was with him, to whom he shewd
His guide by Sea: and sayd: Oft have you viewd
In one heaven many starres, but never yet
In one starre many heavens till now were met.
See lovely sister, see, now *Hero* shines   165
No heaven but her appeares: each star repines,
And all are clad in clowdes, as if they mournd,
To be by influence of Earth out-burnd.
Yet doth she shine, and teacheth vertues traine,
Still to be constant in Hels blackest raigne,   170
Though even the gods themselves do so entreat them
As they did hate, and Earth as she would eate them.
   Off went his silken robe, and in he leapt;
Whom the kinde waves so licorously cleapt,
Thickning for haste one in another so,   175
To kisse his skin, that he might almost go
To *Heros* Towre, had that kind minuit lasted.
But now the cruell fates with *Ate* hasted
To all the windes, and made them battaile fight
Upon the *Hellespont*, for eithers right   180
Pretended to the windie monarchie.
And forth they brake, the Seas mixt with the skie,
And tost distrest *Leander*, being in hell,

128

As high as heaven; Blisse not in height doth dwell.
The Destinies sate dancing on the waves,   185
To see the glorious windes with mutuall braves
Consume each other: O true glasse to see,
How ruinous ambitious Statists bee
To their owne glories! Poore *Leander* cried
For help to Sea-borne *Venus*; she denied: 190
To *Boreas*, that for his *Atthæas* sake,
He would some pittie on his *Hero* take,
And for his owne loves sake, on his desires:
But Glorie never blowes cold Pitties fires.
Then calde he *Neptune*, who through all the noise   195
Knew with affright his wrackt *Leanders* voice:
And up he rose, for haste his forehead hit
Gainst heavens hard Christall; his proud waves he smit
With his forkt scepter, that could not obay,
Much greater powers then *Neptunes* gave them sway.   200
They lov'd *Leander* so, in groanes they brake
When they came neere him; and such space did take
Twixt one another, loth to issue on,
That in their shallow furrowes earth was shone,
And the poore lover tooke a little breath: 205
But the curst Fates sate spinning of his death
On every wave, and with the servile windes
Tumbled them on him: And now *Hero* findes
By that she felt her deare *Leanders* state.
She wept and prayed for him to every fate,   210
And every winde that whipt her with her haire
About the face she kist and spake it faire,
Kneeld to it, gave it drinke out of her eyes
To quench his thirst: but still their cruelties
Even her poore Torch envied, and rudely beate   215
The bating flame from that deare foode it eate:
Deare, for it nourisht her *Leanders* life,
Which with her robe she rescude from their strife:

129

But silke too soft was, such hard hearts to breake,
And she deare soule, even as her silke, faint, weake   220
Could not preserve it: out, O out it went.
Leander still cald *Neptune*, that now rent
His brackish curles, and tore his wrinckled face ⎤
Where teares in billowes did each other chace,   ⎬
And (burst with ruth) he hurld his marble Mace ⎦   225
At the sterne Fates: it wounded *Lachesis*
That drew *Leanders* thread, and could not misse
The thread it selfe, as it her hand did hit,
But smote it full and quite did sunder it.
The more kinde *Neptune* rag'd, the more he raste   230
His loves lives fort, and kild as he embraste.
Anger doth still his owne mishap encrease;
If any comfort live, it is in peace.
O theevish Fates, to let Blood, Flesh, and Sence ⎤
Build two fayre Temples for their Excellence,   ⎬   235
To rob it with a poysoned influence.   ⎦
Though soules gifts starve, the bodies are held dear
In ugliest things; Sence-sport preserves a Beare.
But here nought serves our turnes; O heaven & earth,
How most most wretched is our humane birth?   240
And now did all the tyrannous crew depart,
Knowing there was a storme in *Heros* hart,
Greater then they could make, & skornd their smart.
She bowd her selfe so low out of her Towre,
That wonder twas she fell not ere her howre,   245
With searching the lamenting waves for him;
Like a poore Snayle, her gentle supple lim
Hung on her Turrets top so most downe right,
As she would dive beneath the darknes quite,
To finde her Jewell; Jewell, her *Leander*,   250
A name of all earths Jewels pleasde not her,
Like his deare name: *Leander*, still my choice,
Come nought but my *Leander*; Of my voice

130

Turne to *Leander*: hence-forth be all sounds,
Accents, and phrases that shew all griefes wounds,   255
Analisde in *Leander*. O black change!
Trumpets doe you with thunder of your clange,
Drive out this changes horror, my voyce faints:
Where all joy was, now shrieke out all complaints.
Thus cryed she, for her mixed soule could tell   260
Her love was dead: And when the morning fell
Prostrate upon the weeping earth for woe,
Blushes that bled out of her cheekes did show
Leander brought by *Neptune*, brusde and torne
With Cities ruines he to Rocks had worne,   265
To filthie usering Rocks that would have blood,
Though they could get of him no other good.
She saw him, and the sight was much much more,
Then might have serv'd to kill her; should her store
Of giant sorrowes speake? Burst, dye, bleede,   270
And leave poore plaints to us that shall succeede.
She fell on her loves bosome, hugg'd it fast,
And with *Leanders* name she breath'd her last.
   Neptune for pittie in his armes did take them,
Flung them into the ayre, and did awake them.   275
Like two sweet birds surnam'd th' *Acanthides*,
Which we call Thistle-warps, that neere no Seas
Dare ever come, but still in couples flie,
And feede on Thistle tops, to testifie
The hardnes of their first life in their last: 280
The first in thornes of love, and sorrowes past,
And so most beautifull their colours show,
As none (so little) like them: her sad brow
A sable velvet feather covers quite,
Even like the forehead cloths that in the night,   285
Or when they sorrow, Ladies use to weare:
Their wings blew, red and yellow mixt appeare,
Colours, that as we construe colours paint

L.E.P.—5*

Their states to life; the yellow shewes their saint,
The devill *Venus*, left them; blew their truth,   290
The red and black, ensignes of death and ruth.
And this true honor from their love-deaths sprung,
They were the first that ever Poet sung.

FINIS

The Progresse of the Soule

INFINITATI SACRUM,

16 Augusti 1601.

Metempsychosis

Poêma Satyricon

EPISTLE

Others at the Porches and entries of their Buildings set their Armes; I, my picture; if any colours can deliver a minde so plaine, and flat, and through light as mine. Naturally at a new Author, I doubt, and sticke, and doe not quickly say, good. I censure much and taxe; And this liberty costs mee more then others, by how much my owne things are worse then others. Yet I would not be so rebellious against my selfe, as not to doe it, since I love it; nor so unjust to others, as to do it *sine talione*. As long as I give them as good hold upon mee, they must pardon mee my bitings. I forbid no reprehender, but him that like the Trent Councell forbids not bookes, but Authors, damning what ever such a name hath or shall write. None writes so ill, that he gives not some thing exemplary, to follow, or flie. Now when I beginne this booke, I have no purpose to come into any mans debt; how my stocke will hold out I know not; perchance waste, perchance increase in use; if I doe borrow any thing of Antiquitie, besides that I make account that I pay it to posterity, with as much and as good: You shall still finde mee to acknowledge it, and to thanke not him onely that hath digg'd out treasure for mee, but that hath lighted mee a candle to the place. All which I will bid you remember, (for I would have no such Readers as I can teach) is, that the Pithagorian doctrine doth not onely carry one soule from man to man, nor man to beast, but indifferently to plants also: and therefore you must not grudge to finde the same soule in an Emperour, in a Post-horse, and in a Mucheron, since no unreadinesse in the soule, but an indisposition in the organs workes this. And therefore though this soule could not move when it was a Melon, yet it may remember, and now tell mee, at what lascivious banquet it was serv'd. And though it could not speake, when it was a spider, yet it can remember, and now tell me, who used it for poyson to attaine dignitie. How ever the bodies have dull'd her other faculties, her memory hath ever been her owne, which makes me so seriously deliver you by her relation all her passages from her first making, when shee was that apple which Eve eate, to this time when shee is hee, whose life you shall finde in the end of this booke.

The Progresse of the Soule

First Song

I

I SING the progresse of a deathlesse soule,
Whom Fate, which God made, but doth not controule,
Plac'd in most shapes; all times before the law
Yoak'd us, and when, and since, in this I sing.
And the great world t'his aged evening,   5
From infant morne, through manly noone I draw.
What the gold Chaldee,' or silver Persian saw,
Greeke brasse, or Roman iron, is in this one;
A worke t'outweare *Seths* pillars, bricke and stone,
   And (holy writt excepted) made to yeeld to none.   10

II

Thee, eye of heaven, this great Soule envies not,
By thy male force, is all wee have, begot.
In the first East, thou now beginst to shine,
Suck'st early balme, and Iland spices there,
And wilt anon in thy loose-rein'd careere   15
At Tagus, Po, Sene, Thames, and Danow dine,
And see at night thy Westerne land of Myne,
Yet hast thou not more nations seene then shee,
That before thee, one day beganne to bee,
And thy fraile light being quench'd, shall long, long out live
   thee.   20

III

Nor holy *Janus* in whose soveraigne boate
The Church, and all the Monarchies did floate;
That swimming Colledge, and free Hospitall
Of all mankinde, that cage and vivarie
Of fowles, and beasts, in whose wombe, Destinie   25
Us, and our latest nephewes did install
(For thence are all deriv'd, that fill this All,)
Did'st thou in that great stewardship embarke
So diverse shapes into that floating parke,
As have beene mov'd, and inform'd by this heavenly
    sparke.   30

IV

Great Destiny the Commissary of God,
That hast mark'd out a path and period
For every thing; who, where wee of-spring tooke,
Our wayes and ends seest at one instant; Thou
Knot of all causes, thou whose changelesse brow   35
Ne'r smiles nor frownes, O vouch thou safe to looke
And shew my story,' in thy eternall booke;
That (if my prayer be fit) I may'understand
So much my selfe, as to know with what hand,
    How scant, or liberall this my lifes race is spand.   40

V

To my sixe lustres almost now outwore,
Except thy booke owe mee so many more,
Except my legend be free from the letts
Of steepe ambition, sleepie povertie,
Spirit-quenching sicknesse, dull captivitie,   45
Distracting businesse, and from beauties nets,
And all that calls from this, and t'other whets,
O let me not launch out, but let mee save

136

Th'expense of braine and spirit; that my grave
   His right and due, a whole unwasted man may have.   50

VI

But if my dayes be long, and good enough,
In vaine this sea shall enlarge, or enrough
It selfe; for I will through the wave, and fome,
And shall, in sad lone wayes a lively spright,
Make my darke heavy Poëm light, and light.   55
For though through many streights, and lands I roame,
I launch at paradise, and saile toward home;
The course I there began, shall here be staid,
Sailes hoised there, stroke here, and anchors laid
   In Thames, which were at Tigrys, and Euphrates waide.   60

VII

For this great soule which here amongst us now
Doth dwell, and moves that hand, and tongue, and brow,
Which, as the Moone the sea, moves us; to heare
Whose story, with long patience you will long;
(For 'tis the crowne, and last straine of my song)   65
This soule to whom *Luther*, and *Mahomet* were
Prisons of flesh; this soule which oft did teare,
And mend the wracks of th'Empire, and late Rome,
And liv'd where every great change did come,
   Had first in paradise, a low, but fatall roome.   70

VIII

Yet no low roome, nor then the greatest, lesse,
If (as devout and sharpe men fitly guesse)
That Crosse, our joy, and griefe, where nailes did tye
That All, which alwayes was all, every where;
Which could not sinne, and yet all sinnes did beare;   75
Which could not die, yet could not chuse but die;
Stood in the selfe same roome in Calvarie,

Where first grew the forbidden learned tree,
For on that tree hung in security
   This soule, made by the Makers will from pulling free.   80

IX

Prince of the orchard, faire as dawning morne,
Fenc'd with the law, and ripe as soone as borne
That apple grew, which this Soule did enlive,
Till the then climing serpent, that now creeps
For that offence, for which all mankinde weepes,   85
Tooke it, and t'her whom the first man did wive
(Whom and her race, only forbiddings drive)
He gave it, she, t'her husband, both did eate;
So perished the eaters, and the meate:
   And wee (for treason taints the blood) thence die and
      sweat.   90

X

Man all at once was there by woman slaine,
And one by one we'are here slaine o'er againe
By them. The mother poison'd the well-head,
The daughters here corrupt us, Rivulets;
No smalnesse scapes, no greatnesse breaks their nets;   95
She thrust us out, and by them we are led
Astray, from turning, to whence we are fled.
Were prisoners Judges, 'twould seeme rigorous,
Shee sinn'd, we beare; part of our paine is, thus
   To love them, whose fault to this painfull love yoak'd us.   100

XI

So fast in us doth this corruption grow,
That now wee dare aske why wee should be so.
Would God (disputes the curious Rebell) make
A law, and would not have it kept? Or can
His creatures will, crosse his? Of every man   105

138

For one, will God (and be just) vengeance take?
Who sinn'd? 'twas not forbidden to the snake
Nor her, who was not then made; nor is't writ
That Adam cropt, or knew the apple; yet
   The worme and she, and he, and wee endure for it.   110

XII

But snatch mee heavenly Spirit from this vaine
Reckoning their vanities, lesse is the gaine
Then hazard still, to meditate on ill,
Though with good minde; their reasons, like those toyes
Of glassie bubbles, which the gamesome boyes   115
Stretch to so nice a thinnes through a quill
That they themselves breake, doe themselves spill:
Arguing is heretiques game, and Exercise
As wrastlers, perfects them; Not liberties
   Of speech, but silence; hands, not tongues, end heresies.   120

XIII

Just in that instant when the serpents gripe,
Broke the slight veines, and tender conduit-pipe,
Through which this soule from the trees root did draw
Life, and growth to this apple, fled away
This loose soule, old, one and another day.   125
As lightning, which one scarce dares say, he saw,
'Tis so soone gone, (and better proofe the law
Of sense, then faith requires) swiftly she flew
T'a darke and foggie Plot; Her, her fate threw
   There through th'earths pores, and in a Plant hous'd
     her anew.   130

XIV

The plant thus abled, to it selfe did force
A place, where no place was; by natures course
As aire from water, water fleets away

From thicker bodies, by this root throng'd so
His spungie confines gave him place to grow: 135
Just as in our streets, when the people stay
To see the Prince, and have so fill'd the way
That weesels scarce could passe, when she comes nere
They throng and cleave up, and a passage cleare,
    As if, for that time, their round bodies flatned were. 140

XV

His right arme he thrust out towards the East,
West-ward his left; th'ends did themselves digest
Into ten lesser strings, these fingers were:
And as a slumberer stretching on his bed,
This way he this, and that way scattered 145
His other legge, which feet with toes upbeare.
Grew on his middle parts, the first day, haire,
To show, that in loves businesse hee should still
A dealer bee, and be us'd well, or ill:
    His apples kindle, his leaves, force of conception kill. 150

XVI

A mouth, but dumbe, he hath; blinde eyes, deafe eares,
And to his shoulders dangle subtile haires;
A young *Colossus* there hee stands upright,
And as that ground by him were conquered
A leafie garland weares he on his head 155
Enchas'd with little fruits, so red and bright
That for them you would call your Loves lips white;
So, of a lone unhaunted place possest,
Did this soules second Inne, built by the guest,
    This living buried man, this quiet mandrake, rest. 160

XVII

No lustfull woman came this plant to grieve,
But 'twas because there was none yet but Eve:

140

And she (with other purpose) kill'd it quite;
Her sinne had now brought in infirmities,
And so her cradled child, the moist red eyes   165
Had never shut, nor slept since it saw light;
Poppie she knew, she knew the mandrakes might,
And tore up both, and so coold her childs blood;
Unvirtuous weeds might long unvex'd have stood;
   But hee's short liv'd, that with his death can doe most
    good.   170

XVIII

To an unfetterd soules quick nimble hast
Are falling stars, and hearts thoughts, but slow pac'd:
Thinner then burnt aire flies this soule, and she
Whom foure new comming, and foure parting Suns
Had found, and left the Mandrakes tenant, runnes   175
Thoughtlesse of change, when her firme destiny
Confin'd, and enjayld her, that seem'd so free,
Into a small blew shell, the which a poore
Warme bird orespread, and sat still evermore,
   Till her enclos'd child kickt, and peck'd it selfe a dore.   180

XIX

Outcrept a sparrow, this soules moving Inne,
On whose raw armes stiffe feathers now begin,
As childrens teeth through gummes, to breake with paine,
His flesh is jelly yet, and his bones threds,
All a new downy mantle overspreads;   185
A mouth he opes, which would as much containe
As his late house, and the first houre speaks plaine,
And chirps alowd for meat. Meat fit for men
His father steales for him, and so feeds then
   One, that within a month, will beate him from his hen.   190

XX

In this worlds youth wise nature did make hast,
Things ripen'd sooner, and did longer last;
Already this hot cocke, in bush and tree,
In field and tent, oreflutters his next hen;
He asks her not, who did so tast, nor when,   195
Nor if his sister, or his neece shee be;
Nor doth she pule for his inconstancie
If in her sight he change, nor doth refuse
The next that calls; both liberty doe use;
   Where store is of both kindes, both kindes may freely
     chuse.   200

XXI

Men, till they tooke laws which made freedome lesse,
Their daughters, and their sisters did ingresse;
Till now unlawfull, therefore ill, 'twas not.
So jolly, that it can move, this soule is,
The body so free of his kindnesses,   205
That selfe preserving it hath now forgot,
And slackneth so the soules, and bodies knot,
Which temperance streightens; freely'on his she friends
He blood, and spirit, pith, and marrow spends,
   Ill steward of himself, himselfe in three yeares ends.   210

XXII

Else might he long have liv'd; man did not know
Of gummie blood, which doth in holly grow,
How to make bird-lime, nor how to deceive
With faind calls, hid nets, or enwrapping snare,
The free inhabitants of the Plyant aire.   215
Man to beget, and woman to conceive
Askt not of rootes, nor of cock-sparrowes, leave:
Yet chuseth hee, though none of these he feares,
Pleasantly three, then streightned twenty yeares
   To live, and to encrease his race, himselfe outweares.   220

XXIII

This cole with overblowing quench'd and dead,
The Soule from her too active organs fled
T'a brooke; A female fishes sandie Roe
With the males jelly, newly lev'ned was,
For they had intertouch'd as they did passe,   225
And one of those small bodies, fitted so,
This soule inform'd, and abled it to rowe
It selfe with finnie oares, which she did fit:
Her scales seem'd yet of parchment, and as yet
 Perchance a fish, but by no name you could call it. 230

XXIV

When goodly, like a ship in her full trim,
A swan, so white that you may unto him
Compare all whitenesse, but himselfe to none,
Glided along, and as he glided watch'd,
And with his arched necke this poore fish catch'd.   235
It mov'd with state, as if to looke upon
Low things it scorn'd, and yet before that one
Could thinke he sought it, he had swallow'd cleare
This, and much such, and unblam'd devour'd there
 All, but who too swift, too great, or well armed were. 240

XXV

Now swome a prison in a prison put,
And now this Soule in double walls was shut,
Till melted with the Swans digestive fire,
She left her house the fish, and vapour'd forth;
Fate not affording bodies of more worth   245
For her as yet, bids her againe retire
T'another fish, to any new desire
Made a new prey; For, he that can to none
Resistance make, nor complaint, sure is gone.
 Weaknesse invites, but silence feasts oppression. 250

XXVI

Pace with her native streame, this fish doth keepe,
And journeyes with her, towards the glassie deepe,
But oft retarded, once with a hidden net
Though with great windowes, for when Need first taught
These tricks to catch food, then they were not wrought   255
As now, with curious greedineese to let
None scape, but few, and fit for use, to get,
As, in this trap a ravenous pike was tane,
Who, though himselfe distrest, would faine have slain
   This wretch; So hardly are ill habits left again.   260

XXVII

Here by her smallnesse shee two deaths orepast,
Once innocence scap'd, and left th'oppressor fast.
The net through-swome, she keepes the liquid path,
And whether she leape up sometimes to breath
And suck in aire, or finde it underneath,   265
Or working parts like mills or limbecks hath
To make the water thinne and airelike, faith
Cares not; but safe the place she's come unto
Where fresh, with salt waves meet, and what to doe
   She knowes not, but betweene both makes a boord or
   two.   270

XXVIII

So farre from hiding her guests, water is,
That she showes them in bigger quantities
Then they are. Thus doubtfull of her way,
For game and not for hunger a sea Pie
Spied through this traiterous spectacle, from high,   275
The seely fish where it disputing lay,
And t'end her doubts and her, beares her away:
Exalted she'is, but to th'exalters good,
As are by great ones, men which lowly stood.
   It's rais'd, to be the Raisers instrument and food.   280

144

XXIX

Is any kinde subject to rape like fish?
Ill unto man, they neither doe, nor wish:
Fishers they kill not, nor with noise awake,
They doe not hunt, nor strive to make a prey
Of beasts, nor their yong sonnes to beare away;   285
Foules they pursue not, nor do undertake
To spoile the nests industrious birds do make;
Yet them all these unkinde kinds feed upon,
To kill them is an occupation,
   And lawes make Fasts, and Lents for their destruction.   290

XXX

A sudden stiffe land-winde in that selfe houre
To sea-ward forc'd this bird, that did devour
The fish; he cares not, for with ease he flies,
Fat gluttonies best orator: at last
So long hee hath flown, and hath flown so fast   295
That many leagues at sea, now tir'd hee lyes,
And with his prey, that till then languisht, dies:
The soules no longer foes, two ways did erre,
The fish I follow,'and keepe no calender
   Of th'other; he lives yet in some great officer.   300

XXXI

Into an embrion fish, our Soule is throwne,
And in due time throwne out againe, and growne
To such vastnesse as, if unmanacled
From Greece, Morea were, and that by some
Earthquake uprooted, loose Morea swome,   305
Or seas from Africks body'had severed
And torne the hopefull Promontories head,
This fish would seeme these, and, when all hopes faile,
A great ship overset, or without saile
   Hulling, might (when this was a whelp) be like this whale. 310

XXXII

At every stroake his brazen finnes do take,
More circles in the broken sea they make
Then cannons voices, when the aire they teare:
His ribs are pillars, and his high arch'd roofe
Of barke that blunts best steele, is thunder-proofe: 315
Swimme in him swallow'd Dolphins, without feare,
And feele no sides, as if his vast wombe were
Some Inland sea, and ever as hee went
Hee spouted rivers up, as if he ment
  To joyne our seas, with seas above the firmament.   320

XXXIII

He hunts not fish, but as an officer
Stayes in his court, as his owne net, and there
All suitors of all sorts themselves enthrall;
So on his backe lyes this whale wantoning,
And in his gulfe-like throat, sucks every thing   325
That passeth neare. Fish chaseth fish, and all,
Flyer and follower, in this whirlepoole fall;
O might not states of more equality
Consist? and is it of necessity
  That thousand guiltlesse smals, to make one great, must
    die?   330

XXXIV

Now drinkes he up seas, and he eates up flocks,
He justles Ilands, and he shakes firme rockes.
Now in a roomefull house this Soule doth float,
And like a Prince she sends her faculties
To all her limbes, distant as Provinces.   335
The Sunne hath twenty times both Crab and Goate
Parched, since first lanch'd forth this living boate;
'Tis greatest now, and to destruction
Nearest; There's no pause at perfection;
  Greatnesse a period hath, but hath no station.   340

146

XXXV

Two little fishes whom hee never harm'd,
Nor fed on their kinde, two not throughly arm'd
With hope that they could kill him, nor could doe
Good to themselves by'his death, (they doe not eate
His flesh, nor suck those oyles, which thence outstreat)   345
Conspir'd against him, and it might undoe
The plot of all, that the plotters were two,
But that they fishes were, and could not speake.
How shall a Tyran wise strong projects breake,
   If wreches can on them the common anger wreake?   350

XXXVI

The flaile-finn'd Thresher, and steel-beak'd Sword-fish
Onely attempt to doe, what all doe wish.
The Thresher backs him, and to beate begins;
The sluggard Whale yeelds to oppression,
And t'hide himselfe from shame and danger, downe   355
Begins to sinke; the Swordfish upward spins,
And gores him with his beake; his staffe-like finnes,
So well the one, his sword the other plyes,
That now a scoffe, and prey, this tyran dyes,
   And (his owne dole) feeds with himselfe all companies.   360

XXXVII

Who will revenge his death? or who will call
Those to account, that thought, and wrought his fall?
Th'heires of slaine kings, wee see are often so
Transported with the joy of what they get,
That they, revenge and obsequies forget,   365
Nor will against such men the people goe,
Because h'is now dead, to whom they should show
Love in that act; Some kinds by vice being growne
So needy'of subjects love, that of their own

They thinke they lose, if love be to the dead Prince
    shown. 370

XXXVIII

This Soule, now free from prison, and passion,
Hath yet a little indignation
That so small hammers should so soone downe beat
So great a castle. And having for her house
Got the streight cloyster of a wreched mouse, 375
(As basest men that have not what to eate,
Nor enjoy ought, doe farre more hate the great
Then they, who good repos'd estates possesse)
This Soule, late taught that great things might by lesse
    Be slain, to gallant mischiefe doth herselfe addresse. 380

XXXIX

Natures great master-peece, an Elephant,
The onely harmlesse great thing; the giant
Of beasts; who thought, no more had gone, to make one
    wise
But to be just, and thankfull, loth t'offend,
(Yet nature hath given him no knees to bend) 385
Himselfe he up-props, on himselfe relies,
And foe to none, suspects no enemies,
Still sleeping stood; vex't not his fantasie
Blacke dreames; like an unbent bow, carelesly
    His sinewy Proboscis did remisly lie: 390

XL

In which as in a gallery this mouse
Walk'd, and surveid the roomes of this vast house,
And to the braine, the soules bedchamber, went,
And gnaw'd the life cords there; Like a whole towne
Cleane undermin'd, the slaine beast tumbled downe; 395
With him the murtherer dies, whom envy sent

To kill, not scape, (for, only hee that ment
To die, did ever kill a man of better roome,)
And thus he made his foe, his prey, and tombe:
    Who cares not to turn back, may any whither come.   400

XLI

Next, hous'd this Soule a Wolves yet unborne whelp,
Till the best midwife, Nature, gave it helpe,
To issue. It could kill, as soone as goe.
Abel, as white, and milde as his sheepe were,
(Who, in that trade, of Church, and kingdomes, there   405
Was the first type) was still infested soe
With this wolfe, that it bred his losse and woe;
And yet his bitch, his sentinell attends
The flocke so neere, so well warnes and defends,
    That the wolfe, (hopelesse else) to corrupt her, intends.   410

XLII

Hee tooke a course, which since, succesfully,
Great men have often taken, to espie
The counsels, or to breake the plots of foes.
To Abels tent he stealeth in the darke,
On whose skirts the bitch slept; ere she could barke,   415
Attach'd her with streight gripes, yet hee call'd those,
Embracements of love; to loves worke he goes,
Where deeds move more then words; nor doth she show
Now much resist, nor needs hee streighten so
  His prey, for, were shee loose, she would not barke, nor
    goe.   420

XLIII

Hee hath engag'd her; his, she wholy bides;
Who not her owne, none others secrets hides.
If to the flocke he come, and Abell there,
She faines hoarse barkings, but she biteth not,
Her faith is quite, but not her love forgot.   425

At last a trap, of which some every where
Abell had plac'd, ended his losse, and feare,
By the Wolves death; and now just time it was
That a quick soule should give life to that masse
    Of blood in Abels bitch, and thither this did passe.   430

XLIV

Some have their wives, their sisters some begot,
But in the lives of Emperours you shall not
Reade of a lust the which may equall this;
This wolfe begot himselfe, and finished
What he began alive, when hee was dead;   435
Sonne to himselfe, and father too, hee is
A ridling lust, for which Schoolemen would misse
A proper name. The whelpe of both these lay
In Abels tent, and with soft Moaba,
    His sister, being yong, it us'd to sport and play.   440

XLV

Hee soone for her too harsh, and churlish grew,
And Abell (the dam dead) would use this new
For the field. Being of two kindes made,
He, as his dam, from sheepe drove wolves away,
And as his Sire, he made them his owne prey,   445
Five yeares he liv'd, and cosen'd with his trade,
Then hopelesse that his faults were hid, betraid
Himselfe by flight, and by all followed,
From dogges, a wolfe; from wolves, a dogge he fled;
    And, like a spie to both sides false, he perished.   450

XLVI

It quickned next a toyfull Ape, and so
Gamesome it was, that it might freely goe
From tent to tent, and with the children play,
His organs now so like theirs hee doth finde,

150

That why he cannot laugh, and speake his minde,   455
He wonders. Much with all, most he doth stay
With Adams fift daughter *Siphatecia*,
Doth gaze on her, and, where she passeth, passe,
Gathers her fruit, and tumbles on the grasse,
    And wisest of that kinde, the first true lover was.   460

XLVII

He was the first that more desir'd to have
One then another; first that ere did crave
Love by mute signes, and had no power to speake;
First that could make love faces, or could doe
The valters sombersalts, or us'd to wooe   465
With hoiting gambolls, his owne bones to breake
To make his mistresse merry; or to wreake
Her angers on himselfe. Sinnes against kinde
They easily doe, that can let feed their minde
    With outward beauty; beauty they in boyes and beasts
    do find.   470

XLVIII

By this misled, too low things men have prov'd,
And too high; beasts and angels have beene lov'd.
This Ape, though else through-vaine, in this was wise,
He reach'd at things too high, but open way
There was, and he knew not she would say nay;   475
His toyes prevaile not, likelier meanes he tries,
He gazeth on her face with teare-shot eyes,
And up lifts subtly with his russet pawe
Her kidskinne apron without feare or awe
    Of nature; nature hath no gaole, though shee have law.   480

XLIX

First she was silly'and knew not what he ment:
That vertue, by his touches, chaft and spent,

Succeeds an itchie warmth, that melts her quite;
She knew not first, now cares not what he doth,
And willing halfe and more, more then halfe loth, 485
She neither puls nor pushes, but outright
Now cries, and now repents; when *Tethlemite*
Her brother, enters, and a great stone threw
After the Ape, who, thus prevented, flew.
  This house thus battr'd downe, the Soule possest a
    new. 490

L

And whether by this change she lose or win,
She comes out next, where th'Ape would have gone in.
Adam and *Eve* had mingled bloods, and now
Like Chimiques equall fires, her temperate wombe
Had stew'd and form'd it: and part did become 495
A spungie liver, that did richly'allow,
Like a free conduit, on a high hils brow,
Life-keeping moisture unto every part;
Part hardned it selfe to a thicker heart,
  Whose busie furnaces lifes spirits do impart. 500

LI

Another part became the well of sense,
The tender well-arm'd feeling braine, from whence,
Those sinowie strings which do our bodies tie,
Are raveld out; and fast there by one end,
Did this Soule limbes, these limbes a soule attend; 505
And now they joyn'd: keeping some quality
Of every past shape, she knew treachery,
Rapine, deceit, and lust, and ills enow
To be a woman. *Themech* she is now,
  Sister and wife to *Caine, Caine* that first did plow. 510

LII

Who ere thou beest that read'st this sullen Writ,
Which just so much courts thee, as thou dost it,
Let me arrest thy thoughts; wonder with mee,
Why plowing, building, ruling and the rest,
Or most of those arts, whence our lives are blest,   515
By cursed *Cains* race invented be,
And blest *Seth* vext us with Astronomie.
Ther's nothing simply good, nor ill alone,
Of every quality comparison,
   The onely measure is, and judge, opinion.   520

from *Nosce Teipsum*

from *Nosce Teipsum*

I

Of Humane Knowledge

WHY did my parents send me to the Schooles,
    That I with knowledge might enrich my mind?
    Since the *desire to know* first made men fools,
    And did corrupt the root of all mankind:

For when God's hand had written in the hearts   5
    Of the first Parents, all the rules of good,
    So that their skill infusde did passe all arts
    That ever were, before, or since the Food;

And when their reason's eye was sharpe and cleere,
    And (as an eagle can behold the sunne)   10
    Could have approcht th' Eternall Light as neere,
    As the intellectuall angels could have done:

Even then to them the *Spirit of Lyes* suggests
    That they were blind, because they saw not ill;
    And breathes into their incorrupted brests   15
    A curious *wish*, which did corrupt their *will*.

For that same ill they straight desir'd to know;
    Which ill, being nought but a defect of good,
    In all God's works the Divell could not show
    While Man their lord in his perfection stood.   20

So that themselves were first to doe the ill,
 Ere they thereof the knowledge could attaine;
 Like him that knew not poison's power to kill,
 Untill (by tasting it) himselfe was slaine.

Even so by tasting of that fruite forbid,   25
 Where they sought *knowledge*, they did *error* find;
 Ill they desir'd to know, and ill they did;
 And to give *Passion* eyes, made *Reason* blind.

For then their minds did first in Passion see
 Those wretched shapes of *Miserie* and *Woe*, 30
 Of *Nakednesse*, of *Shame*, of *Povertie*,
 Which then their owne experience made them know.

But then grew *Reason* darke, that *she* no more,
 Could the faire formes of *Good* and *Truth* discern;
 Battes they became, that *eagles* were before: 35
 And this they got by their *desire to learne*.

But we their wretched of-spring, what doe we?
 Doe not we still taste of the fruit forbid
 Whiles with fond fruitlesse curiositie,
 In bookes prophane we seeke for knowledge hid? 40

What is this *knowledge* but the sky-stolne fire,
 For which the *thiefe* still chain'd in ice doth sit?
 And which the poore rude *Satyre* did admire,
 And needs would kisse but burnt his lips with it.

What is it? but the cloud of emptie raine,   45
 Which when *Jove's* guest imbrac't, hee monsters got?
 Or the false *payles* which oft being fild with paine,
 Receiv'd the water, but retain'd it not!

158

Shortly, what is it but the firie coach
    Which the *Youth* sought, and sought his death withal?   50
    Or the *boye's* wings, which when he did approch
    The *sunne's* hot beames, did melt and let him fall?

And yet alas, when all our lamps are burnd,
    Our bodyes wasted, and our spirits spent;
    When we have all the learnèd *Volumes* turn'd,   55
    Which yeeld mens wits both help and ornament:

What can we know? or what can we discerne?
    When *Error* chokes the windowes of the minde,
    The divers formes of things, how can we learne,
    That have been ever from our birth-day blind?   60

When *Reasone's* lampe, which (like the *sunne* in skie)
    Throughout *Man's* little world her beames did spread;
    Is now become a sparkle, which doth lie
    Under the ashes, halfe extinct, and dead:

How can we hope, that through the eye and eare,   65
    This dying sparkle, in this cloudy place,
    Can recollect these beames of knowledge cleere,
    Which were infus'd in the first minds by grace?

So might the heire whose father hath in play
    Wasted a thousand pound of ancient rent;   70
    By painefull earning of a groate a day,
    Hope to restore the patrimony spent.

The wits that div'd most deepe and soar'd most hie
    Seeking Man's pow'rs, have found his weaknesse such:
    "Skill comes so slow, and life so fast doth flie,   75
    "We learne so little and forget so much.

For this the wisest of all Mortall men
    Said, '*He knew nought, but that he nought did know*';
    And the great mocking-Master mockt not then,
    When he said, '*Truth was buried deepe below.*'   80

For how may we to others' things attaine,
    When none of us his owne soule understands?
    For which the Divell mockes our curious braine,
    When, '*Know thy selfe*' his oracle commands.

For why should wee the busie Soule beleeve,   85
    When boldly she concludes of that and this;
    When of her selfe she can no judgement give,
    Nor how, nor whence, nor where, nor what she is?

All things without, which round about we see,
    We seeke to knowe, and how therewith to doe;   90
    But that whereby we *reason, live and be*,
    Within our selves, we strangers are thereto.

We seeke to know the moving of each spheare,
    And the strange cause of th' ebs and flouds of *Nile*;
    But of that clocke within our breasts we beare,   95
    The subtill motions we forget the while.

We that acquaint our selves with every *Zoane*
    And passe both *Tropikes* and behold the *Poles*,
    When we come home, are to our selves unknown,
    And unacquainted still with our owne *Soules*.   100

We study *Speech* but others we perswade;
    We *leech-craft* learne, but others cure with it;
    We interpret *lawes*, which other men have made,
    But reade not those which in our hearts are writ.

Is it because the minde is like the eye,   105
   Through which it gathers knowledge by degrees—
   Whose rayes reflect not, but spread outwardly:
   Not seeing it selfe when other things it sees?

No, doubtlesse; for the mind can backward cast
   Upon her selfe, her understanding light;   110
   But she is so corrupt, and so defac't,
   As her owne image doth her selfe affright.

As in the fable of the Lady faire,
   Which for her lust was turnd into a cow;
   When thirstie to a streame she did repaire,   115
   And saw her selfe transform'd she wist not how:

At first she startles, then she stands amaz'd,
   At last with terror she from thence doth flye;
   And loathes the watry glasse wherein she gaz'd,
   And shunnes it still, though she for thirst doe die: 120

Even so *Man's Soule* which did God's image beare,
   And was at first faire, good, and spotlesse pure;
   Since with her *sinnes* her beauties blotted were,
   Doth of all sights her owne sight least endure:

For even at first reflection she espies,   125
   Such strange *chimeraes*, and such monsters there;
   Such toyes, such *antikes*, and such vanities,
   As she retires, and shrinkes for shame and feare.

And as the man loves least at home to bee,
   That hath a sluttish house haunted with *Sprites*;   130
   So she impatient her owne faults to see,
   Turnes from her selfe and in strange things delites.

For this few *know themselves*: for merchants broke
  View their estate with discontent and paine;
  And *seas* are troubled, when they doe revoke   135
  Their flowing waves into themselves againe.

And while the face of outward things we find,
  Pleasing and faire, agreeable and sweet;
  These things transport, and carry out the mind,
  That with her selfe her selfe can never meet.   140

Yet if *Affliction* once her warres begin,
  And threat the feebler *Sense* with sword and fire;
  The *Minde* contracts her selfe and shrinketh in,
  And to her selfe she gladly doth retire:

As *Spiders* toucht, seek their webs inmost part;   145
  As *bees* in stormes unto their hives returne;
  As bloud in danger gathers to the heart;
  As men seek towns, when foes the country burn.

If ought can teach us ought, *Afflictions* lookes,
  (Making us looke into our selves so neere,)   150
  Teach us to *know our selves* beyond all bookes,
  Or all the learned Schooles that ever were.

This *mistresse* lately pluckt me by the eare,
  And many a golden lesson hath me taught;
  Hath made my *Senses* quicke, and Reason cleare,   155
  Reform'd my Will and rectifide my Thought.

So doe the *winds* and *thunders* cleanse the ayre;
  So working leas settle and purge the wine;
  So lop't and prunèd trees doe flourish faire;
  So doth the fire the drossie gold refine.   160

Neither *Minerva* nor the learnèd Muse,
   Nor rules of *Art*, nor *precepts* of the wise;
   Could in my braine those beames of skill infuse,
   As but the glance of this *Dame's* angry eyes.

She within *lists* my ranging minde hath brought,   165
   That now beyond my selfe I list not goe;
   My selfe am *center* of my circling thought,
   Onely *my selfe* I studie, learne, and know.

I know my bodie's of so fraile a kind,
   As force without, feavers within can kill;   170
   I know the heavenly nature of my minde,
   But 'tis corrupted both in wit and will:

I know my *Soule* hath power to know all things,
   Yet is she blinde and ignorant in all;
   I know I am one of Nature's little kings,   175
   Yet to the least and vilest things am thrall.

I know my life's a paine and but a span,
   I know my *Sense* is mockt with every thing:
   And to conclude, I know my selfe a MAN,
   Which is a *proud*, and yet a *wretched* thing.   180

II

How the Soul doth exercise her Powers in the Body

BUT as the world's *sunne* doth effects beget,
   Divers, in divers places every day;
   Here *Autumnes* temperature, there *Summer's* heat,
   Here flowry *Spring-tide*, and there *Winter* gray:

Eere *Even*, there *Morne*, here *Noone*, there *Day*, there *Night*; 5
Melts wax, dries clay, mak[e]s flowrs, som quick, som dead;
Makes the *More* black, and th' *Europœan* white,
Th' *American* tawny, and th' *East-Indian* red:

So in our little World: this *soule* of ours,
Being onely one, and to one body tyed, 10
Doth use, on divers objects divers powers,
And so are her effects diversified.

The Vegetative or quickening Power

HER *quick'ning* power in every living part,
Doth as a nurse, or as a mother serve;
And doth employ her *oeconomicke art*, 15
And busie care, her houshold to preserve.

Here she *attracts*, and there she doth *retaine*,
There she *decocts*, and doth the food prepare;
There she *distributes* it to every vaine,
There she *expels* what she may fitly spare. 20

This power to *Martha* may comparèd be,
Which busie was, the *houshold-things* to doe;
Or to a *Dryas*, living in a tree:
For even to trees this power is proper too.

And though the Soule may not this power extend 25
Out of the body, but still use it there;
She hath a power which she abroad doth send,
Which views and searcheth all things every where.

The power of Sense

THIS power is *Sense*, which from abroad doth bring
    The *colour, taste,* and *touch,* and *sent,* and *sound*;   30
    The *quantitie,* and *shape* of every thing
    Within th' Earth's center, or Heaven's circle found.

This power, in parts made fit, fit objects takes,
    Yet not the things, but forms of things receives;
    As when a seale in waxe impression makes,   35
    The print therein, but not it selfe it leaves.

And though things sensible be numberlesse,
    But onely five the *Senses'* organs be;
    And in those five, all things their formes expresse,
    Which we can *touch, taste, feele,* or *heare,* or *see.*   40

These are the windows throgh the which she views
    The *light of knowledge,* which is life's loadstar:
    "And yet while she these spectacles doth use,
    "Oft worldly things seeme greater then they are.

Sight

FIRST, the two *eyes* that have the *seeing* power,   45
    Stand as one watchman, spy, or sentinell;
    Being plac'd aloft, within the head's high tower;
    And though both see, yet both but one thing tell.

These mirrors take into their little space
    The formes of *moone* and *sun,* and every *starre*;   50
    Of every body and of every place,
    Which with the World's wide armes embracèd are:

Yet their best object, and their noblest use,
  Hereafter in another World will be;
  When God in them shall heavenly light infuse,   55
  That face to face they may their *Maker* see.

Here are they guides, which doe the body lead,
  Which else would stumble in eternal night;
  Here in this world they do much knowledge *read*,
  And are the casements which admit most light: 60

They are her farthest reaching instrument,
  Yet they no beames unto their objects send;
  But all the rays are from their objects sent,
  And in the *eyes* with pointed angles end:

If th' objects be farre off, the rayes doe meet   65
  In a sharpe point, and so things seeme but small;
  If they be neere, their rayes doe spread and fleet,
  And make broad points, that things seeme great withall.

Lastly, nine things to *Sight* requirèd are;
  The *power* to see, the *light*, the *visible* thing,   70
  Being not too *small*, too *thin*, too *nigh*, too *farre*,
  Cleare space, and *time*, the forme distinct to bring.

Thus we see how the *Soule* doth use the eyes,
  As instruments of her quicke power of sight;
  Hence do th' Arts *opticke* and faire *painting* rise: 75
  Painting, which doth all gentle minds delight.

Hearing

Now let us heare how she the *Eares* imployes:
  Their office is the troubled ayre to take,

Which in their mazes formes a sound or noyse,
Whereof her selfe doth true distinction make.   80

These wickets of the *Soule* are plac't on hie
   Because all sounds doe lightly mount aloft;
   And that they may not pierce too violently,
   They are delaied with turnes, and windings oft.

For should the voice directly strike the braine,   85
   It would astonish and confuse it much;
   Therefore these plaits and folds the sound restraine,
   That it the organ may more gently touch.

As streames, which with their winding banks doe play,
   Stopt by their creeks, run softly through the plaine;   90
   So in th' Eares' labyrinth the voice doth stray,
   And doth with easie motion touch the braine.

It is the slowest, yet the daintiest *sense*;
   For even the *Eares* of such as have no skill,
   Perceive a discord, and conceive offence;   95
   And knowing not what is good, yet find the ill.

And though this *sense* first gentle *Musicke* found,
   Her proper object is *the speech of men*;
   But that speech chiefely which God's heraulds sound,
   When their tongs utter what His Spirit did pen.   100

Our *Eyes* have lids, our *Eares* still ope we see,
   Quickly to heare how every tale is proovèd;
   Our *Eyes* still move, our *Eares* unmovèd bee,
   That though we hear quick we be not quickly movèd.

Thus by the organs of the *Eye* and *Eare*,   105
   The *Soule* with knowledge doth her selfe endue;

"Thus she her prison, may with pleasure beare,
"Having such prospects, all the world to view.

These conduit-pipes of knowledge feed the Mind,
    But th' other three attend the Body still;   110
    For by their services the *Soule* doth find,
    What things are to the body, good or ill.

Taste

THE *bodie's* life with meats and ayre is fed,
    Therefore the *soule* doth use the *tasting* power,
    In veines, which through the tongue and palate spred,   115
    Distinguish every relish, sweet and sower.

This is the bodie's *nurse*; but since man's wit
    Found th' art of *cookery*, to delight his *sense*;
    More bodies are consum'd and kild with it,
    Then with the sword, famine, or pestilence.   120

Smelling

NEXT, in the nosthrils she doth use the *smell*:
    As God the *breath of life* in them did give,
    So makes He now this power in them to dwell,
    To judge all ayres, whereby we *breath* and *live*.

This *sense* is also mistresse of an *Art*,   125
    Which to soft people sweete perfumes doth sell;
    Though this deare Art doth little good impart,
    "Sith they smell best, that doe of nothing smell.

And yet good *sents* doe purifie the braine,
   Awake the fancie, and the wits refine;   130
   Hence old *Devotion, incense* did ordaine
   To make mens' spirits apt for thoughts divine.

Feeling

LASTLY, *the feeling power*, which is Life's root,
   Through every living part it selfe doth shed;
   By sinewes, which extend from head to foot,   135
   And like a net, all ore the body spred.

Much like a subtill spider, which doth sit
   In middle of her web, which spreadeth wide;
   If ought doe touch the utmost thred of it,
   Shee feeles it instantly on every side.   140

By *Touch*, the first pure qualities we learne,
   Which quicken all things, *hote, cold, moist* and *dry*;
   By *Touch, hard, soft, rough, smooth*, we doe discerne;
   By *Touch, sweet pleasure*, and *sharpe paine*, we try.

THESE are the outward instruments of Sense,   145
   These are the guards which every thing must passe
   Ere it approch the mind's intelligence,
   Or touch the Fantasie, *Wit's looking-glasse*.

The Imagination or Common Sense

AND yet these porters, which all things admit,
   Themselves perceive not, nor discerne the things;   150
   One *common* power doth in the forehead sit,
   Which all their proper formes together brings.

For all those *nerves,* which *spirits of Sence* doe beare,
   And to those outward organs spreading goe;
   United are, as in a center there,   155
   And there this power those sundry formes doth know.

Those outward organs present things receive,
   This inward *Sense* doth absent things retaine;
   Yet straight transmits all formes shee doth perceive,
   Unto a higher region of the *braine.*   160

The Fantasie

Where *Fantasie,* neere *hand-maid* to the mind,
   Sits and beholds, and doth discerne them all;
   Compounds in one, things divers in their kind;
   Compares the black and white, the great and small.

Besides, those single formes she doth esteeme,   165
   And in her ballance doth their values trie;
   Where some things good, and some things ill doe seem,
   And neutrall some, in her *fantasticke* eye.

This busie power is working day and night;
   For when the outward *senses* rest doe take,   170
   A thousand dreames, fantasticall and light,
   With fluttring wings doe keepe her still awake.

The Sensitive Memorie

Yet alwayes all may not afore her bee;
   Successively, she this and that intends;
   Therefore such formes as she doth cease to see,   175
   To *Memorie's* large volume shee commends.

The *lidger-booke* lies in the braine behinde,
    Like *Janus'* eye, which in his poll was set;
    The *lay-man's tables, store-house of the mind,*
    Which doth remember much, and much forget.   180

Heere *Sense's apprehension*, end doth take;
    As when a stone is into water cast,
    One circle doth another circle make,
    Till the last circle touch the banke at last.

The Passions of Sense

BUT though the *apprehensive power* doe pause,   185
    The *motive* vertue then begins to move;
    Which in the heart below doth PASSIONS cause,
    Joy, griefe, and *feare,* and *hope,* and *hate,* and *love.*

These passions have a free commanding might,
    And divers actions in our life doe breed;   190
    For, all acts done without true Reason's light,
    Doe from the passion of the *Sense* proceed.

But sith the *braine* doth lodge the powers of *Sense,*
    How makes it in the heart those passions spring?
    The mutuall love, the kind intelligence   195
    'Twixt heart and braine, this *sympathy* doth bring.

From the kind heat, which in the heart doth raigne,
    The *spirits* of life doe their begining take;
    These *spirits* of life ascending to the braine,
    When they come there, the *spirits of Sense* do make.   200

These *spirits of Sense*, in Fantasie's High Court,
    Judge of the formes of *objects*, ill or well;

And so they send a good or ill report
Downe to the heart, where all affections dwell.

If the report bee *good*, it causeth *love*,   205
   And longing *hope*, and well-assurèd *joy*:
   If it bee *ill*, then doth it *hatred* move,
   And trembling *feare*, and vexing *griefe's* annoy.

Yet were these naturall affections good:
   (For they which want them, *blockes* or *devils* be)   210
   If *Reason* in her first perfection stood,
   That she might Nature's passions rectify.

III

O ignorant poor man! what doest thou beare
   Lockt up within the casket of thy brest?
   What jewels, and what riches hast thou there!
   What heavenly treasure in so weake a chest!

Looke in thy *soule*, and thou shalt *beauties* find,   5
   Like those which drownd *Narcissus* in the flood:
   Honour and *Pleasure* both are in thy mind,
   And all that in the world is counted *Good*.

Thinke of her worth, and think that God did meane,
   This worthy mind should worthy things imbrace;   10
   Blot not her beauties with thy thoughts unclean,
   Nor her dishonour with thy passions base;

Kill not her *quickning power* with surfettings,
   Mar not her *Sense* with sensualitie;
   Cast not her serious wit on idle things: 15
   Make not her free-*will*, slave to vanitie.

And when thou think'st of her *eternitie*,
   Thinke not that *Death* against her nature is,
   Thinke it a *birth*; and when thou goest to die,
   Sing like a swan, as if thou went'st to blisse.   20

And if thou, like a child, didst feare before,
   Being in the darke, where thou didst nothing see;
   Now I have broght thee *torch-light*, feare no more;
   Now when thou diest, thou canst not hud-winkt be.

And thou my *Soule*, which turn'st thy curious eye,   25
   To view the beames of thine owne forme divine;
   Know, that thou canst know nothing perfectly,
   While thou art clouded with this flesh of mine.

Take heed of *over-weening*, and compare
   Thy peacock's feet with thy gay peacock's traine;   30
   Study the best, and highest things that are,
   But of thy selfe an humble thought retaine.

Cast downe thy selfe, and onely strive to raise
   The glory of thy Maker's sacred Name;
   Use all thy powers, that Blessed Power to praise,   35
   Which gives thee power to *bee*, and *use the same*.

FINIS

Cynthia

The 11th: And Last Booke
of the Ocean to Scinthia

Sufficeth it to yow my joyes interred,
in simpell wordes that I my woes cumplayne,
yow that then died when first my fancy erred,
joyes under dust that never live agayne.
If to the livinge weare my muse adressed,   5
or did my minde her own spirrit still inhold,
weare not my livinge passion so repressed,
as to the dead, the dead did thes unfold,
sume sweeter wordes, sume more becuming vers,
should wittness my myshapp in hygher kynd,   10
but my loves wounds, my fancy in the hearse,
the Idea but restinge, of a wasted minde,
the blossumes fallen, the sapp gon from the tree,
the broken monuments of my great desires,
from thes so lost what may th' affections bee,   15
what heat in Cynders of extinguisht fiers?
Lost in the mudd of thos hygh flowinge streames
which through more fayrer feilds ther courses bend,
slayne with sealf thoughts, amasde in fearfull dreams,
woes without date, discumforts without end,   20
from frutfull trees I gather withred leves
and glean the broken eares with misers hands,
who sumetyme did enjoy the waighty sheves
I seeke faire floures amidd the brinish sand,
all in the shade yeven in the faire soon dayes   25
under thos healthless trees I sytt alone,

wher joyfull byrdds singe neather lovely layes
nor Phillomen recounts her direfull mone.
No feedinge flockes, no sheapherds cumpunye
that might renew my dollorus consayte, 30
while happy then, while love and fantasye
confinde my thoughts onn that faire flock to waite;
no pleasinge streames fast to the ocean wendinge
the messengers sumetymes of my great woe
but all onn yearth as from the colde stormes bendinge 35
shrinck from my thoughts in hygh heavens and below.
Oh, hopefull love my object, and invention,
Oh, trew desire the spurr of my consayte,
Oh, worthiest spirrit, my minds impulsion,
Oh, eyes transpersant my affections bayte, 40
Oh, princely forme, my fancies adamande,
devine consayte, my paynes acceptance,
Oh, all in onn, oh heaven on yearth transparant,
the seat of joyes, and loves abundance.
Out of that mass of mirakells, my Muse, 45
gathered thos floures, to her pure sences pleasinge
out of her eyes (the store of joyes) did chuse
equall delights, my sorrowes counterpoysinge.
Her regall lookes, my rigarus sythes suppressed,
small dropes of joies, sweetned great worlds of woes, 50
one gladsume day a thowsand cares redressed.
Whom Love defends, what fortune overthrowes?
When shee did well, what did ther elce amiss?
When shee did ill what empires could have pleased?
No other poure effectinge wo, or bliss. 55
Shee gave, shee tooke, shee wounded, shee apeased.

The honor of her love, love still divisinge,
woundinge my mind with contrary consayte,
transferde it sealf sumetyme to her aspiringe,
sumetyme the trumpett of her thoughts retrayt. 60

178

To seeke new worlds, for golde, for prayse, for glory,
to try desire, to try love severed farr,
when I was gonn shee sent her memory
more stronge then weare ten thowsand shipps of warr,
to call mee back, to leve great honors thought,   65
to leve my frinds, my fortune, my attempte,
to leve the purpose I so longe had sought
and holde both cares, and cumforts in contempt.
Such heat in Ize, such fier in frost remaynde,
such trust in doubt, such cumfort in dispaire,   70
mich like the gentell Lamm, though lately waynde,
playes with the dug though finds no cumfort ther.
But as a boddy violently slayne
retayneath warmth although the spirrit be gonn,
and by a poure in nature moves agayne   75
till it be layd below the fatall stone
or as the yearth yeven in cold winter dayes
left for a tyme by her life gevinge soonn
douth by the poure remayninge of his rayes
produce sume green, though not as it hath dunn   80
or as a wheele forst by the fallinge streame
although the course be turnde sume other way
douth for a tyme go rounde uppon the beame
till wantinge strenght to move, it stands att stay.
So my forsaken hart, my withered minde,   85
widdow of all the joyes it once possest,
my hopes cleane out of sight with forced wind
to kyngdomes strange, to lands farr of addrest,
alone, forsaken, frindless onn the shore
with many wounds, with deaths cold pangs inebrased   90
writes in the dust as onn that could no more
whom love, and tyme, and fortune had defaced,
of things so great, so longe, so manefolde
with meanes so weake, the sowle yeven then departing
the weale, the wo, the passages of olde   95

and worlds of thoughts discribde by onn last sythinge,
as if when after Phebus is dessended
and leves a light mich like the past dayes dawninge,
and every toyle and labor wholy ended
each livinge creature draweth to his restinge   100
wee should beginn by such a partinge light
to write the story of all ages past
and end the same before th' aprochinge night.
Such is agayne the labor of my minde
whose shroude by sorrow woven now to end   105
hath seene that ever shininge soonn declynde
so many yeares that so could not dissende
but that the eyes of my minde helde her beames
in every part transferd by loves swift thought
farr of or nire, in wakinge or in dreames   110
imagination stronge their luster brought
such force her angellike aparance had
to master distance, tyme, or crueltye,
such art to greve, and after to make gladd,
such feare in love, such love in majestye.   115
My weery lymes, her memory imbalmed,
my darkest wayes her eyes make clear as day,
what stormes so great but Cinthias beames apeased?
What rage so feirce that love could not allay?
Twelve yeares intire I wasted in this warr,   120
twelve yeares of my most happy younger dayes,
butt I in them, and they now wasted ar,
of all which past the sorrow only stayes.
So wrate I once and my mishapp fortolde,
my minde still feelinge sorrowfull success   125
yeven as before a storme the marbell colde
douth by moyste teares tempestious tymes express,
so fealt my hevy minde my harmes att hande
which my vayne thought in vayne sought to recure;
att middell day my soonn seemde under land   130

when any littell cloude did it obscure
and as the Isakells in a winters day
when as the soonn shines with unwounted warme
so did my joyes mealt into secreat teares
so did my hart desolve in wastinge dropps 135
and as the season of the yeare outweares
and heapes of snow from of the mountayn topps
with suddayne streames the valles overflow
so did the tyme draw on my more dispaire
then fludds of sorrow and whole seas of wo 140
the bancks of all my hope did overbeare
and dround my minde in deapts of missery.
Sumetyme I died sumetyme I was distract,
my sowle the stage of fancies tragedye.
Then furious madness wher trew reason lackt 145
wrate what it would, and scurgde myne own consayte.
Oh, hevy hart who can thee wittnes beare,
what tounge, what penn could thy tormentinge treat
but thyne owne mourning thoughts which present weare,
what stranger minde beleve the meanest part 150
what altered sence conceve the weakest wo
that tare, that rent, that peirsed thy sadd hart.
And as a man distract, with trebell might
bound in stronge chaynes douth strive, and rage in vayne,
till tyrde and breathless, he is forst to rest, 155
fyndes by contention but increas of payne,
and fiery heat inflamde in swollen breast.
So did my minde in change of passion
from wo to wrath, from wrath returne to wo,
struglinge in vayne from loves subjection. 160
Therfore all liveless, and all healpless bounde
my fayntinge spirritts sunck, and hart apalde,
my joyes and hopes lay bleedinge on the ground
that not longe since the highest heaven scalde,
I hated life and cursed destiney 165

the thoughts of passed tymes like flames of hell
kyndled a fresh within my memorye
the many deere achivements that befell
in those pryme yeares and infancy of love
which to describe weare butt to dy in writinge. 170
Ah those I sought, but vaynly, to remove
and vaynly shall, by which I perrish livinge.
And though strong reason holde before myne eyes
the Images, and formes of worlds past
teachinge the cause why all thos flames that rize 175
from formes externall, cann no longer last,
then that thos seeminge bewties hold in pryme
Loves ground, his essence, and his emperye,
all slaves to age, and vassals unto tyme
of which repentance writes the tragedye. 180
But this, my harts desire could not conceve
Whose love outflew the fastest fliinge tyme,
A bewty that cann easely deseave
th' arrest of yeares, and creepinge age outclyme,
a springe of bewties which tyme ripeth not, 185
tyme that butt workes onn frayle mortallety,
a sweetness which woes wronges outwipeth not,
whom love hath chose for his devinnitye,
A vestall fier that burnes, but never wasteth,
that looseth nought by gevinge light to all 190
that endless shines eachwher and endless lasteth
blossumes of pride that cann nor vade nor fall.
Thes weare thos marvelous perfections,
the parents of my sorrow and my envy,
most deathfull and most violent infections, 195
Thes be the Tirants that in fetters tye
their wounded vassalls, yet nor kill nor cure,
but glory in their lastinge missery
that as her bewties would our woes should dure
thes be th' effects of pourfull emperye. . . 200

Yet have thes wounders want which want cumpassion,
yet hath her minde sume markes of humayne race,
yet will shee bee a wooman for a fashion,
So douth shee pleas her vertues to deface
and like as that immortall pour douth seat   205
an element of waters to allay
the fiery soonn beames that on yearth do beate
and temper by cold night the heat of day
so hath perfection which begatt her minde
added therto a change of fantasye   210
and left her the affections of her kynde
yet free from evry yevill but crueltye.

But leve her prayse, speak thow of nought but wo,
write on the tale that Sorrow bydds the tell,
strive to forgett, and care no more to know   215
thy cares ar known, by knowinge thos to well,
discribe her now as shee apeeres to thee,
not as shee did apeere in dayes fordunn,
in love thos things that weare no more may bee
for fancy seildume ends wher it begunn.   220

And as a streame by stronge hand bounded in
from natures course wher it did sumetyme runn
by sume small rent or loose part douth beginn
to finde escape, till it a way hath woone,
douth then all unawares in sunder teare   225
the forsed bounds and raginge, runn att large,
in th'auncient channells as they wounted weare,
such is of weemens love the carefull charge,
helde, and mayntaynde with multetude of woes,
of longe arections such the suddayne fall,   230
onn houre deverts, onn instant overthrowes,
for which our lives, for which our fortunes thrale,
so many yeares thos joyes have deerely bought,

183

of which when our fonde hopes do most assure
all is desolvde, our labors cume to nought, 235
nor any marke therof ther douth indure,
no more then when small dropps of rayne do fall
uppon the parched grounde by heat up dried,
no coolinge moysture is percevde att all
nor any shew or signe of weet douth byde. 240
But as the feildes clothed with leves and floures,
the bancks of roses smellinge pretious sweet,
have but ther bewties date, and tymely houres,
and then defast by winters cold, and sleet,
so farr as neather frute nor forme of floure 245
stayes for a wittnes what such branches bare,
butt as tyme gave, tyme did agayne devoure
and chandge our risinge joy to fallinge care,
So of affection which our youth presented
when shee that from the soonn reves poure and light 250
did but decline her beames as discontented
convertinge sweetest dayes to saddest night,
all droopes, all dyes, all troden under dust
the person, place, and passages forgotten
the hardest steele eaten with softest ruste, 255
the firme and sollide tree both rent and rotten,
thos thoughts so full of pleasure and content
that in our absence weare affections foode
ar rased out and from the fancy rent
in highest grace and harts deere care that stood, 260
ar cast for pray to hatred, and to scorne,
our deerest treasors and our harts trew joyes
the tokens hunge onn brest, and kyndly worne
ar now elcewhere disposde, or helde for toyes,
and thos which then our Jelosye removed 265
and others for our sakes then valued deere,
the on forgot, the rest ar deere beloved,
when all of ours douth strange or vilde apeere.

Thos streames seeme standinge puddells which, before,
wee saw our bewties in, so weare they cleere.   270
Bellphebes course is now observde no more,
that faire resemblance weareth out of date,
our Ocean seas are but tempestius waves
and all things base that blessed wear of late. . . .
And as a feilde wherin the stubbell stands   275
of harvest past, the plowmans eye offends,
hee tills agayne or teares them up with hands
and throwes to fire as foylde and frutless ends
and takes delight another seed to sow. . . .
so douth the minde root up all wounted thought   280
and scornes the care of our remayninge woes,
the sorrowes, which themsealvs for us have wrought,
ar burnt to Cinders by new kyndled fiers,
the ashes ar dispeirst into the ayre,
the sythes, the grones of all our past desires   285
ar cleane outworne, as things that never weare. . .

With youth, is deade the hope of loves returne,
who lookes not back to heare our after cryes,
wher hee is not, hee laughts at thos that murne,
whence hee is gonn, hee scornes the minde that dyes,   290
when hee is absent hee beleves no words,
when reason speakes hee careless stopps his ears,
whom hee hath left hee never grace affords,
but bathes his wings in our lamentinge teares.

Unlastinge passion, soune outworne consayte   299
wheron I built, and onn so durelesse trust,
my minde had wounds, I dare not say desaite,
weare I resolvde her promis was not Just.
Sorrow was my revendge, and wo my hate,
I pourless was to alter my desire,   300
my love is not of tyme, or bound to date

my harts internall heat, and livinge fier
would not, or could be quencht, with suddayn shoures.
My bound respect was not confinde to dayes
my vowed fayth not sett to ended houres,   305
I love the bearinge and not bearinge sprayes
which now to others do ther sweetnes send,
th'incarnat, snow driven white, and purest asure,
who from high heaven douth on their feilds dissend
fillinge their barns with grayne, and towres with treasure. 310
Erringe or never erringe, such is Love,
as while it lasteth scornes th'accompt of thos
seekinge but sealf contentment to improve,
and hydes if any bee, his inward woes,
and will not know while hee knowes his own passion   315
the often and unjust perseverance
in deeds of love, and state, and every action
from that first day and yeare of their joyes entrance.

But I unblessed, and ill borne creature,
that did inebrace the dust, her boddy bearinge   320
that loved her both, by fancy, and by nature,
that drew yeven with the milke in my first suckinge
affection from the parents brest that bare mee,
have found her as a stranger so severe
improvinge my mishapp in each degree   325
But love was gonn, So would I, my life weare.
A Queen shee was to mee, no more Belphebe,
a Lion then, no more a milke white Dove,
a prissoner in her brest I could not bee
shee did untye the gentell chaynes of love   330
Love was no more the love of hydinge
all trespase, and mischance, for her own glorye.
It had bynn such, it was still for th'ellect,
but I must bee th'exampell in loves storye
this was of all forpast the sadd effect. . . .   335

186

But thow my weery sowle and hevy thought
made by her love a burden to my beinge,
dust know my error never was forthought
or ever could proceed from sence of lovinge.
Of other cause if then it had proceedinge 340
I leve th'excuse syth Judgment hath bynn geven
the lymes devided, sundred and a bleedinge
cannot cumplayne the sentence was uneyevunn
This did that natures wounder, Vertues choyse
the only parragonn of tymes begettinge 345
Devin in wordes angellicall in voyse
that springe of joyes, that floure of loves own settinge
Th'Idea remayninge of thos golden ages
that bewtye bravinge heavens, and yearth imbalminge
which after worthless worlds but play onn stages, 350
such didsst thow her longe since discribe, yet sythinge,
that thy unabell spirrit could not fynde ought
in heavens bewties, or in yearths delighte
for likeness, fitt to satisfy thy thought.
Butt what hath it avaylde thee so to write? 355
Shee cares not for thy prayse, who knowes not thers.
Its now an Idell labor and a tale
tolde out of tyme that dulls the heerers eares,
a marchandise whereof ther is no sale.
Leve them, or lay them up with thy dispaires, 360
she hath resolvde, and Judged thee longe ago,
thy lines ar now a murmuringe to her eares
like to a fallinge streame which passinge sloe
is wount to nurrishe sleap, and quietnes.
So shall thy paynfull labors bee perusde 365
and draw on rest, which sumetyme had regard
but thos her cares, thy errors have excusde,
they dayes foredun have had ther dayes reward,
so her harde hart, so her estranged minde
in which above the heavens, I once reposed 370

L.E.P.—7 187

so to thy error have her eares inclined,
and have forgotten all thy past deservinge,
holdinge in minde butt only thyne offence
and only now affecteth thy depravinge
and thincks all vayne that pleadeth thy defence. 375
Yet greater fancye bewtye never bredd,
a more desire the hart bludd never nourished,
her sweetness and affection never fedd
which more in any age hath ever floryshedd.
The minde and vertue never have begotten 380
a firmer love, since love on yearth had poure,
a love obscurde, but cannot be forgotten
to great and stronge for tymes Jawes to devoure,
contayninge such a fayth as ages wound not,
Care, wackfull ever of her good estate, 385
feare, dreadinge loss, which sythes, and joyes not
a memory, of the joyes her grace begate,
a lastinge gratfullness, for thos cumforts past
of which the cordiall sweetness cannot dye
thes thoughts knitt up by fayth shall ever last, 390
thes, tyme assayes, butt never can untye.
Whose life once lived in her perrellike brest,
whose joyes weare drawne but from her happines,
whose harts hygh pleasure, and whose minds trew rest
proceeded from her fortunes blessedness, 395
who was intentive, wakefull, and dismayde,
in feares, in dreames, in feeverus Jelosye,
who longe in sylence served, and obayed
with secret hart, and hydden loyaltye,
which never change to sadd adversetye, 400
which never age, or natures overthrow,
which never sickness, or deformetye,
which never wastinge care, or weeringe wo,
If subject unto thes she could have bynn. . . .

Which never words, or witts mallicious, 405
which never honors bayte, or worlds fame,
atchyved by attemptes adventerus,
or ought beneath the soonn, or heavens frame,
can so desolve, dissever, or distroye
the essentiall love, of no frayle parts cumpounded, 410
though of the same now buried bee the joy
the hope, the cumfort, and the sweetness ended,
but that the thoughts, and memories of thees
worke a relapps of passion, and remayne
of my sadd harte the sorrow suckinge bees 415
the wrongs recevde, the scornes perswade in vayne. . . .
And though thes medcines worke desire to end
and ar in others the trew cure of likinge,
the salves that heale loves wounds and do amend
consuminge woe, and slake our harty sythinge, 420
they worke not so, in thy minds long deseas,
externall fancy tyme alone recurethe
all whose effects do weare away with ease.
Love of delight while such delight indureth
stayes by the pleasure, but no longer stayes. . . . 425
But in my minde so is her love inclosde
and is therof not only the best parte
but into it the essence is disposde. . . .
oh love (the more my wo) to it thow art
yeven as the moysture in each plant that growes, 430
yeven as the soonn unto the frosen ground,
yeven as the sweetness, to th' incarnate rose,
yeven as the Center in each perfait rounde,
as water to the fyshe, to men as ayre
as heat to fier, as light unto the soonn. 435
Oh love it is but vayne, to say thow weare,
ages, and tymes, cannot thy poure outrun. . . .
Thow art the sowle of that unhappy minde
which beinge by nature made an Idell thought

begonn yeven then to take immortall kynde   440
when first her vertues in thy spirrights wrought. . . .
from thee therfore that mover cannot move
because it is becume thy cause of beinge,
what ever error may obscure that love
what ever frayle effect of mortall livinge,   445
what ever passion from distempered hart,
what absence, tyme, or injuries effect,
What faythless frinds, or deipe dissembled art
present, to feede her most unkynde suspect.
Yet as the eayre in deip caves under ground   450
is strongly drawne when violent heat hath rent
great clefts therin, till moysture do abound,
and then the same imprisoned, and uppent,
breakes out in yearthquakes teringe all asunder,
So in the Center of my cloven hart,   455
my hart, to whom her bewties wear such wounder
Lyes the sharpe poysoned heade of that loves dart,
which till all breake and all desolve to dust
thence drawne it cannot bee or therin knowne.
Ther, mixt with my hart bludd, the fretting rust   460
the better part hath eaten, and outgrown. . . .
Butt what of thos, or thes, or what of ought
of that which was, or that which is, to treat?
What I possess is butt the same I sought,
my love was falce, my labors weare desayte,   465
nor less then such they ar esteemde to bee,
a fraude bought att the prize of many woes,
a guile, wherof the profitts unto mee—
coulde it be thought premeditate for thos?
wittnes thos withered leves left on the tree   470
the sorrow worren face, the pensive minde,
the externall shews what may th' internall bee
cold care hath bitten both the root, and rinde, ...

190

Butt stay my thoughts, make end, geve fortune way,
harshe is the voice of woe and sorrows sounde,   475
cumplaynts cure not, and teares do butt allay
griefs for a tyme, which after more abounde
to seeke for moysture in th' arabien sande
is butt a losse of labor, and of rest.
The lincks which tyme did break of harty bands   480
words cannot knytt, or waylings make a new,
seeke not the soonn in cloudes, when it is sett. . . .
On highest mountaynes wher thos Sedars grew
agaynst whose bancks, the trobled ocean bett,
and weare the markes to finde thy hoped port,   485
into a soyle farr of them sealves remove
on Sestus shore, Leanders late resorte,
Hero hath left no lampe to Guyde her love,
Thow lookest for light in vayne, and stormes arise,
Shee sleaps thy death that est thy danger syth-ed,   490
strive then no more, bow down thy weery eyes,
eyes, which to all thes woes thy hart have guided.
Shee is gonn, Shee is lost, shee is found, shee is ever faire.
Sorrow drawes weakly, wher love drawes not too,
woes cries, sound nothinge, butt only in loves eare.   495
Do then by Diinge, what life cannot doo. . . .
Unfolde thy flocks, and leve them to the feilds
to feed on hylls, or dales, wher likes them best,
of what the summer, or the springe tyme yeildes,
for love, and tyme, hath geven thee leve to rest.   500
Thy hart, which was their folde, now in decay
by often stormes, and winters many blasts
all torne and rent, becumes misfortunes pray,
falce hope, my shepherds staff now age hath brast.
My pipe, which loves own hand, gave my desire   505
to singe her prayses, and my wo uppon,
dispaire hath often threatned to the fier
as vayne to keipe now all the rest ar gonn.

Thus home I draw, and deaths longe night drawes onn.
Yet every foot, olde thoughts turne back myne eyes,   510
constraynt mee guides as old age drawes a stonn
agaynst the hill, which over wayghty lyes
for feebell armes, or wasted strenght to move.
My steapps are backwarde, gasinge on my loss,
my minds affection, and my sowles sole love,   515
not mixte with fances chafe, or fortunes dross.
To god I leve it, who first gave it me,
and I her gave, and she returned agayne,
as it was herrs, so lett his mercies bee,
of my last cumforts, the essentiall meane.   520
  But be it soo, or not, th' effects, ar past,
  her love hath end, my woe must ever last.

*The End of the Boockes, of the Oceans Love to Scinthia, and the
Beginninge of the* 12 *Boock, Entreatinge of Sorrow*

My dayes delights, my springetyme joies fordunn,
which in the dawne, and risinge soonn of youth
had their creation, and weare first begunn,

do in the yeveninge, and the winter sadd,
present my minde, which takes my tymes accompt   5
the greif remayninge of the joy it had.

my tymes that then rann ore them sealves in thes
and now runn out in others happines
bringe unto thos new joyes, and new borne dayes,

so could she not, if shee weare not the soonn,   10
which sees the birth, and buriall, of all elce,
and holds that poure, with which shee first begunn,

levinge each withered boddy to be torne
by fortune, and by tymes tempestius,
which by her vertu, once faire frute have borne,   15

knowinge shee cann renew, and cann create
green from the grounde, and floures, yeven out of stonn,
by vertu lastinge over tyme and date,

levinge us only woe, which like the moss,
havinge cumpassion of unburied bones,   20
cleaves to mischance, and unrepayred loss,

for tender stalkes

Prothalamion

L.E.P.—7*

Prothalamion

1

CALME was the day, and through the trembling ayre,
Sweete breathing *Zephyrus* did softly play
A gentle spirit, that lightly did delay
Hot *Titans* beames, which then did glyster fayre:
When I whom sullein care,   5
Through discontent of my long fruitlesse stay
In Princes Court, and expectation vayne
Of idle hopes, which still doe fly away,
Like empty shaddowes, did aflict my brayne,
Walkt forth to ease my payne   10
Along the shoare of silver streaming *Themmes*,
Whose rutty Bancke, the which his River hemmes,
Was paynted all with variable flowers,
And all the meades adornd with daintie gemmes,
Fit to decke maydens bowres,   15
And crowne their Paramours,
Against the Brydale day, which is not long:
   Sweete *Themmes* runne softly, till I end my Song.

2

There, in a Meadow, by the Rivers side,
A Flocke of *Nymphes* I chaunced to espy,   20
All lovely Daughters of the Flood thereby,
With goodly greenish locks all loose untyde,
As each had bene a Bryde,
And each one had a little wicker basket,
Made of fine twigs entrayled curiously,   25
In which they gathered flowers to fill their flasket:

197

And with fine Fingers, cropt full feateously
The tender stalkes on hye.
Of every sort, which in that Meadow grew,
They gathered some; the Violet pallid blew,   30
The little Dazie, that at evening closes,
The virgin Lillie, and the Primrose trew,
With store of vermeil Roses,
To decke their Bridegromes posies,
Against the Brydale day, which was not long: 35
   Sweete *Themmes* runne softly, till I end my Song.

3

With that I saw two Swannes of goodly hewe,
Come softly swimming downe along the Lee;
Two fairer Birds I yet did never see:
The snow which doth the top of *Pindus* strew,   40
Did never whiter shew,
Nor *Jove* himselfe when he a Swan would be
For love of *Leda*, whiter did appeare:
Yet *Leda* was they say as white as he,
Yet not so white as these, nor nothing neare;   45
So purely white they were,
That even the gentle streame, the which them bare,
Seem'd foule to them, and bad his billowes spare
To wet their silken feathers, least they might
Soyle their fayre plumes with water not so fayre,   50
And marre their beauties bright,
That shone as heavens light,
Against their Brydale day, which was not long:
   Sweete *Themmes* runne softly, till I end my Song.

4

Eftsoones the *Nymphes*, which now had Flowers their fill,   55
Ran all in haste, to see that silver brood,
As they came floating on the Christal Flood,

Whom when they sawe, they stood amazed still,
Their wondring eyes to fill.
Them seem'd they never saw a sight so fayre, 60
Of Fowles so lovely, that they sure did deeme
Them heavenly borne, or to be that same payre
Which through the Skie draw *Venus* silver Teeme,
For sure they did not seeme
To be begot of any earthly Seede, 65
But rather Angels or of Angels breede:
Yet were they bred of *Somers-heat* they say,
In sweetest Season, when each Flower and weede
The earth did fresh aray,
So fresh they seem'd as day, 70
Even as their Brydale day, which was not long:
    Sweete *Themmes* runne softly, till I end my Song.

5

Then forth they all out of their baskets drew
Great store of Flowers, the honour of the field,
That to the sense did fragrant odours yield, 75
All which upon those goodly Birds they threw,
And all the Waves did strew,
That like old *Peneus* Waters they did seeme,
When downe along by pleasant *Tempes* shore
Scattred with Flowres, through *Thessaly* they streeme, 80
That they appeare through Lillies plenteous store,
Like a Brydes Chamber flore:
Two of those *Nymphes*, meane while, two Garlands bound,
Of freshest Flowres which in that Mead they found,
The which presenting all in trim Array, 85
Their snowie Foreheads therewithall they crownd,
Whil'st one did sing this Lay,
Prepar'd against that Day,
Against their Brydale day, which was not long:
    Sweete *Themmes* runne softly, till I end my Song. 90

6

Ye gentle Birdes, the worlds faire ornament,
And heavens glorie, whom this happie hower
Doth leade unto your lovers blisfull bower,
Joy may you have and gentle hearts content
Of your loves couplement: 95
And let faire *Venus*, that is Queene of love,
With her heart-quelling Sonne upon you smile,
Whose smile they say, hath vertue to remove
All Loves dislike, and friendships faultie guile
For ever to assoile. 100
Let endlesse Peace your steadfast hearts accord,
And blessed Plentie wait upon your bord,
And let your bed with pleasures chast abound,
That fruitfull issue may to you afford,
Which may your foes confound, 105
And make your joyes redound,
Upon your Brydale day, which is not long:
    Sweete *Themmes* run softlie, till I end my Song.

7

So ended she; and all the rest around
To her redoubled that her undersong, 110
Which said, their bridale daye should not be long.
And gentle Eccho from the neighbour ground,
Their accents did resound.
So forth those joyous Birdes did passe along,
Adowne the Lee, that to them murmurde low, 115
As he would speake, but that he lackt a tong,
Yet did by signes his glad affection show,
Making his streame run slow.
And all the foule which in his flood did dwell
Gan flock about these twaine, that did excell 120
The rest, so far, as *Cynthia* doth shend
The lesser starres. So they enranged well,

Did on those two attend,
And their best service lend,
Against their wedding day, which was not long: 125
   Sweete *Themmes* run softly, till I end my song.

8

At length they all to mery *London* came,
To mery London, my most kyndly Nurse,
That to me gave this Lifes first native sourse:
Though from another place I take my name,   130
An house of auncient fame.
There when they came, whereas those bricky towres,
The which on *Themmes* brode aged backe doe ryde,
Where now the studious Lawyers have their bowers,
There whylome wont the Templer Knights to byde,   135
Till they decayd through pride:
Next whereunto there standes a stately place,
Where oft I gayned giftes and goodly grace
Of that great Lord, which therein wont to dwell,
Whose want too well, now feeles my freendles case: 140
But Ah here fits not well
Olde woes but joyes to tell
Against the bridale daye, which is not long:
   Sweete *Themmes* runne softly, till I end my Song.

9

Yet therein now doth lodge a noble Peer,   145
Great *Englands* glory and the Worlds wide wonder,
Whose dreadfull name, late through all *Spaine* did thunder,
And *Hercules* two pillors standing neere,
Did make to quake and feare:
Faire branch of Honor, flower of Chevalrie,   150
That fillest *England* with thy triumphes fame,
Joy have thou of thy noble victorie,
And endlesse happinesse of thine owne name

That promiseth the same:
That through thy prowesse and victorious armes,   155
Thy country may be freed from forraine harmes:
And great *Elisaes* glorious name may ring
Through al the world, fil'd with thy wide Alarmes,
Which some brave muse may sing
To ages following,   160
Upon the Brydale day, which is not long:
    Sweete *Themmes* runne softly, till I end my Song.

10

From those high Towers, this noble Lord issuing,
Like Radiant *Hesper* when his golden hayre
In th'*Ocean* billowes he hath Bathed fayre,   165
Descended to the Rivers open vewing,
With a great traine ensuing.
Above the rest were goodly to be seene
Two gentle Knights of lovely face and feature
Beseeming well the bower of anie Queene,   170
With gifts of wit and ornaments of nature,
Fit for so goodly stature:
That like the twins of *Jove* they seem'd in sight,
Which decke the Bauldricke of the Heavens bright.
They two forth pacing to the Rivers side,   175
Received those two faire Brides, their Loves delight,
Which at th'appointed tyde,
Each one did make his Bryde,
Against their Brydale day, which is not long:
    Sweete *Themmes* runne softly, till I end my Song.   180

FINIS

NOTES

57. HERO AND LEANDER

THE FIRST SESTIAD

SESTIAD: Hero lived in Sestos; Chapman, on the anology of 'Iliad' from 'Ilios', coined this term for each book. One name of Musaeus' poem is Σηστιας.
Argument. l.2. phane. fane: temple.

l.6. implie: include.

l.3. Seaborderers: 1629 + Seaborders 1598.

l.4. hight: called.

ll.5–50. BM has noted that there is only one unequivocal reference to Hero's flesh in the description—*l.42*—whereas Leander, *ll.51–90*, is described as nakedly desirable.

l.6. This is Marlowe's invention.

l.7. burning throne: the sun.

l.9. lawne: a kind of fine linen.

l.10. drawne: embroidered.

l.15. staine: This is not a realistic detail. This odd decoration endows Hero with a somewhat sinister aspect.

ll.31–6. The grotesquerie of this is deliberate.

l.45. Venus Nun: priestess of Venus, but a paradox that embodies the poet's comic and essentially hostile view of Hero. The association of nuns and whores was an Elizabethan commonplace; some prostitutes were known as 'abbesses'.

l.47. she . . .she: i.e. Hero.

l.49. her: Nature's.

l.50. Marlowe has his tongue in his cheek; but this nevertheless reinforces his hostile view of female beauty.

l.52. Musaeus: See Introduction, p. 14.

l.59. Cinthia: the Moon.

l.61. Circes wand: used by the enchantress to change men to beasts: hence, 'arousing lust'.

l.65. Pelops: Pelops' father Tantalus served him as stew to the Gods; Demeter ate a shoulder.

l.70. But this is exactly what Marlowe is irreverently up to.

l.73. his: Narcissus'.

l.77. wilde Hippolytus: was dedicated to Artemis and the enemy of Venus, and hence in this context impervious to female beauty but not to male. Marlowe had previously, *Amores*, II, 4, *l.*32, called him 'chastest'. There is throughout his part of the poem a suggestion that 'chastity' is essentially a male attribute.

*l.*80.   *uplandish:* rural.

*ll.*83–4.   Compare Shakespeare, Sonnet 20.

*l.*90.   *thrall:* slave.

*l.*99.   *melancholie earth:* the earth is the humour associated with the humour of melancholy.

*l.*101.   Phaethon persuaded his father Helios to allow him to drive the chariot of the sun across the heavens for one single day; looking down at the stars he felt dizzy, lost control, and his chariot threatened to burn up the earth (creating the Libyan desert). Zeus, to save the earth, killed him with a thunderbolt, and his scorched body fell into the River Eridanus.

*l.*107.   *starre:* the moon.

*l.*108.   *thirling carre:* whirling, spinning chariot.

*l.*111.   *over-rules the flood:* holds sway over the sea.

*ll.*113–130. This description of the havoc created by Hero, though comic, is calculated to alarm.

*l.*114.   *Wretched Ixion's shaggie footed race:* Ixion murdered his father-in-law Eioneus and was purified of this crime by Zeus. He attained immortality; but then tried to seduce Hera. Zeus created Nephele, a phantom, to deceive Ixion, and of the resultant union the 'shaggy-footed' centaurs—half-horses, half-men —were born. Ixion was then bound to a wheel of fire in hell. The centaurs were brutishly lustful.

*l.*134.   *they:* Hero and Leander.

*l.*136.   *discoloured:* variegated.

*l.*137.   *Proteus:* A god of the sea who is able to change himself into whatever shape he desires.

*l.*138.   *livelie:* lifelike. *Sea agget:* 'agate with green wave-like markings' (*O.E.D*).

*l.*139.   *Bacchus:* Roman name for Dionysus in his aspect as God of wine and revelry.

*ll.*143–156.   This matter-of-fact, mock-realistic, pleased tone is new in sixteenth-century poetry: there is no Christian awe at pagan evil, but plenty of casual pleasure in the facts. The pictures in the crystal pavement emphasize the bisexuality of the Gods (in *ll.*148 and 154–5).

*l.*147.   *sisters:* Juno's.

*l.*148.   *Idalian Ganimed:* Ganymede, son of Tros the founder of Troy, was a boy so beautiful that Jove snatched him up to be his cupbearer. 'Idalian' refers either to Mount Ida or to Idalium in Cyprus.

*l.*149.   Jove wooed Europa in the form of a bull.

*l.*150.   As Jupiter Pluvialis, the sender of rain.

*ll.*151–2.   This story is to be found in the eighth book of the *Odyssey*, and was retold by Ovid, *Metamorphoses*, pp. 98–9. Vulcan (Hephaestus) caught Mars (Ares) and his wife Venus (Aphrodite) in *flagrante delicto*, and with the aid of his assistants, the Cyclops, he flung an invisible iron net around them.

ll.154–5. Cyparissus loved a sacred stag, which he killed in error. He died of grief and was turned into a cypress tree. Despite LCM and MM, there is nothing in Ovid, *Metamorphoses*, pp. 227–8, about Sylvanus, a rustic Roman deity and form of Pan, loving the youth. But Apollo mourned for him.

l.158. The turtle dove was a symbol of constancy, as in Shakespeare's *The Phoenix and the Turtle*.

l.159. vaild: bowed.

ll.167–174. Kocher, pp. 313–4, quotes these lines as of 'extreme interest as [an expression] of Marlowe's own opinions'. This may be so, but as LCM points out, *ll.169–70* are a paraphrase of a passage from Sir Thomas Hoby's translation of Castiglione's *Il Cortegiano:* '. . . at . . . combats and games . . . it is seene that the lookers on many times beare affeccion without any manifest cause why. . . .'

l.168. will: A pun in which the usual sense is subordinated to that of 'lust'.

ll.180–1. Marlowe's emphasis upon Hero's deliberate hypocrisy and its inflaming effects on Leander should be noted.

l.184. hardly: with difficulty.

l.185. parled: spoke.

l.186. amazed: bewildered, and therefore rendering lovers incapable of speech.

l.189. Acheron: a river in Hades.

l.197. Sophister: (i) specious reasoner, (ii) second- or third-year undergraduate at sixteenth-century Cambridge.

ll.199–294. This passage is, ostensibly, a summary of several traditional arguments against virginity. They are most famously found in Milton's *Comus*, but are there represented as wholly sinful. Some of the same arguments are to be found in the most factitious of Shakespeare's sonnets, 1–18. The whole passage, which becomes progressively more ridiculous, is an elaborately artificial send-up of the kind of psychologically absurd Aristotelian disputations that undergraduates were supposed to conduct. None of the arguments used by Leander, most of which are individually annotated, is more absurd or casuistic than ones seriously employed at the time; *mishapen stuffe:* deformed people, i.e. in this instance, one whose mental cruelty contradicts her physical beauty.

l.210. bending: turning, i.e. the perfume (accent is on second syllable) follows Hero wherever she goes.

l.212. nunne: priestess.

l.214. flaring: brightly coloured; gaudy.

ll.215–222. Alert readers will note that the argument is as specious as Hero's

205

attitude is hypocritical. Leander's notion of his 'duty' (see *l.*221) is to defile Hero's 'divinity and purity'. In his accumulation of such details Marlowe cynically mocks the strict conventions of the courtship game by revealing the psychological realities that underlie it.

*l.*223. Another specious argument, with a casually insolent look at Christian doctrine: on the theologically proper analogy that heaven has deeper purposes than merely to be enjoyed (in an ocular sense), Hero is being persuaded to allow herself to be enjoyed (in a sexual sense).

*l.*230. A delicate way of reiterating the age-old, if possibly unjust, commonplace that if they are not loved physically women become shrewish.

*l.*233. *use*: with a pun on the sense of 'lust'.

*l.*247. *faire jem, sweet in the losse alone*: virginity is sweet only in the losing of it (a male generalization not universally borne out by female reports on the subject).

*ll.*249–54. The argument, psychologically a deliberately absurd one, parodying both a current allegorical, Christian manner of dealing with pagan material (see Introduction, p. 16), and of the sort of logic produced by men in the throes of lust, is: 'If virginity were bequeathable, then all the Gods would rush down to claim it, producing such strife that it would destroy human order; therefore the Gods have wisely seen to it that men and women experience sexual enjoyment.' Marlowe at least glances here at the sexual fascination exercised by virginity.

*l.*255. *One is no number:* A technical matter first raised by Aristotle in his *Metaphysics* and *Physics*.

*ll.*257–8. In marriage you can experience the proper 'singleness', of unity; *never-singling:* who never separates.

*ll.*265–6. 'We value ugly [base—or, here, probably merely commonplace] women for the sake of their child-bearing capacities ["for the stampes sake"]; we value *you* for the pleasure you give us when we make the actual impression'.

*ll.*267–8. Aristotle had said that in the sexual act women received 'perfection' from men, while men received 'imperfection'. This was later taken up, without regard to its context, by certain 'reverend fathers', whose abstractly anti-sexual earnestness is now parodied by Marlowe by being put to profane use, in Leander's argument.

*l.*270. *essence:* philosophical term for any entity, visible or abstract.

*l.*273. *mold:* form. A reference to Platonic 'ideas': virginity, the argument goes, is not even a Platonic 'idea'.

*l.*278. Leander now appeals to the doctrine of Original Sin in order to persuade Hero of the non-virtuousness of her 'virtue'.

*ll.*283–4. 'Do you seek immortality by remaining chaste while aware that some have slandered even Diana [Goddess especially revered by women]?'

l.296.   *tralucent:* translucent.

l.298.   *trace:* go.

l.301.   *Dorick musicke.* The Doric mode was simple, solemn and appropriate to heroic action. LCM, and MM following him, complain that 'Soft Lydian airs' (as in Milton's *L'Allegro*) would be more suitable. But Leander, despite his grasp of theological and scholastic disputation, is sexually a dolt and may conceive of love-making as a heroic activity.

l.303.   *Idiot:* ignorant person; *she:* Venus.

l.309.   *shake hands:* not a charming euphemism for his real intentions but, more comically, an announcement of what he seriously expects. Hero knows better.

l.311.   *so:* in such a way.

l.312.   *put:* repelled; *mo:* more.

l.321.   *Flint-brested Pallas:* armour-clad Pallas Athene was a traditional enemy of Venus.

l.325.   *avarice:* miserliness (of hoarding your virginity).

l.326.   *nice:* coy, i.e. sexually 'proper'.

l.328.   'Beauty on its own is destroyed if it is hoarded', i.e. not given out to 'use'.

ll.329–30.   The meaning is: 'He used these and many other persuasions, upon which she conceded what she had already decided to concede'.

l.332.   *jarre:* argue; wrangle.

l.342.   *her:* herself.

l.346.   *whist:* silent.

l.352.   *swannes and sparrowes:* both sacred to Venus.

l.356.   *apish:* stupid.

l.360.   *anger:* at her own revelation of eagerness.

ll.361–2.   *mooving severall waies . . . instant:* in the Ptolemaic system of astronomy, in which the earth was the fixed centre of the universe, the planets moved in their own orbit but were also carried along by the rotation of the other spheres; *assaies:* attempts.

ll.365–6.   A characteristically Marlovian image, throwing a bitterly cynical light upon both 'heaven' and the nature of 'innocence': heaven is represented as itself lusting for a type of innocence that only ten lines previously has been knowingly alluding to a 'better' way of spending the night than in discourse with an old woman. . . .

l.370.   *emptie aire:* presumably the etherial realm above the 'lower air'.

l.377.   *destinies:* the Fates.

l.378.   *Laden . . . griefe:* because of his own angry impulse, described in *ll*.369–72.

l.380.   *Both:* Hero and Leander.

l.382.   This line occurs in Marlowe's play *The Tragedie of Dido Queen of Carthage*, II, i, *l*.231.

l.383.   *Love:* i.e. Cupid.

ll.386ff.   MM, following LCM, thinks that this tale may have been 'suggested (but no more)' by the Mercury-Herse episode in Ovid's *Metamorphoses*, 69–72; *Jove-borne Mercury:* Mercury was the son of Jupiter and Maia.

l.388.   *Inchaunted Argus:* see *Metamorphoses*, pp. 45–8.

ll.389.   *carelesse:* untended.

l.390.   *seem'd to skorne:* she only appeared to scorn it: the implication is that she knew it looked better 'careless'; *it:* adornment.

l.392.   *glose:* flatter.

l.398.   *snakie rod:* Mercury's caduceus. Mercury, messenger of the Gods, was the patron of heralds, and carried a golden staff, around the top of which serpents were entwined; it was regarded as a symbol of power. Doubtless a phallic allusion is involved.

l.402.   *her fancie to assay:* 'assail or make trial of her love-sentiment' (LCM); 'it means something like "provoke images (of love) in her mind"' (MM). Both cite one obsolete use of 'assay' given in *O.E.D*: 'assail with love-proposals'. I think the phrase means, essentially, 'incite her to feel lust for him': *fancie* combines the senses of 'imagination', 'whim' and 'amorous inclination' into something suggestive of the physical; 'assay' combines the early (Middle English) sense of 'try by touch' with that cited by LCM and MM. Mercury's 'smooth speech' would have played on the country girl's own 'too too' advanced knowledge of her charms (*l*.395).

l.411.   *new Elisium:* The physical goal, i.e. orgasm, of lovers (and others) has very frequently been described as 'paradise', 'Elysium', and so on. Marlowe wittily describes Mercury's goal as a 'new' Elysium: as son of Jove he knows the old one.

l.418.   *to heare his tale:* this is not a story, but a series of persuasive arguments such as those employed by Leander in an earlier passage (*ll*.199–294). As BM has pointed out, Marlowe is clearly concerned, both in the earlier passage and in this only apparently irrelevant interpolation, with the persuasive powers of rhetoric. See Introduction, p. 20.

l.420.   *pleasure* 1598 (1); *pleasures* 1598 (2).

l.425.   *wanting no excuse:* 'availing herself of any pretext' is LCM's explanation, and MM quotes him. But it could mean 'not requiring any pretext', as in the Whitman idiom.

l.426.   *as women use:* as women usually do.

l.434.   *Hebe Joves cup fil'd:* Hebe preceded Ganymede in the office of cup-bearer to the Gods.

l.437.   *He:* Jove; *inly:* inwardly, hence 'furiously'.

ll.447–8.   The Fates, or spinners, spun out for mortals their thread of mortality.

l.449.   *engins:* these, like this story, seem to have been products of Marlowe's

208

imagination. The sense is that the Fates, in their love for Mercury, offered him their control over human destiny.

l.452. *his fathers seat:* Jove's own father, Saturn.

l.456. *Ops:* the Greek Rhea, consort of Saturn.

l.458. *Stigian:* hellish; *Emprie:* empery; dominion.

l.459. *blessed time:* the reign of Saturn was proverbially regarded as the Golden Age.

ll.465–70. Mercury represented learning. This is an oblique, cautious and humorous statement of Marlowe's dislike of Christianity, which suppressed learning and inculcated ignorance. The association between learning and poverty was, naturally, a commonplace.

l.472. *boore:* clown, ignorant person.

l.473. *angrie sisters:* the Fates.

l.475. *Midas brood:* the ass-eared rich. The two most famous tales of Midas, son of Gordius, are (i) that having been granted his wish that everything he touched should turn to gold, he was forced to wash in the river Pactolus in order to return to his former non-gilding state, so that he might eat and drink; (ii) that he was awarded ass's ears by Apollo for deciding against him in a lute-contest.

l.477. *in aspiring:* inaspiring 1598; not ambitious for money, power or the 'Honor' attained by *'Midas* brood'.

l.478. As MM suggests, Marlowe must be alluding to the intellectuals of his age 'and their continental adventures'. Ralegh comes immediately to mind; so does Marlowe himself. *discontent:* discontented.

l.480. *surpris'd:* captivated.

l.481. *the loftie servile clowne:* highly placed boor, unworthy of his freedom. Marlowe thus characterizes the establishment of his time, from which we may conclude that not all things have changed.

l.483. *muse not:* don't wonder that; *sped:* succeeded.

THE SECOND SESTIAD

ARGUMENT. l.1. *of love takes deeper sence:* 'feels love more deeply' (LCM).

    l.2. *Her love:* Leander.

    l.7. *aspire:* aspire to.

l.1. *By this:* We are resuming at the point where Hero is no longer able to control her desire, and has even betrayed it (I, *l.*357).

l.9. *light:* wanton.

l.12. *traine:* allure.

l.13. *a novice:* in the sexual ways of women.

l.17. *graces:* the three Graces bestowed, among other attributes, beauty.

l.20. *pointed:* appointed.

209

l.25. *and . . . denied:* actually on this occasion it was. The reference is to love-talk.

l.26. *affied:* betrothed.

l.28. *what he did she willingly requited:* In view of Hero's ultimate reservations at this stage, we must suppose that Leander 'did' nothing too drastic.

l.32. *pais'd:* poised.

l.44. Cf. II, *ll*.8–9. An allusion to the nervousness frequently felt by women— when, like Hero, they are intent on 'yielding'—that they are going too far with the game (as when Leander, being a 'novice', did not go after her at *ll*.11–14).

l.46. *Salmacis:* The nymph Salmacis wooed Hermaphroditus: see *Metamorphoses, ll*.101–4. The implied comparison of Leander and Hermaphroditus is significant. When Salmacis approaches Hermaphroditus amorously, he blushes, 'for he did not know what love was'.

l.49. *slake:* diminish.

l.51. Aesop's cock, in the fable, rejects the jewel for a barleycorn, i.e. Leander does not understand what is being offered to him; the parallel with the cock even suggests that what is being offered is valueless to him. 'Cock', for penis, was then extant (it occurs in Shakespeare): this makes the passage even more explicit.

l.55. *creatures wanting sence:* inanimate objects; as LCM suggests, Marlowe in *ll*.55–8 is comparing love to the phenomenon of magnetism.

l.56. *appetence:* 'the action of seeking for, desire; appetite, passion' (*O.E.D.*).

l.58. *lep:* leap.

l.61. *rude:* ignorant; *raw:* immature; with a glance at the earlier Middle English meaning, 'in a natural state'.

l.65. *clung:* used transitively.

ll.66–72. The essence here is that Hero, even while she struggled, taught Leander 'what to do'.

l.71. *cunningly:* skilfully, dexterously.

l.73. *by:* off.

l.75. *tree of Tantalus:* the tree, in Hades, for whose fruit Tantalus vainly grasped.

l.87. *steeds:* the horses that draw the chariot of the Sun.

l.100. *As pittying these lovers, downeward creepes:* 'in order that their love may be kept secret by darkness' (LCM).

l.105. *Cupids myrtle:* Marlowe translated the last couplet of Ovid's opening 'elegy' thus: '*Elegian* Muse, that warblest amorous laies,/Girt my shine browe with Sea-banke Mirtle sprays'. MM adds: 'Leander, after all, is an Ovidian love-poet'.

l.107. *heare:* hair.

l.116. *reeking:* fuming.

210

l.118. *aire:* LCM notes that this is one of 'the recognized sixteenth-century spellings of "heir" ', but MM retains the 1598 reading, explaining 'The simile is curious, but the reference is surely to the displacement of air from its proper "sphere", in the Ptolemaic conception.' Obviously a pun is involved: there is no need to reject the original reading.

l.120. *Alcides like:* Hercules-like.

l.123. *in a Dyameter:* 'The distinction here implied appears to be between the sun shining down from its highest altitude and shining sideways or obliquely ['lat'rally']. The sun is thought of as being farther away at the meridian than before or after it reaches that point, though more powerful in its heat-giving capacity' (LCM).

ll.129–30. Because he was separated from Hero, Leander's looks gave his love away (it should not be forgotten that the love was forbidden).

l.132. *descride:* given away.

l.135. *apparantly:* clearly.

ll.141–4. Cf. *Ovid's Elegies*, III, iv, *ll*.13–16: 'I saw a horse against the bitte stiffe-neckt,/ Like lightning go, his strugling mouth being checkt./When he perceivd the reines let slacke, he stayde,/And on his loose mane the loose bridle laide./

l.144. *Checkes:* stamps upon.

l.146. 'What thing now will Leander dare not do?'

l.154. *lively:* briskly.

l.155. *saphir visag'd god:* Neptune [Greek Poseidon]; *prowd:* experienced an erection.

l.156. *capring Triton:* Neptune usually called upon his son Triton to blow his conch to soothe the waves (e.g. Ovid, *Metamorphoses*, *l*.38); here, LCM rather naïvely suggests, 'Marlowe seems to make it . . . a consequence of Neptune's joy or pride'.

ll.157–8. A joke: Neptune has mistaken Leander for the legendary catamite of the Gods.

l.159. *striv'd:* struggled against (temptation as well as Neptune).

l.164. *sort:* manner; *shipwracke:* shipwrecked.

l.166. Marlowe postulates a homosexual rivalry, over Ganymede, between Neptune and his brother.

l.170. *he:* Leander.

ll.171–4. This is not meant to be taken seriously; it is, in fact, an excellent example of the mock heroic.

l.179. *Helles bracelet:* Helle was daughter of Athamas and the phantom Nephele (see I, *l*.144, n.). She felt giddy, lost her hold of the winged golden ram on whose back she was riding, and was drowned in the straits between Europe and Asia, now called Hellespont in her honour. There is a late mythographic tradition, noted by LCM, in which Helle was saved by Neptune and bore him a son; this is strengthened by the fact that the winged golden ram was the offspring of Poseidon and Theophane.

l.182. bewrayd: revealed.

l.187. threw: the grammar demands 'throw'.

ll.192–3. You . . . Neptune: This was certainly an 'in' joke.

ll.194–201. 'The relationship of this passage to *Edward II* could hardly be clearer. Gaveston, who might 'have swum from France/And like *Leander* gaspt upon the sande', proposes to sway the pliant king by exactly the same means' (BM). Cf., *Edward II*, I, i, *ll.*58–66:

> Like *Sylvan* Nimphes my pages shall be clad,
> My men like Satyres grazing on the lawnes,
> Shall with their Goate feete daunce an antick hay.
> Sometime a lovelie boye in *Dians* shape,
> With haire that gilds the water as it glides,
> Crownets of pearle about his naked armes,
> And in his sportfull hands an Olive tree,
> To hide those parts which men delight to see,
> Shall bathe him in a spring, . . .

l.200. up-staring Fawnes: fawns were woodland creatures like the satyrs, and as lustful. '*Up-staring*' [upstarting 1609–37, 1826] is difficult in this context; perhaps it means 'showing the whites of their eyes in amazed lust'.

l.203. Thetis glassie bower: the sea (where Thetis dwelt).

ll.209–12. This couplet, if nothing else, should convince anyone who doubts Marlowe's comic intentions in this episode.

l.212. darting: 'throwing as a dart' (LCM).

l.217. obdurat: accented on second syllable.

l.218. hinds: literally, 'rustics'; here, 'people'.

l.220. he: i.e. Neptune himself.

l.223. fancie to surprize: see I, *l.*402, n.; I, *l.*480, n.

l.226. deepe perswading Oratorie failes: and, in this case, much else: see II, *ll.*159–60; II, *ll.*181–190.

l.229. albeit: although.

l.234. Sailors carrying Arion the musician back from a festival were jealous of the prizes he had won, and so forced him to jump overboard. But his music had attracted a school of dolphins, one of which saved him from drowning; *crooked:* curved.

l.242. lawne: see I, *l.*9, n. Hero had now, in modern parlance, put on a negligée.

l.246. Though, 1598 (2): Through 1598 (1).

l.250. cherely: gladly.

l.255. Whose: i.e. her lukewarm place's; *fet:* fetched.

212

*ll.*256–8. *higher set . . . boules:* 'The meaning intended here is "higher than the thoughts of Mars as he carouses, etc." ' (LCM).

*l.*258. *drerie:* bloody.

*l.*261. Actaeon spied Diana bathing in a stream, whereat she changed him into a stag. See Ovid, *Metamorphoses*, pp. 78–9.

*l.*266. *darksome:* dark.

*l.*270. *She the Harpey playd:* The Harpies, beautiful in the early myths, were later represented as hideous woman-faced birds, huge-clawed, always white with hunger, stinking and all-devouring. MM has an excellent note: 'Hero may be said to be withdrawing the banquet of herself'. This whole account of Leander's third encounter with Hero contrasts with the farcical preceding episode in which Neptune chases the lovely boy: the description of Hero's shifts and changes before succumbing to Leander is comparatively serious in its realism.

*ll.*273–8. LCM is probably correct when he identifies the 'globe' with Hero's body as a whole. ('The veins or "lines" make the poet think of the lines on a globe-map; in the parenthesis the comparison is justified by the suggestion that Leander uses the globe, or body, as a mariner might, for guidance in sailing to new regions. The idea of the globe also perhaps calls up that of Sisyphus' rolling block of marble'); but the notion of the breasts is suggested by the 'rising yu'rie mount'; and these do, of course, play their part in the journey 'to regions full of blis'. I think there is this physical basis for the whole metaphor; the comparison with Sisyphus, who pushed a rock to the top of a mountainside only to have it always roll back, is peculiarly appropriate in the physio-psychological circumstances.

*l.*274. *empal'd:* surrounded.

*ll.*279–300. The order of 1598 is patently wrong: *l.*278 is followed by *ll.*291–300, which is then followed by *ll.*279–90. Singer (ed. 1821) followed *l.*278 by *ll.*289–300, and this by *ll.*279–88. The present order was proposed by TB and is followed by LCM and MM. One modern editor, the always highly eccentric Ridley (ed. 1955), follows Singer. Presumably the mistake came about through the misplacement of a leaf of Marlowe's original MS.

*l.*280. *some thing:* 1598 (1); *some things:* 1598 (2). Modernizing editors, i.e. LCM, MM, etc., emend to 'something', an example of why modernization is so often simply another form of emendation. The 'some thing' was, of course, that he loved her.

*l.*284. *alarme:* call to arms, i.e. action.

*l.*285. *the truce was broke:* the truce, of *l.*278, was broken; and not only, of course, the truce.

*l.*288. *pray:* prey.

*l.*289. *wring:* press, in order to hold firmly onto.

*ll.*291–3. The metaphor is based on the notion of the continual combinations and separations of the elements under the influences of Love and Strife. Marlowe got this, which was familiar material, from Aristotle's *Metaphysics*. *ll*.298–300. MM states that this is a reference to 'the twelfth and last labour of Hercules'; but this must be a misprint for the eleventh labour: the Hesperides, Atlas' daughters, pilfered apples from the tree that they were entrusted to guard, so the ever-watchful dragon Ladon was set to coil around it. Hercules' task was to bring apples from this tree. The reference here is, of course, to sexual pleasure.

l.305. *Ericine:* Venus, who had a sanctuary at Eryx in Sicily.

l.314. *cling'd:* see II, *l*.65, n.

l.320. *glymse:* glyms; gleams. The only known form of this word is 'glyms' or 'glims'.

l.326. *Dis:* Roman God of wealth: Greek 'Pluton' (the original God) derives from 'ploutos', wealth; Latin 'Dis' derives from 'dives', rich.

ll.327–8. 'These images combine Apollo's attributes of sun-god and patron of music. . . .' (MM).

l.329. *Hesperus:* the evening-star (which is of course also the morning-star, Venus; but the two were distinguished in mythology).

l.330. *day bright-bearing:* conj. LCM day Bright-bearing 1598.

l.334. *dang'd:* 1598 (1); hurld 1598 (2). Possibly the latter, which means the same, is Chapman's alteration.

CHAPMAN'S DEDICATION
Heading.
Lady Walsingham: wife of Sir Thomas Walsingham.

l.2. *strange instigation:* probably a double pun in which a 'mysterious inspiration' is yoked to a 'commission from outside'.

l.5. *common:* commonly.

l.7. *Shewed:* 1598 Chapman may, as LCM suggests, have written 'showered'.

l.8. *Mony-Monger:* seeker after profit; *concluded:* included.

ll.10–12. *But he. . . ridiculous lover:* LCM thought that Chapman, who is clearly referring here to hypocritical puritans (who 'shun trifles', i.e. frivolities), was alluding specifically to his comedy *An Humorous Days Mirth*, in which puritanism is satrized, and which was performed before 10 March 1598.

l.12. *trifle:* MM thinks that the repetition of this word 'suggests [Chapman's] pretentious stance as a poet'. But he misses the irony. See the following notes.

l.15. *uncourtly and sillie:* not fawning, and homely: but the pun involving the usual meaning of 'silly' points up the grave irony of the whole paragraph.

l.19. *adjoynde . . . honour:* 'contentment has been added [joined on to] my desire for your true honour' (the 'true', pretending to be merely rhetorical, emphasizes Chapman's own sense of 'honour', as opposed to the usual concept of it).

214

l.22. meere: Another unmistakable indication of the ironic nature of the whole dedication: virtues ('good parts') could hardly be regarded as 'mere' under any *truly* honourable circumstances. Later, in James I's reign, much sexual scandal attached itself to Lady Audrey Walsingham, such as that she was the mistress of the crippled Sir Robert Cecil: doubtless 'good parts' is yet another pun: the phrases 'sweet inclination' and 'happines of your proceedings' reinforce the suggestion.

ll.25–27. then if . . . presents: The 'others' may include her husband Sir Thomas, whose 'horns' (indicating his cuckolded status) are only smoothed out by 'sensualitie and presents'. However, that Lady Audrey had already started on her career as tart is only conjectural.

l.25. then: than.

l.26. Ensignes: badges; *state:* high rank; *sowrenes:* moroseness; peevishness.

l.28. in figure of the other unitie. Chapman's dedication is to Lady Walsingham; Blount's, of the whole poem, is to Sir Thomas.

l.29. rejoyned: joined in another way.

l.31. circulare: 'Chapman frequently describes the perfect or complete life as circular. . . . The platonic conception of the circle as the perfect form is common in Renaissance criticism . . .' (PPB).

THE THIRD SESTIAD

Argument: l.4. Thesme: a coinage from Greek θεσμός.

l.6. improving: reproving; this obsolete verb was derived from Latin 'improbare', to blame, disapprove.

l.10. Waies: weighs (her state).

ll.1–2. New Light . . . ensue. The poem begins with the dawning of a new day—and a change in the fortune of the lovers. Chapman is also carefully pointing out that he is not trying to finish Marlowe's poem as the dead poet himself would have finished it, but that he is taking over from him in his own person.

l.3. lest: least; *hard:* arduous (for the lovers in the story); *grave and hie.* Cf. Ben Jonson, *The Poetaster*, Epilogue . . . 'Leave me! There's something come into my thought,/That must and shall be sung high and aloof,/Safe from the wolf's black jaw, and the dull ass's hoof.'

l.6. became: were suitable to.

l.7. High: lively; *sharpe plights:* 'eager or keen conditions, states' (LCM).

l.8. staid: sober; sedate; *censure:* judge (but not necessarily adversely).

l.9. That being enjoyd aske judgement: 'that, having been experienced, now invite judgement' (cf. 'censure' of preceding line).

ll.9–10. now we praise,/As having parted: 'now we appraise [these delights] as things that have past'. There is a pun, involving the familiar sense of praise, which pays tribute to Marlowe: Chapman is turning another way. *l.*10. *Evenings crowne the daies*. This is proverbial; 'crowne' is sometimes replaced by 'praise'. e.g.: from Hall's *Contemplations* (1612–15): 'The evening praises the day, and the chief grace of the theatre is in the last scene. "Be faithful to the death, and I will give thee a crown of life".' Essentially, this merely caps the preceding statement ('now we praise/As having parted') with a proverb. Almost certainly also current was the proverb, 'The evening praises the day, and the morning a frost' (first collected by the poet, George Herbert, in his *Outlandish Proverbs*, 1640).

*l.*12. i.e. Strange attires have their source in Pied Vanity.

*l.*13. *lisping:* cunningly ingratiating.

*l.*14. *Relentfull:* enervating; languishing.

*l.*16. 'Desist from lust by heeding the example of what these two went through'.

*ll.*17–19. Leander arose with the sun.

*l.*22. *Epethite:* epithet.

*l.*23. *enamourd waves:* waves (personifying Neptune) enamoured of Leander.

*l.*24. Phoebus deliberately gilded (shone upon) Leander's limbs.

*l.*24. (margin) *vertue:* power.

*l.*27. *had to stay:* did not wait.

*l.*28. *joy:* enjoy.

*l.*32. *dispend:* squander wastefully.

*ll.*35–6. The essence of this couplet, and the preceding nine lines, is that Leander had been guilty of unconsidered, 'unceremonius', sensuality. He had not considered his sexual actions; nor, therefore, had he considered Hero. *l.*35. *graven in sence:* rooted in lust.

*l.*36. 'Nothing can last unless it is preserved by virtue [best understood here as meaning "right, loving behaviour"]'.

*l.*40. i.e. her skin has a delicious colour; *damaske:* colour of the damask rose.

*l.*42. *whose mixture and first fire:* 'her nature in its complexity and her simple essence' (LCM), i.e. her whole self and her passion.

*l.*43. *limit:* keep in proper proportion; *both Love's deities:* Venus and Cupid.

*l.*46. *earth-exempted minde:* a mind free from gross materialism.

*l.*48. *like earth:* wholly materialistically.

*l.*49. *ranke:* swaggeringly crude.

*ll.*50–58. This passage is adapted from a Latin translation, by Xylander, of Plutarch's *Moralia*, very frequently used by Chapman.

*ll.*50–52. The meaning is: no true value may be attached to the things-in-themselves that remove hunger and thirst or cover nakedness. The thinking. as in the next six lines, is Neoplatonic.

*l.*53. *what doth plentifully minister:* those actions that liberally dispense.

*l.*55. *orderd:* arranged; *desire:* sexual desire.

216

l.56. *to aspire:* to experiment.

l.57. *moyst:* fruitful.

l.58. *carving:* ornament.

l.59. *Ceremonie:* cf. Argument, *l.4* and n.

ll.60–64. The sense is: that valid men and valid actions arise from the sort of right use of sensuality that has already been described.

l.60. *Times golden Thie:* 'Time's *order* is the harmony of creation, a harmony expressed in terms of the intervals of the musical scale by Pythagoras. Chapman combines this tradition with the legend that Pythagoras had a golden thigh, to make a striking image' (MM).

l.64. *The use of time is Fate:* We control our destinies by the proper use of time.

l.66. *This prize of love:* Leander.

l.67. *unlades:* unloads.

l.68. *composde:* gathered together; *stelth:* Leander's behaviour, described in the preceding lines, is seen as denying his own humanity; hence his 'stealth'.

l.72. *seasde:* seized; taken possession of. The sense, as LCM observes, is near to the legal one, which is still extant: the emphasis is upon the materialist, i.e. the purely lustful, nature of Leander's enterprise.

l.74. *like a shower:* he was wet from the sea.

l.75–76. *that . . . skin:* the streams of water had to 'die' for love when they dropped off him.

l.89. *virtuall:* powerful.

l.90. *weere:* absolutely; *insensuall:* without sense.

l.96. *prefer:* proffer.

l.99. *characters:* letters.

l.106. *his other secret fire:* his lust; this is 'another' fire than the generalized 'flame' of *l.88,* above.

l.109. *twentie:* as in III, *l.243,* this is used vaguely, to mean 'many'.

l.110. *Rainbow views:* Rainbow views 1598; this means 'views of the rainbow'.

l.112. *Ceremonie.* This is the 'Thesme' (Chapman's invention) of the Argument, and of *l.59,* above. We have to understand her as regulating the proper use of time, etc., advocated above. See Introduction, p. 25.

l.113. *heaven with her descended:* 'Either abstract or in the sense of all . . . of the gods' (LCM); the point is that all goodness is invested in what Ceremony represents.

l.115. *bench of Deities:* 'the gods assembled for judgement' (LCM).

l.123. *disparent Pentackle:* a diversely coloured, magical five-sided charm. Cf. Chapman, *The Shadow of Night,* 515–16, 'Then in thy deere, and Isie Pentacle,/Now execute a Magicke miracle'.

l. 125. 'She looked differently to each person.'

217

l.126.   'She had an evil and a benign aspect.'

ll.127–8.   'Men were happy and good when they looked on her gracious aspect; when they saw the other, they were evil and unhappy.'

l.129.   *snakie:* tortuous; difficult; *each observed law:* of Ceremony.

l.130.   *Policie:* prudence; sagacity.

l.131.   *Mathematique:* prismatic; also, 'possessing astrological powers'.

l.133.   *Confusion . . . death:* i.e. the resultant heat burns Confusion to death.

l.136.   *sightly figures:* attractive appearances.

l.137.   *Her:* Ceremony's.

l.142.   *Howrs and Graces:* the Horae, or Seasons, sisters of the Fates, whose names are Lawfulness, Justice and Peace; and the Graces, who bestowed beauty.

l.151.   *civill:* 'orderly', in the sense that has already been enumerated. Chapman does not mean that lovers ought to go through a formal ceremony. His part of this poem is about the consequences of lust unattended by love; but he does use the formalities to symbolize conditions imposed by observation of Ceremony.

l.156.   *part:* behaviour.

l.158.   *close and flatly:* 'secretly and crudely' (LCM); *O.E.D.* gives 'plainly, bluntly; decisively 1562; absolutely, completely 1577' for 'flatly'.

l.163.   *with utmost powre:* energetically and solemnly.

l.170.   *Astonisht.* This combines a number of senses: 'stunned' (as with a blow); 'bewildered'; 'surprised' or 'stupefied'. The implication is that Leander has left her 'unceremoniously', and that she is 'abasht' and 'blushing'; it is not only that she has broken her vows.

l.173.   *of:* on.

l.175.   *het:* heated.

ll.176–7.   Hero was, it must be remembered, a priestess of Venus.

l.180.   *figur'd:* prefigured; foreshadowed.

l.182.   Chapman means that he fails if his conclusion of the poem is merely sensual.

ll.183–98.   This is the famous, and very characteristic, passage in which Chapman describes his inspiration.

l.183.   *thou:* CFTB how 1598; now 1826; *thou . . . fire:* Chapman is addressing his inspiration.

l.184.   *proper to my soule:* 'It is the peculiar property of his genius' (LCM).

l.186.   *unspheared:* not limited to the personality of its owner.

ll.187–8.   *Time . . . Motion.* Motion and Time are simultaneous, so Chapman means 'with no delay at all'. *Clime:* region.

l.189.   *his:* Marlowe's; *free:* of the body; also, probably, 'open-hearted'; *living subject:* body (the bodily manifestation, the substance, of his 'free soul')

218

' "subject" as used here is a technical Aristotelian term, and is used of the body as "subject" to the soul' (DJG).

l.190. *Pyerean:* sacred to the Muses, who were born at Pieria near Mount Olympus. The Castalian spring of Mount Parnassus was sacred to them.

l.191. *drunke to me:* toasted me with (his part of the poem).

l.193. *Confer:* consult; he exhorts his inspiration to consult with Marlowe's soul; i.e. his continuation is to be regarded as organic; *my pledge:* my conclusion of the poem.

l.194. *sleepe:* oblivion.

l.195. *his late desires:* Chapman does not mean, of course, that Marlowe asked him to finish *Hero and Leander*—Marlowe's sudden death precludes that possibility. Here we should take 'desires' as meaning 'poetic intentions'. *tender:* respect.

l.196. *to light surrender:* to surrender to the light, i.e. to publish; but Chapman also sees Marlowe's poetry as 'light', as distinct from his own 'dark' involute procedures.

l.197. *willing:* a pun; the primary sense is 'making an act of the will'. Chapman, whose intelligence has been consistently underrated and misunderstood, knew that his conclusion would be undervalued, and was 'willing' that this should be so, thus, the following words:

l.198. *loves ... passions ... societie* carry on this secondary sense. The primary sense is that Chapman does not intend his conclusion to be sensuous: 'Chapman is willing that it shall not be concerned with the loves and passions and intercourse of Hero and Leander' (LCM).

ll.199–210. In this passage Hero's state of mind is compared to the town of Cadiz newly taken by foreign troops.

l.204. '*Th' Iberian citie:* Cadiz, which had fallen to the English under Essex in June 1596.

l.205. *guide:* guidance.

l.206. 'At just the time when the certainty of peace had assured her of strength'.

l.209. *Turrets:* a symbol for the whole town; also for 'breasts'; *waste:* waist. Cf. Shakespeare's sexual puns in sonnet 'The expence of spirit [semen] in a waste [vagina] of shame'. And cf. III, *l.324.*

ll.211–12. *that ... chid:* took Hero by force instead of love. The precedent is in Marlowe: see I, *l.*300, and n. The reference is, as MM notes, to Leander's arguments against chastity; more fundamentally, it is against the essentially loveless method of his conquest.

l.214. *Confusion:* See III, *l.*133.

l.215. *that:* so that.

l.217. *by wonder:* by magic.

l.221. *enjoyer:* a native (of the conquered city).

*l.*222.   *Supplying:* replacing.

*l.*223.   *expugned:* captured.

*ll.*227–8.   'She suffered as the honest mother of equally honest thoughts, which wished their mother dead'.

*l.*229.   *their:* her 'thoughts'.

*l.*230.   *the race:* (i) the course of events; (ii) the brood of thoughts; *prefers:* promotes.

*l.*232.   *extreames:* miseries; griefs.

*l.*234.   *intire:* within.

*ll.*235–8.   *For . . . us.* The sense of this passage, in which Chapman, as elsewhere, anticipates the metaphysical poets, is: 'for, as a mirror is a lifeless eye that within itself reflects externals, so the eye is a living mirror that reveals thoughts and feelings'. *In-formes:* Chapman's coinage: inner 'forms': images, likenesses, shapes.

*ll.*238–50.   PPB notes that this, like III, *ll.*50–58, is 'taken largely' from a passage in Xylander's Plutarch.

*l.*240.   *them:* the clouds.

*l.*241.   *rorid:* dewy.

*l.*242.   *event:* send forth.

*l.*243.   *a tender twentie-coloured eie:* i.e. a rainbow.

*l.*246.   *circulare:* Cf. Chapman's dedication, *l.*31, and n.

*ll.*244–50.   LCM quotes from Chapman's play *Bussy d'Ambois* (?1604), III, i, *ll.*78–82: 'Our bodies are but thick clouds to our souls,/Through which they cannot shine when they desire:/When all the stars, and even the sun himself,/ Must stay the vapours times that he exhales/ Before he can make good his beams to us'. The passage means that the soul manifests itself in the eye, which affects the facial expression.

*l.*251.   *this event:* this power of the soul to shine forth (in the face); *uncourtly:* unsophisticated; with the implication of 'unspoiled'.

*l.*252.   'Would reveal her inner guilt in her face'.

*l.*254.   *forge . . . listed:* 'counterfeit whatever looks she liked'.

*l.*257.   The sense is that she was glad to disclaim any pride in the art of deception.

*l.*258.   *Pandar:* procurer.

*l.*259.   *Moones:* the moon's light is deceitful because it is borrowed; furthermore, it looks as though it is still full when in reality it is waning: a hit at the false beauties of the court, 'mutton dressed as lamb'.

*l.*261.   *Lapwing:* deceitful—because this bird is supposed to lure people from its nest by crying loudest when farthest from it: see *l.*262 below.

*l.*262.   *vow:* 'avow (the existence of)' (LCM).

*l.*263.   'Picks up the image of the "Lapwing faces". Those men are fools who are deceived by false expressions, and every fowl of the moors can teach them

220

all they think there is to learn.' (PPB) There is a pun involved between 'fooles' and 'fowle', which could doubtless be pronounced identically.

ll.265–7. custome . . . offence: Habit is the final seizure that attacks lives without moral quality and anaesthetizes conscience.

l.266. beddred: bedridden.

l.268. brazde not: [custome] did not make brazen.

l.275. affayres: of utterance and concealment.

ll.275–6. keeps . . . effects: 'simultaneously holds back and throws forth two contrary emotions [or thoughts]'.

l.278. this one vice: dissimulation.

l.280. 'governs both what we do and what we say.' This links up with *ll.265–7* (see n.): we get so used to dissimulating that ultimately neither our actions nor our thoughts and feelings are real.

l.281. conceits: notions; *foyld:* agitated; also, perhaps, drove into a trap.

l.282. discoursive: wildly and confusedly rushing about.

ll.284–5. The 'worldly cinctures' [girdles] are the 'thoughts' of *l.225*: pangs of conscience, or, to express it in Chapman's Neoplatonic manner, knowledge of imperfections that threaten the moral quality of life. She cannot avoid their reproaches, because she is a priestess of Venus ('a heavenly flame incompast her').

l.286. Phane: fane: temple.

l.287. impulsive: LCM (and MM following him) suggests 'penetrating', a meaning not recorded in *O.E.D.* I think it means 'determining to action; impelling' (which is recorded): consequently Hero takes a robe, etc., at *l.292.*

l.290. pierst: which pierced.

l.292. was nigh: that was nigh.

l.293. Cypres: a fabric originally brought from Cyprus, and used extensively for mourning. But a typically learned pun is involved here: 'cy pres', from the French 'si près'=so near, was a legal term meaning 'as near as practicable': Hero had actually lost her virginity, so she mourned for it 'as nearly as was practicable'. This is reinforced by the phrase 'heavie to the death' and the word 'sigh' in 291: 'death' meant 'orgasm' (from 'to die'=to come, sexually).

l.297. hart-bowing: 'to which her heart was bowed, or which was bent towards her heart'; but I think what is meant is that she was 'on her knees', supplicatory, towards her heart.

l.299. that, and that: 'her (right) hand, and her (left) hand'.

l.300. disgrace: not, primarily, 'ignominy', but in the earlier sense of 'adverse fortune; misfortune'. The first meaning is also implied, however.

l.301. She was sitting in an 'unshapeful' garment, so that her true shape could not be discerned. This is a characteristic paradox: '*her* shape could not be seen, although, the sight of her ['her sight'] was itself a form [like an 'Embrion', 'scorched statue', 'wretched soul']. . . .'

l.302. *Embrion:* embryo.

l.307. *imitating eye:* 'endeavouring eye' i.e. an eye trying to see. This even now not obsolete (I have heard it in rural Sussex) dialectical usage originally arose from a confusion, as evinced in 'he's imitating to walk'.

l.309. *Through her black vaile:* to be taken with 'see', *l*.307.

ll.310–11. *then . . . With:* then her thoughts [wit, ingenuity] set to work upon; *her Goddess wrath:* the wrath of Venus; *fame:* reputation.

l.312. *enginous:* wily (in the sense of having recourse to 'engines' = artifices). The modern word is 'ingenious'.

l.315. *Joves sons club:* Hercules' club, which he cut from a wild olive tree, and with which he despatched the Cithaeronian Lion, and other beasts. It is Hero's 'strong passion' that is like this club. *strook:* struck.

l.316. 'and forced her to swoon with a piteous shriek'.

ll.317–19. 'her shriek made her frightened attendant [cf. Marlowe's 'dwarfish beldame, I, *l*.353] shriek'; *sence:* here, 'lust; sexual desire; sexuality'; the root of 'sensuality'.

l.320. *calde againe:* recalled.

l.322. *lay:* had lain.

l.323. *blood:* (i) feeling; (ii) passion; lust.

l.324. *Ebd with Leander:* 'Had been ebbing, with her esteem for Leander' (LCM). Also: 'her lust had been quiescent'.

l.325. *sprites:* spirits. Cf. III, *l*.209.

l.327. 'With those austere notions to which she had [previously] paid too much heed'.

l.330. *his thought:* the thought of him.

l.334. *deserv'd in her:* deserved with regard to her. There is of course a sexual meaning implicit in the phrase 'in her'.

l.335. *fresh heat:* newly heated.

ll.336–7. *Neptunes skyes/How her star wandred:* Leander, 'her star', wanders (swims to her) in the sea ('Neptunes skyes').

l.343. *slick-tongde:* sleek; smooth-tongued.

l.348. A genuine ambiguity: this means (i) Fame spits out news for the dogs (other gossips) to eat as their 'fee' for hunting for it (ii) Fame spits out news fit (meet) only for dogs.

l.350. *Presume:* sued in the modern sense; *what . . . bow:* this, of course, is lack of sexual activity.

l.361. *when . . . ever:* as LCM observes (although he is apparently not open to the suggestion that a poet can mean two things simultaneously) 'ever' means 'always', but also 'whenever', this being split by 'we live loosely'.

l.364. Since they are 'one', there can be no 'yielding'.

l.367. *when t'is gone:* when love has passed.

l.373. *this sphere:* this world.

222

l.374. searching: searching for.

l.378. 'Even our fear of falling is overcome by our ambition to climb up'.

l.383. she: 1826; *he:* 1598.

l.385. straight: strait: grudging (here, 'over-spiritual').

l.388. weight: weighty.

l.389. logick: means of convincing in argument.

l.390. proofes of dutie: proofs that the duties [the laws of Neoplatonic love] had been observed.

l.391. a skilfull glance: a gleam incorporating the skill of its original: a microcosm of heaven.

l.392. imperance: 'commandingness' (PPB).

l.396. supples: softens; makes supple.

l.398. Trouping: assembling.

l.402. Turnd to: (i) returned to; (ii) transformed to.

ll.403–4. that loves ... harme!: she deprecates that love's own basis in sensation itself destroys it.

l.407. Parts: goes away.

l.408. renownes his kinde: celebrates and makes famous all men.

l.409. Orbiculer: orbicular: circular. This is an adjective, but we can be sure that Chapman himself gave it the initial capital: cf. III, *l.*246, n. LCM comments 'He belongs to any point touched by his orbit (*l.*410)' and compares Chapman, *Chabot,* I, i, *ll.*188–9: 'And therefore our soul motion is affirmed/ To be like heavenly nature's, circular'.

l.413. mine ... mine: As MM observes, there is a pun involved, on 'mine' as a source of wealth.

ll.416–7. 'Rich, fruitful love links two personalities together—and their properties; it is also like the alchemists' elixir of life, or quintessence, in that while it binds together it purifies [separates out the impure from the pure]'.

l.419. ever sent to mee: 'sent to be mine forever' (LCM).

THE FOURTH SESTIAD

Argument: l.1. in sacred habit: in her priestly robes.

    l.4. ostents: portents; *threaten her estate:* foretell her doom.

    l.6. counterfeit: portrait.

    l.7. Ciprides: 'Venus, to whom Cyprus was sacred' (LCM).

    l.9. Ecte: see IV, *l.*269, n.

    l.11. Leucote: see IV, *l.*233, n.

    l.12. excuse: justify.

    l.14. Eronusis: see IV, *l.*305, n.

    l.5. exhibite: offer up.

    l.6. Those: her hair and rent robe.

    l.9. sort: manner.

*l.*10.   *them:* the hair and robe.

*l.*11.   *as quite:* as completely; *loves holy fire:* her duty as priestess of Venus, as contrasted with her unholy love for Leander.

*l.*12.   *they:* the relics; *inspire:* generate; breathe life into.

*l.*14.   *secret sacred deedes:* her worship of Venus.

*l.*16.   *figur'd chast desire:* represented properly ordered sexual pleasure: chaste lust.

*l.*18.   *Queene-light of the East:* 'Referring to the moon-goddess, Artemis or Selene' (LCM): 'Venus as the morning star' (MM). Surely MM is correct, giving regard to the context.

*l.*20.   *Peristera:* περιστερά = dove.

*l.*24.   *clime:* see III, *l.*188, n.

*l.*25.   *Her:* Hero's.

*l.*27.   *Sustainde:* supported; *subtile:* of fine texture (and therefore revealing).

*l.*28.   *as it:* as if it; *assaile:* attack (touch), and with a sensual play on the sense of 'woo'.

*l.*29.   *Their different concord:* 'the harmony her differing parts made'.

*l.*31.   The 'veil' did not cover because, if you had been there you could have seen through it.

*l.*32.   *heart-piercing parts:* those parts that appealed most keenly both to the emotions (heart) and to the 'vital centre'.

*l.*33.   *as it did shadow:* 'it' refers to the veil; 'shadow' is used in the following senses: (i) conceal; (ii) suggest; (iii) 'protect from blame, punishment or wrong'; (iv) to symbolize: 'shadow forth', cf. 'adumbrate', *l.*31.

*l.*34.   *all-love-deserving Paradise:* the whole of her nakedness.

*l.*35.   *It:* the veil.

*ll.*37–55.   'This description of Hero's scarf . . . is emblematic, "figuring" a mental state . . .' (MM).

*l.*37.   *On:* over; *of wondrous frame:* 'wonderfully designed and made' (LCM).

*l.*43.   *rested:* remained; *bashfully:* combines the familiar sense with the now obsolete 'daunted' (by her Goddess' authority).

*l.*45.   *This:* the scarf.

*ll.*47–8.   She began the embroidering of the sea (*l.*49) since her affair with Leander.

*ll.*50–1.   *where . . . goods* alluding to the proverbial saying, used by both Shakespeare and Chapman himself in their plays, 'Do not put your all in one vessel'. Perhaps this originated in the Latin: 'Uni navi ne committas omnia'. PPB gives Erasmus' adaptation as Chapman's source: 'Ne uni navi facultates'.

*ll.*56–7.   'Even inanimate things [like Hero's embroidery] may be made to live by art. But men [things rational] die through neglect of it'.

*l.*59.   Chapman has developed this metaphor out of Skelton's 'But when I sat sowing his beke,/Methought, my sparow Phillyp Sparow did speke,/ And

224

opened his prety byll,/ Saynge, 'Mayd, ye are in wyll/ Agayne me for to kyll,/ Ye prycke me in the head'.

*l.*61.   *as . . . cited:* 'as though she had been called by some accident'.

*l.*62.   *dead things griefs:* cf. senceles, *l.*56.

*l.*63.   *They kill:* they kill both themselves and their friends.

*l.*71.   *still:* constantly.

*l.*74.   *queintly:* ingeniously.

*l.*76.   *conceited:* ingenious.

*l.*78.   *her:* the moon.

*l.*79.   *figur'd:* represented; *affects:* emotions.

*l.*80.   *Nature . . . bodie:* Nature as represented by the moon.

*ll.*84–89.   This is adapted from Theocritus, Idyll I: '. . . an ancient fisherman . . . the old man drags a great net for his cast, as one that labours stoutly. Thou woulds't say that he is fishing with all the might of his limbs, so big the sinews swell all about his neck' (tr. Andrew Lang, 1896).

*l.*90.   *sped:* provided with.

*l.*93.   *instinct:* prompting.

*ll.*96–107.   This passage, too, is adapted from the same Idyll of Theocritus: '. . . on the rough wall a little lad watches the vineyard, sitting there. Round him two she-foxes are skulking, and one goes along the vine-rows to devour the ripe grapes, and the other brings all her cunning to bear against the scrip shepherd's bag and vows she will never leave the lad, till she strand him bare and breakfastless. But the boy is plaiting a pretty locust-cage with stalks of asphodel . . . and less care of his scrip has he, and of the vines, than delight in his plaiting'.

*l.*103.   *theeveries did devide:* they divided the task of thieving (not the spoils) between them.

*l.*105.   *overslip:* neglect.

*l.*108.   *her:* Hero's.

*l.*111.   *her judgement conquer destinies:* (i) her own judgement acquire the judgement of Destiny; (ii) her judgement comprehends the secrets of two destinies: hers and Leander's.

*l.*112.   *formes:* Platonic forms.

*l.*113.   'If only they could be given physical actuality'.

*l.*116.   i.e. sewing.

*l.*117.   *yasty:* Bartlett, after Kathleen Tillotson; yas 1598; eyas 1821; 'yes' is clearly wrong; 'eyas', meaning 'young hawk', was also used as an adjective to mean 'youthful, vital'; 'yasty', a form of 'yeasty', was used by Chapman in his Homer: it means here 'turbid; frothy; restless; in a ferment'.

*l.*118.   *plied:* (i) occupied; (ii) stranded (like the 'silks').

*l.*120.   *own-built citties:* the cities they have woven, as distinct from real cities.

225

l.121.   *Pinniond:* 'Affection is to be shown bound, and the binding material is to be stories and songs . . .' (LCM).

l.121.   *Arachnean.* For the story of Arachne, see Ovid, *Metamorphoses*, pp. 134–8.   Arachne vied with Athena in the art of weaving, and was transformed into a spider. Here the adjective refers to a very fine and elaborately woven silk.

l.123.   *odours:* substances that emit odours.

l.130.   *ostents:* see *Argument*, *l*.4, n.; *too neere success:* all too near event: i.e. Leander's final swim.

l.131.   *moving beauties:* Hero and Leander; *motionlesse:* dead.

ll.140–5.   The sense is: Leander was so beautiful that Nature had endowed his beauty with the power of light [a notion important in Chapman's poetry], the understanding of which confers knowledge of the number and proportion; Nature did this to show that art was subordinate to her, and that in devoting themselves to purely abstract study men renounce Nature and become immersed in spiritual gloom. All this is very much of a piece with Chapman's previous poem, *Ovid's Banquet of Sence* (1595), whose theme is that men must proceed to the spiritual through the physical.

l.146.   *accident:* event.

ll.146–7.   *which . . . historie:* 'of which, because she gloried in it, Hero could not fail to tell the story; *or*, of which the story could not fail to be told because of Hero's glory or noble reputation' (LCM).

l.151.   *prize:* 1598; price: LCM value.

l.153.   *continent:* what it contained.

l.154.   *approv'd:* confirmed.

l.158.   *pull:* extract.

l.161.   *conceits:* 1598 conceit LCM (i) ideas; (ii) notions; (iii) whims—I cannot find much justification for LCM's gloss, 'imagination'.

l.162.   *for the time:* a characteristic stroke of humour; *cease:* cause to cease.

l.165.   *dreadfulst Comet:* portent of disaster; *doubt:* dread.

ll.166–7.   *it . . . mad:* the mentally disturbed frequently have extreme difficulty in sleeping.

l.168.   *barbarous eyes:* i.e. eyes belonging to cruelly savage people.

l.169.   *sprung:* caused to spring up.

l.174.   *confirmd:* assured.

l.176.   *sillie:* see Chapman's dedication, *l*.19.

l.178.   *Policie:* cunning; expediency.

l.182.   *these:* her desires; *forego:* precede.

ll.184–6.   *Yet . . . god:* She was not aware that she gave her desires precedence over the gods, but she did know that her desires made Leander her god; *self:* own.

ll.186–9.   It was less serious, sinful ('lesse nought') to give up the gods in her formal, external, deliberately cultivated life than in her actual life—for it is in the latter that they exercise their true function.

l.190. brain-bald: devoid of brains.

l.191. i.e. the great sin is in the hypocritical practice of the outward forms of religion.

l.195. Her love would give her conscience no time to operate.

ll.196–7. 'Great men who employ smaller ones to act for them must support them even in their worst deeds.'

l.198. This is the whole point: love is of itself a good cause, but Hero is acting irresponsibly in it. She is Love's priestess, and she should provide her love with proper 'ceremony'.

l.199. attones: reconciles.

l.200. then: formerly.

l.201. now she must live with men: now that, being in love, she must live in the world (not as a priestess).

l.203. when . . . lest: when she was least ('lest') aware of it (cf. IV, *ll.*183, 195).

l.204. proceed . . . divine: go on being a priestess.

l.209. terror: terribleness.

ll.210–17. As MM notes, a 'set piece of satiric attack on the shortcomings of the clergy'.

l.213. scuse: excuse; *slubbered:* performed hurriedly.

l.215. sweat: fume; rage; *affayres:* matters.

l.216. cut out: I think MM's gloss 'determined' refers to the secondary sense. LCM's 'supplanted' is the primary sense.

l.218. repaire: restore.

l.219. to sacrifice: to the business of the (interrupted) sacrifice.

l.222. Chapman is alluding to the tradition that the Cyclops were assistants of Vulcan.

l.225. with: at.

l.227. pheres: feres: companions.

l.231. Aedone: a typical Chapman coinage, from $\dot{\eta}\delta ov\dot{\eta}$ = pleasure.

l.232. ruffoot: ruff-foot: 'having feet adorned with ruffs, frills of feathers' (LCM). *Chrests:* another coinage from $\chi\rho\eta\sigma\tau\acute{o}s$ = good, and crista = tuft.

l.235. Proyne: form of 'preen' = 'dress up with minute nicety' (*O.E.D.*).

l.236. Leucote: coinage, from $\lambda\epsilon v\kappa\acute{o}\tau\eta s$ = whiteness. She is a swan.

l.237. Dapsilis: coinage, from $\delta a\psi\iota\lambda\acute{\eta}s$ = bounteous.

l.244. yew: representing unhappiness.

l.245. th' icie wreath: the 'Crowne of Isickles' of IV, *l.*15.

l.247. be trew: obey.

l.249. lightnes: unchastity.

ll.250–1. thou . . . counterfeit: 'you have become a part of the world [i.e. a lover: cf. IV, 201] through breaking your vows'.

227

*l.*252. *pide:* pied: variegated, and thus symbolizing deceit.

*l.*253. i.e. Hero must use the mould of deceit when she puts on—coins—her countenance as a priestess.

*l.*254. *for:* instead of.

*l.*255. *mayd:* virgin; *cosoned:* cozened: cheated.

*l.*256. Hero will have an incongruous real expression behind her false one. *antike:* (i) incongruous; (ii) grotesque; (iii) grinning; (iv) cheating.

*l.*258. *since:* used in both senses.

*l.*261. *cleare:* extenuate.

*l.*264. *savor* 1598, PPB favor 1629+: '. . . the phrase has a close parallel in *Ovid's Banquet of Sence* [by Chapman], 31, 3, where Chapman speaks of the nose as 'the sensor of his savor' (PPB). She also points to a passage in Sylvester's translation of Du Bartas in which the nose is called a 'conduit'. MM finds this unconvincing, and sneers: 'Did Hero have a nose-bleed?' But the 1598 reading is at least as convincing as the emendation, and should therefore be given preference. If 'favor' is correct then it means 'countenance'.

*l.*267. *Epicedians:* singers of funeral odes (epicides).

*l.*268. *As:* as if.

*l.*269. *Ecte:* a coinage from οἶκτος = pity.

*l.*271. *broken:* weeping. Chapman had used this word before, in *The Shadow of Night:* '. . . leave the glasses of the hearers eyes/Unbroken'.

*l.*275. *for . . . much:* for what she herself (Venus) had practised.

*l.*288. *inforced:* torn out: 'enforced' could mean 'having been subjected to force' (PPB).

*l.*290. *For:* in; *aspect:* accented on second syllable.

*l.*292. *pants:* palpitations.

*l.*294. *twentie fashiond:* cf. III, *l.*243; *brakes:* either toothed instruments or levers: it is not clear which.

*l.*300. *Cares:* 'Caria, in south-west Asia Minor' (MM).

*l.*302. *Arachnes web:* the one she wove to challenge Athena; cf. IV, *l.*121.

*l.*304. *More hold:* more to catch hold of.

*l.*305. *Eronusis:* a coinage, from ἔρως—love and, probably, νουσίζω = to make sick. The latter word is used by Aristotle in *Problemata*, which Chapman probably knew—as Marlowe certainly did.

*l.*308. *sleight:* 'by cunning use' (LCM and MM); but I think the word here probably simply means 'skill'.

*l.*316. *her:* Hero; *delighted:* delightful.

*l.*324. *upbrayd:* reproach.

*l.*327. *light demeanour:* unchaste behaviour.

*l.*330. *Phoebes:* Diana's.

*l.*334. *the . . . verse:* Apollo; *undanted:* undaunted: spirited.

*l.*336. *Anademe:* wreath, from ἀνάδημα.

l.338.   fat: dense.
l.346.   Persian shield: like Perseus' mirror.
l.347.   successe: outcome.
l.349.   haples: luckless.

THE FIFTH SESTIAD

Argument. l.1.   date: duration.
   l.2.   incenst: incited; stirred up to.
   l.4.   longs: i.e. 'is to long for'.
   l.5.   recovers: obtains; but with a play on the usual sense.
   l.7.   crew: the company with the betrothed lovers.
   l.12.   Teras: see V. *l.62,* n.

l.2.   Olympiad: period of four years (between the Olympic Games).
l.5.   Aurora: Diana.
l.7.   Set: sat; *list:* wished.
l.12.   full of note: eminent; well known.
l.14.   heavie humors . . . steepe: the rheum of tiredness that saturated their eyes.
l.17. i.e. that were foolish enough to try to pursue business despite their sleepiness.
l.19.   smotherd: i.e. the ground was covered with people who grovelled.
l.22.   frame: encompassing.
l.25.   parted: departed.
ll.27-8. cf. IV, *ll.62-3.*

l.32.   Alcmane: Alcman: name of the earliest Greek choral lyric poet known to us. He lived in Sparta *c.* 650. *Mya:* 'Mya is the name of an ancient Spartan poetess. Chapman seems to have picked up both names from Suidas' Lexicon' (MM). (This latter has now been renamed as the *Suda.*)
l.43.   Ayre: (i) aria; (ii) the air.
l.44.   her: music's.
l.46.   led after by the Graces: the Graces came first.
l.50.   t'abide: to endure.
l.51. i.e. that compassion might be important in (i) the determination of (ii) the operation of, her destiny.
l.58.   constrained: forced out. Johnson's definition of 'to constrain' in his *Dictionary,* 1755, was 'to produce in opposition to nature'; *O.E.D.* restricts this sense to before 1725.
l.62.   Teras: from τέρας = sign; portent; *Ebon:* ivory: a mistake made by at least one other poet besides Chapman.
l.64.   consort: accompany.
l.65.   gaysome: full of gaiety.
l.66.   Elegies: perhaps, as LCM suggests, used vaguely for 'short poems', as in the title of Marlowe's translations of Ovid's *Amores,* which, however, were

229

written in elegiac metre. However, in view of the function of Teras here—see especially V, *ll*.489–90—there is a strong hint of the other sense.

l.71.　*vertue:* 'occult efficacy or power'; *his beames:* Apollo was the sun God.

l.77.　*Silvane:* sylvan: creature of the woods.

l.78.　*estate:* dignity.

l.79.　*forewent:* preceded.

l.82.　*perfect . . . grow:* born fully developed and therefore incapable of growing.

　　　The tale of Teras: MM states that the source of this tale is Servius' commentary on Virgil's *Aeneid*, but suggests that Chapman found it in Cartari's *Imagines Deorum*. For the fullest discussion of this see DJG.

l.91.　*Hymen:* Roman God of marriage.

l.98.　*your:* the bridal pair.

l.101.　*responsible:* LCM and MM suggest 'responsive'; but this sense is not in *O.E.D.*; it seems to mean 'morally accountable for his actions', which fits well into the immediate and into Chapman's general context.

l.104.　*invade:* 'take possession of' (MM).

ll.105–7.　*which . . . eye:* the physical beauties of the lovers match their spiritual attributes. The 'affections' are 'yet unseen' because they, unlike Hero and Leander, have not consummated their love.

ll.109–10.　Lovers were as well matched as the colour and configuration of Hymen's face.

l.115.　*consorted:* accompanied.

l.119.　*Eucharis:* from $\epsilon\ddot{\upsilon}\chi\alpha\rho\iota\varsigma$ = pleasing.

l.122.　*transmission:* conveyance (of his 'heart' to her 'white brest').

l.123.　*estate:* rank.

l.124.　*passing:* excelling; *interminate:* boundless.

l.128.　*prove:* try.

l.141.　*gat:* got.

l.142.　*To his best prayes:* 1598 i.e. he attained the highest praise. 'Prayes' was an accepted form of 'praise', so that there is no need for the universally accepted emendation, 'prayers', of 1821.

l.154.　*extreame:* very strong; accented on first syllable. The contiguity of the two long sounds is intended to reinforce the meaning.

l.166.　*Ceres Eleusina:* the Eleusinian Mysteries: held at Eleusis to celebrate Ceres (Demeter).

l.169.　*enforst:* enforced: carried off.

l.171.　*yellow . . . skie:* the stars.

l.177.　*watch:* wakefulness.

l.178.　*Morpheus:* God of sleep.

l.182.　*O . . . in:* the (heavenly) virgins were in the hell of anticipating the robbers' waking, etc.

l.188.   *remorse:* pity.

l.193.   *one . . . wine:* 'if one, to cheer another, should call for wine'.

l.206.   *Proteus:* see I, *l*.137.

l.207.   *Inggl'd:*   ingled: coaxed,   wheedled.   Modern   editors   read 'Juggled'.

ll.211–12.   *he . . . burnd.* This is subtler than is at first apparent. What Chapman means is that Hymen—prototype of a proper lover—learned to love by having to wait. Hero and Leander had not waited. As he writes at V, *l*.227: 'And where Loves forme is, love is, love is forme'.

ll.223–4.   *forme . . . spirits:* carries the form [the Platonic form: see below, V, *l*.227, n.] of the flower over into her mind.

l.227.   *Love is forme.* This does not primarily mean, as LCM asserts, that 'love is beauty of form', though LCM's gloss is acceptable as a secondary meaning when we have understood the main sense. It once again alludes to the Platonic, more strictly Socratic, doctrine of 'form': in this doctrine, 'love' is an enterprise that is more than the mere enterprise of collecting examples of it, i.e. as a 'form' that it has an objective existence, and is indeed—with all the other forms—divine. Such forms may be discerned, as is explained by a modern interpreter of Plato, by 'the eye of the mind'.

l.232.   *divided cheekes:* divided by the conflict of her emotions (between her rank and her desire; her shyness and her lust); this phrase is either unfortunate, or, more likely, deliberately physically suggestive.

l.235.   *Zephire:* Zephyr: the West wind.

l.236.   *broke:* broken.

l.245.   *the lower place:* (i) marriage, which is inferior to virginity; (ii) Hymen's inferior status; (iii) the vagina, which is the place for love, not 'female pride'.

l.246.   *contents:* pleasures; *moves:* 'A singular verb for a composite plural is common in Elizabethan English' (LCM).

ll.247–9.   This reluctance of Hymen's beauty and valour is not his own: it refers to Eucharis' reluctance to allow them to operate upon her.

l.247.   *With:* here to be understood as meaning 'as well as; on the side of'.

l.248.   *scarce . . . favour:* 'despite the distinction of having Love as a comrade-in-arms'.

l.249.   *fameles:* undistinguished.

l.250.   *Action . . . good:* i.e. there was still reluctance in Eucharis' mind, because Hymen took no action.

l.253.   *bribde, but incorrupted:* 'There is a concentration of thought in 'bribde but incorrupted' which it would be hard to find in Spenser, Sidney, or the young Shakespeare' (CSL).

ll.257–8.   *That . . . out:* Protean Love turns himself into her 'roughest frownes', which are thus expelled; i.e. they turn into love.

ll.258–60.   *and . . . deitie.* Teras is reinforcing the point that the important

231

aspect of love is marriage, by which he means 'ceremony'; hence, here, Love makes the actual God of *marriage* 'King of his thoughts'.

*l.*259. *Emperie:* dominion.

*l.*260. *his:* Hymen's, Love's and man's.

*l.*265. *plat:* plot.

*l.*268. *crosse:* thwart.

*ll.*269–70. *And . . . force.* The sense is: And in the way people usually return kindnesses when the law does not force them to be just. . . .

*l.*272. *bestowne:* given in marriage: 'bestow' could have this specific meaning until the early eighteenth century.

*l.*274. *prove:* discover.

*ll.*275–6. 'Whether, if he restored every one of the virgins to their homes and former reputations, he should be able to marry Eucharis'.

*l.*278. *The riper sort:* the more mature ones.

*l.*279. *so farre deriv'd:* coming from so far away.

*l.*280. *brave:* worthy.

*l.*281. *carriage:* burden.

*l.*282. *Occurrents:* news.

*l.*284. *all . . . complement:* all of them together.

*ll.*285–6. *but . . . them.* He must excuse them from running the risk of further harm (left alone in the grove, while Hymen went to Athens).

*l.*287. *Adoleshes:* 1598; Adolesches 1606+; Adoleshe is formed from

*l.*286. *wit:* idea; notion.

αδολέσχης = talker; gossipper.

*l.*289. *neither:* 1598; nether 1637+; the latter was a form of the former.

*l.*291. *Since it:* her tongue; *it must go,* i.e. keep nagging.

*l.*293. *quicknes:* vitality.

*l.*296. *one:* 1821; *on:* 1598.

*l.*298. *fa'st:* faced.

*l.*301. *this lovely Beautie:* either the bride who is hearing this tale, or Hymen.

*l.*303. *which:* to which.

*l.*306. *rent:* split.

*l.*308. *in their joyes:* at the unraped girls' return; *them:* the lovers and their coming wedding.

*l.*310. *quick:* living.

*l.*311. *firmament:* (i) the girls attending Eucharis (already called stars); (ii) the jewelled heads of their hairpins.

*l.*312. *Godhead-proving:* 'able to make her husband into a god' (MM).

*l.*313. *she lookt in her command:* she looked what she was: in the central position.

*l.*314. *forme-giving:* cf. V, *l.*227 and n.; *Cyprias:* Venus.

*l.*319. *by:* along.

*l.*321. *efficient right:* proper function.
*l.*323. *od disparent:* this is tautological.
*l.*326. *one:* i.e. one part.
*ll.*335–40. LCM quotes Sir Thomas Browne, *Garden of Cyprus:* 'The Conjugal Number, which ancient Numerists made out by two and three, the first parity and imparity'.
*l.*339. *For . . . is:* cf. I, *l.*255, n.
*ll.*339–40. *but . . . number:* 'but one is the source of numbers'.
*l.*342. *rock:* distaff: the staff upon which the flax or wool was wound.
*l.*343. *Weathers:* wether's: ram's.
*l.*344. *peece.* I think that what LCM calls 'the depreciatory significance now usually attached to the feminine meaning', which he (and MM) asserts is not present, is certainly present here; but it need not be.
*l.*355. *disparent:* different.
*l.*358. *one selfe:* one and the same.
*ll.*359–69. These lines were suggested by two different passages from Xylander's *Plutarch.*
*l.*360. *which . . . invented:* 'which custom was first instituted' (LCM).
*l.*361. *ingenerate:* produce.
*l.*364. *For humane race:* for the perpetuation of the human race.
*l.*375. *Agneia:* ἀγνεία=chastity.
*l.*381. *Phemonoe:* priestess of Apollo.
*l.*386. *Confits:* comfits: sugar-plums or the like.
*l.*387. *other some:* some others.
*l.*392. *Minerva's knot:* symbol of chastity.
*l.*395. *eternisde:* eternized: deified.
*l.*398. An example of Chapman's humour.
*l.*400. *affectionate blood:* feelings of affection.
*l.*401. *so true feeling:* such precise knowledge of (because they had experienced the 'dissolution' of Minerva's knot).
*l.*404. *her:* 1698; *their* 1826+.
*l.*405. *joyed:* (i) enjoyed; (ii) gave pleasure to; (iii) honoured.
*ll.*407–8. i.e. the moon rose. As C. S. Lewis has pointed out, CSL 69, this is 'successfully Bartasian': writing in the style of the French poet Guillaume de Salluste Du Bartas (1544–1590), whose technique consisted in 'representing things great and superhuman in the most humdrum and anthropomorphic terms. Du Bartas was influentially translated into English by Joshua Sylvester (1563–1618) in 1590 and 1605—and, less influentially and completely by the future King James I in *His Majesties Poeticall Exercises at vacant houres* (1591). Chapman probably knew him in French; but translations had been appearing since 1584.
*l.*407. *Saffron mirror:* the moon.

l.408.   *Tellus:* the earth; *decks her:* beautifies herself.

l.414.   *occurrents:* see V, *l*.282, n.

l.416.   *she . . . tell:* she failed to tell.

l.418.   *well-spoken:* verbally gifted; *take such a toy:* fall into such a tantrum.

l.420.   *for meere free love:* i.e. casually, because it was 'ready to attach itself to any object'—(LCM).

ll.421–4.   'The meaning of this little fable is . . . Adolesche tries to play the part played by the tale-bearer . . . in an affair of courtly love, but fails because marriage comes in between her and her hopes. Chapman is pointing out that marriage settles the old problem of the [tale-bearer]'—CSL, 68.

l.426.   *Torchie:* 'lit with torches'; *sprung:* brought forth.

l.428.   *line:* proceedings.

l.434.   *sheaves . . . fire:* the stars.

l.440.   *outfacing face:* 'face that outfaces others'—LCM.

l.449.   *bals of Discord:* the golden apples of Atalanta's race: see *Metamorphoses*, pp. 240–4. PPB quotes from Chapman's *Euthymiae Raptus:* '. . . and holde every strife/To other ends . . . As bals cast in our Race. . . .'

l.451.   *Day . . . here:* (i) day is here reduced to its essence; (ii) Day (personified) is absent-minded—i.e. not able to join in the spirit of things—here.

l.453.   *thee:* day.

l.454.   *let . . . thee:* Thetis, mother of Achilles, wished to make her son immortal, so laid him in a fire at night to purge away his mortality ('refine' him).

l.463.   *right:* 1598, MM rite LCM the original puns on both senses.

l.470.   *expansure:* expanse. This seems to be Chapman's own word; he used it elsewhere.

l.475.   *parted:* divided.

l.485.   *staring up:* standing on end.

l.494.   *stood:* encountered; bare the brunt of.

THE SIXTH SESTIAD

Argument. l.2.   as the messenger of the Fates, Leucote orders the winds to remain calm.

l.4.   *compleate:* accent on first syllable.

l.7.   *Ate:* derision; guilt: daughter of Zeus and Eris (discord): makes men blind so that they become guilty through ignorance.

l.10.   *surprise:* catastrophe.

l.13.   *whose just ruth:* 'proper compassion for whom' (MM).

l.14.   *Acanthides:* see VI, *l*.276, n.

l.3.   *humorous:* (i) capricious; (ii) moist.

234

*l.*7. *yet:* as yet.

*l.*18. *obsequious:* (i) cringing; sycophantic; (ii) having to do with death. Chapman's 'too' beautifully hints at the sinister second meaning.

*l.*19. *fleering:* grinning; tittering; smiling obsequiously upon; secretly gibing at.

*l.*20. *warping:* weaving; devising; *sleight:* cunning trick; legerdemain.

*l.*21. *devotes:* devotions: 'acts implying devotion' (LCM). He disguises his 'rottenness' (treacherous nature) with these pretended devotions.

*l.*22. he writes down ('pricks') falsely obsequious music as an accompaniment to his victim's melody. A prick was a dot used in musical notation (hence the often used 'pricksong', with the opportunities it provides for sexual punning); descant is an accompaniment to a plainsong. This striking metaphor emphasizes the elaborateness of the fate's malefic sycophancy.

*ll.*23–4. *and . . . heart:* these words are bracketed to indicate that the oaths are internal.

*ll.*25–6. ' "Hand" is the subject of the verbs, "leave" and "leapes". However charming his gesture of throwing a kiss, the hand does not follow through, but leaps to his own lips, remaining there' (PPB). The fate is represented as loving itself.

*l.*27. *queane:* whore; tart.

*l.*28. *sharpe at:* keenly pursuing (to entice).

*ll.*28–9. *and . . . shewes:* his grotesque actions mean nothing (i.e. are totally insincere).

*l.*29. *repayre:* renew; revitalize: i.e. the only purpose of the fate's obsequiousness is to feed itself.

*l.*30. *fawnes:* fawnings.

*ll.*30–31. *takes . . . shoulder:* i.e. with falsely affectionate familiarity.

*l.*31. *whips:* moves violently.

*l.*32. *he:* Leander.

*l.*33. *backward humblesse:* cringing humility.

*l.*35. *Eurus:* the East wind.

*l.*36. *Levant:* Chapman meant either Eastern countries in general, or the Eastern Mediterranean; if the former then the '*Negros*' are simply black people living beneath the rising sun; if the latter—and this seems to be very unlikely— then they must be Egyptians, Arabs or Turks.

*l.*38. *shewes:* the subject is Leucote.

*l.*40. *fennie Notus:* Notus is the South wind, which brings damp: hence 'fennie'.

*l.*41. *in folds:* folded.

*l.*45. *Zephire:* West wind.

*l.*46. *snake-foote Boreas:* the second-century A.D. Greek geographer and historian, whose work Chapman knew either directly or through various mythographers, described the North Wind, Boreas, as having serpents' tails for feet.

l.47. *his ravisht love:* Orithyia, daughter of Erechtheus, King of Athens, whom Boreas carried off while she was dancing by a river. See Ovid, *Metamorphoses,* pp. 153–4.

l.52. *comfortable:* delightful.

l.53. *Torch:* i.e. candle; *curious price:* choice esteem.

l.59. *prize:* esteem: identical with the 'price' of *l.53.*

l.60. *true Glasse:* truthful mirror: i.e. 'faithful metaphor for'.

l.61. 'No man can do good without thereby wasting away his own substance.' *consumes:* wastes away (intransitive).

l.62. *thou:* the torch; *for good:* for being good.

l.64. *pinde:* pined: wasted away; *deedles:* without action. The sense of the line is: Perform good actions and you starve; be a good person in yourself and be disgraced. Both kinds of good are doomed.

l.65. 'Unless we [the common run of humanity] can profit from people, we allow them to starve'.

l.66. *these:* i.e. the following.

l.69. *proper vertue:* an illusion to the Neoplatonic doctrine that each thing's perfection is achieved when it becomes the form that is also its cause. 'Nature' is seen as the raw material upon which the soul works.

l.71. *one life:* i.e. that of chastity.

l.72. *free:* unwedded.

l.74. *milde:* 'soft; referring to the wax softened by the torch's heat' (LCM).

ll.76–7. Chapman's comment makes it clear that Hero's argument is false: 'it is not the rightness or wrongness of anything that we are concerned with, but the delight it brings us' (DJG). We lament our grief itself, not the cause of it—which may lie in our failure to observe virtue. I take the primary sense of *l.77* to be: No 'proper virtue' (see VI, *l. 69,* above) may thus be discovered (*gleande:* gleaned); only the pleasure or displeasure ('delight') that it affords us. But it also means: 'The proper virtue, real purpose, of anything may only be discovered by "its proper fruition" [LCM]'.

l.79. *my verse ended:* i.e. that the story I have to tell did not remain to be told.

ll.80–2. *She . . . Yet . . .* She was the priestess of love, yet she thus broke her vows (in lighting Leander's way to her).

l.80. *rule:* guiding principle.

l.81. *parts:* gifts.

l.82. *further forth:* than Hero's (brightness).

l.83. i.e. the lesser brightness of Hero was of truer worth for the oncoming Leander.

l.86. Leander's sexual potency was awakened by the anticipation of her lust for him.

*l.*87. A conceit characteristic of Chapman.

*l.*88. Only men governed by the external aspects of things ('shewes') kiss fire (i.e. Hero's torch, cf. VI, *ll.*84–5 above).

*l.*89. *figure:* symbolize; represent.

*l.*96. *arguments:* representations; *shewes:* tokens.

*l.*98. *addrest:* offered.

*l.*101. *His:* its; *no misers nuptiall joyes:* i.e. these were (nervously) lavish.

*l.*107. *made . . . surmisde:* made him think himself so rich (in happiness).

*ll.*109–33. As MM observes, this is a satiric attack on a contemporary type; it may be related to the satires of Hall, Marston and Donne, all of which were current when Chapman was writing his continuation of *Hero and Leander.*

*l.*109. *full of forme:* full of outward refinements. Cf. Marston, *The Scourge of Villanie* (1599), Satyre VII, 17–20: Ho *Linceus!*/Seest thou yon gallant in the sumptuous clothes,/ How brisk, how spruce, how gorgiously he showes,/ Note his French-herring bones, but note no more. . . .'

*l.*111. *most:* usually; *brought up:* (i) considered as above contempt; discussed; (ii) vomited.

*l.*112. *our Metropolis:* London.

*l.*115. The 'heat' here is that of war: Chapman had, like Ben Jonson, almost certainly fought in the Low Countries. The gallant is scoffed at as a mere tourist.

*l.*116. *rampires:* dykes; *yet:* still: i.e. he is continually effusive about them.

*l.*117. *for . . . discourse:* ironic for 'in order to improve his conversation with you'; *with mouthes is heard:* i.e. practising pompous speeches.

*l.*118. *with his very beard:* PPB suggests that this means 'aggressively, rudely'. I think it means that the man speaks offensively close to his listener, so touching him with his beard.

*l.*120. *Rhene:* the Rhineland.

*l.*124. *contends:* which tries.

*l.*128. *reach:* (i) stretch of water; (ii) 'a single stretch or spell of movement' (*O.E.D.*); (iii) contrivance.

*l.*129. *halfe a burdbolts shoote:* half the distance covered by the kind of blunt, light arrow used for murdering birds: i.e. a very short distance. *coyle:* fuss.

*l.*132. *vacantrie:* emptiness; idleness; insignificance.

*l.*139. *favour:* beauty.

*l.*142. *disease:* 1598 CFTB; decease 1826–1885; dis-ease LCM, MM. This puns on all the possible senses, 'disease' having been an accepted spelling of 'decease'.

*l.*144. *cockhorse:* As PPB observes, this is a noun (= 'an exalted position') used as modifier: it has the sense here of 'upstart'.

*l.*148. *deserts:* good (not, here, evil) qualities.

*l.*149. *close:* secret.

*l.*153. *fainde:* feigned.

*l.*154. *meane:* way.

*l.*156. i.e. Leander looked for Hero.

*l.*162. *His guide by Sea:* Hero's torch.

*l.*171. *entreat:* treat.

*l.*172. *as:* as if.

*l.*174. *licorously:* lustfully; *cleapt:* clipped. This alludes to Neptune's lust for Leander, cf. Marlowe's II, *ll.*173–4.

*l.*176. *go:* walk.

*ll.*180–1. *eithers right/Pretended:* each one claimed the right.

*l.*182. *brake:* burst out.

*l.*186. *braves:* boasts.

*l.*188. *Statists:* politicians.

*l.*191. *Atthaeas:* another form of Orithyia (see VI, *l.*42), which Chapman may have coined from $'A\tau\theta\acute{\iota}s$ = Attica.

*l.*198. *heavens hard Christall:* the crystalline surface of the heavenly sphere.

*l.*204. *earth:* i.e. the ocean bed; *shone:* shown.

*l.*208. *now:* now that.

*l.*209. *that:* refers to the force of the winds; *state,* 1598 state CFTB, LCM, MM. But LCM concedes that 1598 'may be right: now that she finds she wept.'

*l.*215. *envied:* hated.

*l.*216. *bating:* (i) fluttering (a term of falconry); (ii) burning lower; *eate:* ate.

*l.*218. She protected the flame from the winds with her robe.

*l.*226. *Lachesis:* Greek $\Lambda\acute{\alpha}\chi\epsilon\sigma\iota s$ = disposer of lots. One of the Fates. The thread of life is spun on Clotho's spindle, measured by the rod of Lachesis, and about to be snipped by Atropos' shears. Chapman would have known from Homer's *Iliad* that men claim that they can, to some extent, control their fates by avoiding unnecessary dangers. . . .

*l.*230. *raste:* rased: demolished.

*ll.*237–8. 'Even though spiritual talents are let starve, bodies are usually preserved, even ugly ones like that of the bear which is preserved for the game of bear-baiting' (PPB).

*l.*243. *skornd their smart:* scorned the suffering they could inflict.

*l.*248: *so most downe right:* 'So completely in a downward position' (LCM).

*ll.*254–6. *be . . . Analisde in:* analysed: 'find their definition in'; 'be reduced to their elements in': cf. Chapman, *Peristeros: or the male Turtle:* 'She was to him th' *Analisde* World of Pleasure'.

*l.*257. *clange.* Almost certainly a variant spelling of 'clang', which derives, through Latin clangere = to resound, from Greek $\kappa\lambda\alpha\gamma\gamma\acute{\eta}$ = noise of trumpets or screaming of birds. Both forms occur in Marlowe's translation of the first book of Lucan.

238

l.260. *mixed.* LCM suggests 'confused', but points out that *O.E.D.* gives no instance of this use before 1872. MM suggests that 'Chapman may have been thinking of the various "faculties" of the soul, in which case "mixed" would have the sense of complete or whole'. Since the meaning of 'confused' was colloquial it could have been orally current in Elizabethan times. Chapman had already put special emphasis on Hero's confusion: see III, *ll.*292–305, n.

l.265. *he:* Neptune; *usering:* usuring: exacting; greedy (like a money lender).

ll.266. *that . . . blood.* As LCM suggests, this connection of usury with the exaction of blood may well refer to *The Merchant of Venice.*

*ll.*274–91. For comment on this passage, see Introduction, pp. 22–3.

l.276. *Acanthides:* from ἀκανθίς = goldfinch and ἀκανθα = thistle. Many species of goldfinch do feed on thistle-seed: they are often known as thistle-finches. *O.E.D.*'s earliest instance of 'thistlewarp' is 1606. The Latin name of this bird is *carduelis elegans.* It has no blue in it; but Chapman doubtless intended, as DJG suggets, the blue sheen of black.

l.282. *And so:* i.e. to compensate.

l.283. *so little:* 'small as they are' (MM).

l.285. *forehead cloths:* probably used to prevent wrinkling.

l.288. *construe:* interpret.

l.293. *the first:* Musaeus was thought of as the first poet: see Introduction, p. 14.

THE TEXT

Marlowe's part (i.e. the first two Sestiads) of *Hero and Leander* was entered in the Stationer's Register on 28 September 1593 by John Wolf, as 'a booke intituled HERO and LEANDER beinge an amorous poem devised by CHRISTOPHER MARLOW'. If Wolf published an edition there is no trace of it. Since the poem was subsequently so popular, it seems likely that some hard evidence of such an edition would exist between 1593 and 1598. There are in fact some echoes of it in the period 1595–8; but this implies no more than that it had been widely circulated in manuscript.

In 1598 there appeared first, Marlowe's part of the poem, published by Edward Blount—designated as 1598 (1)—and then the complete work, 'Begun by Christopher Marloe; and finished by George Chapman', published by Paul Linley—1598 (2). No succeeding edition has any independent textual authority.

The first part of this text is based on 1598 (1) collated with 1598 (2); the four last Sestiads are based on the latter alone. Where corrections have been made, the original readings are noted. A few notable emendations not accepted in my text, which is conservative, have been recorded. The fullest accounts of the text are in CFTB, LCM, PPB. 1598 (2)'s additions to 1598 (1), such as Chapman's 'Arguments', are enclosed in square brackets, but not otherwise noted. '1598' used in notes to I and II means '1598 (1) and 1598 (2) in common'; in notes to III, IV, V, VI, it means, of course, simply 1598 (2).

Other editions of *Hero and Leander*, sometimes referred to in the notes by date, appeared in 1600, 1606, 1609, 1613, 1617, 1622, 1629 and 1637.

133. THE PROGRESSE OF THE SOULE

Infinitati Sacrum: In keeping with the generally fantastic tone of the poem, Donne dedicates it to 'the infinite'.

EPISTLE

Here Donne, full of confidence in his ability to complete it, set out his intentions for the whole epic—or, rather, mock-epic.

*l.*1. *Others . . .* refers to his proposed frontispiece.

*l.*2. *through light:* transparent.

*l.*3. *sticke:* hesitate.

*l.*4. *taxe:* censure; dispute.

*l.*6. *sine talione:* without expecting the same kind of treatment in return. The *lex talionis* decreed punishment in kind. The phrase *sine talione* is from Martial.

*ll.*8–9. *like . . . write.* The Trent Council had decided that no books on sacred subjects were to be published without the author's name. WM calls this, unaccountably, 'a malicious deduction': it seems rather to stem from common sense and a shrewd awareness of the nature of censors and committees.

*ll.*10–11. *Now . . . debt:* he means to be original.

*ll.*16. *for . . . teach:* this satire is to be for the sophisticated only.

*ll.*19. *Mucheron:* mushroom.

*ll.*19–20. *since . . . this:* the soul is willing to occupy a body and to exercise all three of its faculties; but the type of body it occupies (man, animal, vegetable) determines ('workes') the sort of life it will lead. Hence the soul when in a melon could not move, but because it had the faculty of observation, could describe the kind of dinner at which it was eaten.

*ll.*24. *her memory . . . owne:* the soul remembers its whole history.

*l.*26. *eate:* ate; *shee:* the soul; *hee:* that (presumably male) person.

THE PROGRESSE OF THE SOULE

*l.*1. *I sing.* The routine epic opening. Cf. the opening of Vergil's *Aeneid:* 'Arma virumque cano'.

240

l.2.   WM points out a possible inconsistency with *l*.31; but I think this means only that while God is ultimately responsible for how things will be, he does not decree exactly how they shall become so: there are an infinite number of ways of arriving at the same result.

l.3.   *the law:* given by God to Moses.

l.5.   *aged evening:* refers to a common contemporary notion that Donne certainly enjoyed, whether he believed it or not: that the world was in decay.

ll.7–8.   Cf. *Elegy on Mistress Boulstred*, *ll*.23–4: 'Thou hast, and shall see dead, before thou dyest,/ All the foure Monarchies, and Antichrist'. Another reference to the decay of the world, this time to the notion of the degeneration of the world from a golden age, through silver and brass ages, to an iron one.

ll.9–10. This boastful note sets the generally mocking tone. Seth's children, according to Josephus, built two pillars, one of brick and one of stone, upon which they inscribed all their knowledge: these were to survive the deluge.

l.11.   *eye of heaven:* the sun.

l.16.   *Danow:* the Danube.

l.17.   *Westerne . . . Myne:* America and the Western Indies.

l.21.   *holy Janus.* WM cites 'We call *Noah, Janus,* because hee had two faces, in this respect, That hee looked into the former, and onto the later world, he saw the times before, and after the flood' from Donne's *Sermons.* There were learned precedents for calling Noah 'holy'. But Janus was proverbially double-faced.

l.22.   *Monarchies,* see *ll*.7–8, n.

l.23.   *Colledge:* Noah was supposed by some to have taught while on the ark. *Hospitall:* place of refuge.

l.24.   *vivarie:* vivarium: a place specially prepared for keeping animals.

l.26.   *latest nephewes:* original forebears ('nephew' could mean 'descendent').

l.30.   *heavenly sparke:* the soul, and hero of this epic.

l.31.   *Commissary:* deputy.

l.33.   *tooke:* derived.

l.41.   *lustres:* periods of five years each: from Latin, *lustrum*. Donne, as he says, was twenty-nine when he wrote this poem.

l.42.   *Except:* unless.

l.43.   *letts:* hindrances.

l.45.   *Spirit-quenching:* 'The "spirit" destroyed by sickness is (as in *l*.49) the refined and vitalizing part of the blood, by means of which the soul is able to act upon and through the organs of the body. Cf. "The Ecstasy", *ll*.61–62. . . .' (WM). Pronounce 'spirit', *spright*.

l.47.   *t'other whets:* other incitements to action.

l.52.   *this sea:* this poem.

l.55.   *light, and light:* both lively (not 'heavy') and radiant.

241

l.56. *streights:* (i) narrow sea-passages that the soul negotiates; (ii) difficulties in writing this poem.

l.57. WM paraphrases: 'I begin my poem in Eden and bring its story to England at the end'. However, the 'at' may also be understood in the sense of 'towards'.

l.59. *hoised:* raised: in nautical terms, 'set'.

l.60. Paradise was located in Mesopotamia.

l.61. *this greate soule:* that person in whom the soul was to end up in modern times: see Introduction, pp. 31–3.

l.66. *Mahomet:* pronounce 'Mah'met'.

l.70. *a . . . roome.* The soul is first seen by Donne as being in the apple on the tree of knowledge. Therefore it was 'low', merely vegetable; and 'fatal' because Eve plucked it and brought 'knowledge' into the world.

ll.71–80. The soul's first place, the argument runs, was far from being low if Christ's Cross stood in the same place as the tree of knowledge had once stood. Donne invents this hypothesis to state a characteristic paradox: the soul is 'made by the Makers will from pulling free', and yet, like the apple, it was plucked.

l.82. *ripe . . . borne:* WM cites a passage from the *Sermons*: 'In paradise, the fruits were ripe, the first minute'. This whole stanza is a neat and orthodox statement of the doctrine of the fall: Satan, once upright but made to crawl for his offence, gave the apple to Eve, who gave it to Adam; they were then expelled (made mortal), and corrupted us so that we suffer for the sinfulness that is in us.

l.90. *die:* 'The wages of sin is death'.

ll.91–3. The apple of the tree of knowledge gave Adam and Eve sexual consciousness: now women 'slay' us again here by tempting us to sexuality. *The mother:* Eve; *well-head:* Adam.

l.94. *Rivulets:* we men, descendents of Adam.

l.97. *turning:* returning.

ll.98–100. 'If we men could become judges, as God is, we should think it very hard that we should be forced to suffer for woman's crime; as it is, part of our actual suffering is to love women, whose sin actually caused it'. This is an attack, very playful, on God—or simplistic religion—as well as on women.

ll.101–2. This is bitterly ironic; its target is, as above, simplistic or tyrannical religiosity.

ll.105–6. *Of . . ./. . . take?* 'Can God justly revenge himself on all men for the sake of one man's transgression?' I do not believe that Donne, in listing this and other traditional rabbinical speculations, was entirely serious. His criticism is here directed at the capacity of the *Genesis* myth to explain the difficulties of humanity.

*ll.*111–120.   Considering Donne's own highly speculative nature, we cannot take this entirely at its face value: there is some more irony, if rueful, here: it comes out particularly obviously in 'Not liberties/Of speech, but silence; hands, not tongues, end heresies'. Donne's own family was 'heretic': his uncle Jasper Heywood, a Jesuit, was imprisoned in the Tower and was lucky not to have been executed—he died abroad; his brother Henry died of the plague in Newgate, where he was awaiting trial for harbouring a Roman Catholic priest, who was hanged, drawn and quartered.

*l.*121.   *gripe:* grip.

*l.*125.   *one . . . day:* 'two days old, but fully mature (cf. *l.*82)' WM.

*l.*129.   *foggie:* marshy; boggy: mandrakes were supposed to grow in marshy places.

*l.*130.   *th'earths pores:* 'The earth was supposed to have pores like those in the human skin' (WM).

*l.*131.   *abled:* enabled. Now that this plant (the mandrake) has obtained a soul, it can act as it desires. WM quotes a short passage from one of Donne's sermons: '[The soul] must act, but what this body will give it leave to act, according to the Organs, which this body affords it'.

*l.*134.   *throng'd:* squeezed. The mandrake pushed the water away from itself in order to gain a denser medium in which to grow.

*l.*137.   *Prince:* used here, as elsewhere, for 'Princess', i.e. Elizabeth.

*ll.*141–50.   The mandrake, or mandragora, was the subject of many myths and legends. Because its root often forked into two and took the appearance of a little man, it was endowed with life, and supposed to scream when it was uprooted. It was also supposed to have aphrodisiac properties. In fact it is poisonous, like most so-called aphrodisiacs, whose action is to inflame the sexual membranes. In *l.*148 Donne refers to these aphrodisiac properties, and playfully makes the mandrake into a pubically hairy little lover on its own account. Like the poppy, it was also a soporific (see *l.*167 below).

*l.*142.   *digest:* divide.

*l.*150.   *apples:* the mandrake was known as the loveapple, owing to its aforesaid aphrodisiac properties.

*l.*150.   *force . . . kill:* Donne refers to a legend that the mandrake, while it kindles lust, inhibits conception.

*l.*159.   *guest:* the soul: see *l.*131 n.

*ll.*161–70.   Eve tore up this mandrake, in order to quieten the proverbially weeping Cain.

*l.*169.   *Unvirtuous:* medicinally useless.

*ll.*171–80.   The soul, after four days as inhabitant of the mandrake, enters a sparrow's egg. The sparrow was a symbol of lechery. The soul has now gained the faculty of movement.

*ll.*201–10.   The problem of why incest is morally 'wrong' has puzzled and

L.E.P.—9*

fascinated men since antiquity. The most convincing anthropological reason is that marriage between close kin would have led to impossible divisions of, and therefore disputes over, authority. Donne is being baldly ironic (in the face of authoritarian 'horror') in *l*.203: he is drawing characteristic attention to an unsolved problem.

l.202.   *ingresse:* enter (the flesh of).

l.204.   *jolly:* 'over-confident' (WM).

l.206.   Donne frequently referred, more or less playfully, to the belief that sexual over-indulgence led to a shortening of life: cf. *Loves Alchymie*, *ll*.11–12.

l.208.   *streightens:* strengthens.

l.209.   *spirit:* a pun involving the meaning 'semen', cf. Shakespeare, Sonnet 129, *l*.1.

ll.211–15.   *Else ... aire.* Had this sparrow not exhausted himself with venery, he might have lived a long life: mankind at this stage of history had not learned the various ways of ensnaring birds.

ll.216–7.   'Men and women did not then use roots or sparrows as aphrodisiacs': i.e. the sparrow was safe from capture for these purposes (being lecherous, its dung, eggs and flesh were later sought out as aphrodisiacs).

l.218.   *these:* mankind's means of ensnaring him.

l.219.   *then:* than; *streightned:* sexually temperate, with a pun involving the meaning of the word at *l*.208, above.

l.227.   *inform'd:* invested with form and life.

l.243.   *digestive fire:* cf. Davies, II, *l*.18, and n. This is a polite way of saying that the soul was excreted by the swan, whose digestive processes had broken the fish down.

ll.251–60.   The pike swims through the primitive net which its owner, Adam, has constructed.

ll.261–2.   She saved her own life and that of the fisherman, whom she would have slain. *Once:* for once.

ll.264–8.   Refers to the age-old controversy over how fishes breathed. Faith 'cared not' because this question is a merely factual one: Donne is being ironic at the expense of a type of faith that can ignore facts.

l.266.   *limbecks:* stills.

l.270.   *makes a boord or two:* a nautical term: moves in different directions.

ll.271–3.   *So .../...are:* refers to the phenomenon of refraction.

l.274.   'For sport, and not because it is hungry, an oyster-catcher [a bird].'

l.275.   *traiterous spectacle:* 'deceitful mirror', i.e. what the bird sees is an illusion, see *ll*.271–3: the pike was really smaller.

l.276.   *seely:* foolish; *disputing:* which way to go (which 'boord' to make).

ll.278–80.   'She is exalted (raised on high), but for the good of the one who raised her.' An apt comment on Kings, Queens, Princes—and their favourites.

l.290.   The fishing industry in England declined after the change from Roman

Catholicism, giving rise to a number of unkind jokes by poets and dramatists. The situation became so serious that in 1564 the government made Wednesdays and Saturdays 'fish-days': those who ate meat on those days were fined or imprisoned. The hapless fish here may well stand for people in general, subject to the whims and fancies of the powerful: the answer to the famous question of *l.*281 may well be: 'mankind'.

*l.*294. *Fat . . . orator:* the bird is a most apt advertisement for gluttony: heedless of consequences, it destroys itself.

*l.*298. *soules no longer foes.* The soul of the oyster-catcher would of course have been an enemy of the soul, whose progress this poem traces, in the seized pike; but as soon as these souls leave their respective bodies (which are, as predator and preyed-upon, enemies) they cease from enmity.

*l.*300. *he . . . officer:* because as a bird he preyed on others not for need (hunger) but for sport ('game').

*l.*304. *Morea:* the Peloponnese; *that:* if.

*l.*307. *hopefull Promontories head:* the tip of the Cape of Good Hope.

*l.*308. *hopes:* of conveying the whale's magnitude; with a pun on the 'hopefull' of the preceding line.

*l.*309. *overset:* capsized.

*l.*310. *Hulling:* looking like a hull because its sails are all taken in; *this:* the whale.

*ll.*321–2. *He . . ./. . . net:* The officer, like a lawyer, needs only to stay where he is in order to feed on those who come to him for help.

*l.*323. *enthrall:* enslave.

*ll.*326–30. The whale is clearly compared to the state (rather than, I think, to an individual prince). Cf. the trope underlying Hobbes's *Leviathan.*

*l.*333. *roomefull:* huge.

*ll.*336–7. *The Sunne . . . parched:* twenty years have passed.

*l.*340. *station:* permanency.

*l.*345. *outstreat:* outstretch, i.e. exuded.

*l.*347. *that . . . two:* an apt illustration of Donne's cynical mood.

*l.*349. *projects:* schemes.

*l.*351. *Thresher:* thrasher: tail-lashing shark. The battle described in this stanza was legendary.

*l.*360. *dole:* portion.

*l.*371. The soul is free from the passion of the whale (at being killed by small enemies) because it has left its body. When Donne says that the soul, having got into a mouse, still has some small indignation, he is making fun of the convolutions of theology. *This* soul is playfully permitted some 'human feelings'. WM comments that this is 'an example of the Soul's ability to remember what occurred in a previous incarnation, and "to keep some quality" (*ll.*506–7), usually evil, of the life she formerly led'.

245

*l.*375. *streight cloyster:* limited confines.

*l.*382. Mankind has always loved elephants, and this reflected in their lore. WM quotes Topsell, an Elizabethan naturalist: 'Their love and concord with all mankind is most notorious'.

*l.*385. *no knees:* it is unlikely that Donne himself believed this, which was better known, amongst writers, as a fallacy than as a fact.

*ll.*388–9. *vex't . . . dreames:* i.e. no black dreams troubled his imagination.

*l.*389. *carelesly:* it did not knot its trunk.

*l.*390. *remisly:* (i) foolishly; (ii) limply.

*l.*391. *in:* into.

*l.*398. *roome:* office, i.e. rank.

*l.*404. *Abel:* the first to have a flock of sheep, and therefore considered as the first 'church' and 'king'. Donne's use of the word 'trade' is not complimentary.

*l.*406. *still:* continually.

*l.*419. *Now much resist.* Some MSS and WM *Nor much resist* 1633. The meaning is: 'nor does the sheep-dog now show much resistance'.

*ll.*419–20. *nor . . . goe:* because she is enjoying it.

*l.*421. *engag'd:* (i) bound by obligation; (ii) fascinated; (iii) won over; (iv) entangled.

*ll.*429–30. *that . . ./. . . blood:* The wolf has impregnated the sheep-dog bitch, and so the soul leaves the trapped and slain wolf and enters into its own unborn progeny.

*l.*431. *Some have their wives:* by marrying their daughters; *their sisters some:* by getting their mothers with child, as Oedipus did. Cf. *ll.*201–3, and n.

*ll.*432–40. This delightful passage should not be taken too seriously; the soul by inhabiting first the father and the son, becomes as WM notes, 'the personification of lust': but it is a puzzling ('ridling') lust, because the Schoolmen could not classify it. The mocking tone is unmistakable.

*l.*438. *both these:* the sheep-dog and the wolf.

*l.*439. *Moaba.* Grierson showed that this name, and *Siphatecia* (*l.*457), *Tethlemite* (*l.*509), *Themech* (*l.*509) were drawn from rabbinical mythology. *Moaba* is a mistake for Noaba (Noba), the twin wife of Seth (and therefore Abel's sister). *Siphatecia* telescopes two of Adam's daughters, Zifath and Hekhiah. *Tethlemite* is obscure. *Themech* is a latinization of Temed, Cain's twin wife. Donne is drawing attention to the fact that all the earliest unions, even as recorded in scripture, were incestuous. Theologians had given attention to the problems raised by this, but without humour.

*l.*446. *cosen'd:* cheated.

*l.*447. *hopelesse . . . hid:* no longer hoping that his trickery could remain concealed.

*ll.*449. To the dogs he was a wolf, to the wolves he was a dog.

l.451. *It:* the soul; *toyfull:* amorous: certain apes and baboons were thought of as sexually attracted to human beings.

l.452. *Gamesome:* sportive.

l.455. Laughter, as well as speech and reason, had since antiquity been regarded as distinguishing marks of man.

l.456. *He wonders:* this ape, the first true lover, is given the powers of reason.

l.460. There is of course considerable satirical point in Donne's making of this first (and wisest) 'true', i.e. conventionally love-sick—and 'romantic'—lover into an ape.

ll.461–2. *He was . . ./. . . another:* WM thinks this is in contrast to the 'usual practice' of incest 'before the coming of the law'. It also cynically defines romantic love: the first creature to experience sexual preference was this absurd ape, who in this stanza is pictured as a fashionable Elizabethan lover—who is thus, by implication, condemned as incapable of speech, i.e. inarticulate.

l.465. *the valters sombersalts:* feats on the vaulting-horse, to excite his lady's admiration.

l.466. *hoiting gambolls:* noisily playful leaps and bounds.

l.470. As WM implies, Donne is careful to maintain 'the central convictions' of his 'mature love-poetry': he is finding the shallow and the superficial ridiculous, not love; but there may be some real reservation about the whole notion of 'romantic love'.

l.471. *this:* outward beauty.

l.473. *through-vaine:* thoroughly thoughtless.

ll.474–5. *but . . ./. . . was:* the way was open.

l.480. *nature . . . law:* The artificial, or at least 'non-natural', laws imposed by God and men impose restraints ('gaole'); but the ape lives under the law of nature, and (in a certain view) is therefore free of such restraints. Donne merely blandly and pleasedly draws attention to this paradox, as he does to others equally disturbing to conformist minds.

l.481. *silly:* innocent.

l.482. *That vertue:* innocence; *by his touches chaft and spent:* the ape pleases her by masturbating her: she only knows that she likes this.

l.483. *Succeeds:* follows; *an itchie warmth:* a lustful, nagging desire.

l.493. *mingled bloods:* sexual union was supposed to involve a 'mingling of bloods'.

l.494. *Like Chimiques equall fires:* Like the fires of alchemists, which were required to maintain a constant temperature in order to produce gold. The human embryo was supposed to need such a constant temperature in the womb.

l.502. *well-arm'd:* well protected.

*l.*503.   *sinowie strings:* the nerves and the sinews.

*l.*510.   '. . . Abel was a keeper of sheep, but Cain was a tiller of the ground'—
Genesis 4, 2.

*l.*511.   *sullen Writ:* gloomy record.

*l.*512.   'You will enjoy this poem in exact proportion to your sympathy with
it': e.g. if you find it 'pointless as well as disgusting' (Grierson's phrase) you
will not enjoy it, and it will puzzle and dismay you.

*l.*516.   *cursed Cains race:* Cain, of course, was cursed because he was the first
murderer. Pronounce 'Cain' here as two syllables: 'Cay-in'. Cain's des-
cendents are the children of the world; Abel's successor (*Genesis* 4, 25) Seth's
children are those of 'light'. Donne enjoys stating yet another annoying
paradox: Cain's descendents invented the arts: Seth's 'vexed' mankind with
'Astronomie', i.e. astrology.

*l.*518.   *simply:* only; essentially; purely.

*ll.*518-20.   WM quotes from a sermon in which Donne says that opinion 'is
a middle station, betweene ignorance, and knowledge; for knowledge excludes
all doubting, all hesitation; opinion does not do so; but opinion excludes
indifferency, and equanimity'. This kind of thinking, while not 'orthodox
and . . . mature' (the yoking of these two words is significant) as WM wishes,
is in line with the general, although varying, scepticism of the time.

THE TEXT

This text is that of the posthumous 1633 edition of Donne's poems. The
question of Donne's text is complicated, and for the fullest account the reader
is referred to W. Milgate, *Satires, Epigrams and Verse Letters,* 1967.

155.   FROM NOSCE TEIPSUM

I

As Clare Howard has written, in this introductory section of *Nosce Teipsum*
Davies 'elaborates the concept of an intellectual fall of man'. She quotes from
Calvin: 'Soundness of mind and integrity of heart were at the same time
withdrawn, and it is this which constitutes the corruption of natural gifts.
For although there is still some residue of intelligence and judgement as well
as will, we cannot call a mind sound and entire which is both weak and
immersed in darkness. As to the will, its depravity is well known'.

*ll.*13-16.   'And the serpent said unto the woman. . . . God doth know that in
the day ye eat thereof, then your eyes shall be opened, and ye shall be as gods,
knowing good and evil' (*Genesis,* 3, 4-5).

*l.*19.   *In:* 1622; And: 1599.

248

l.34. This stanza refers back to *l*.10, where Adam and Eve are compared to eagles who can (proverbially) gaze at the sun. Now they are as blind as bats. *Good:* 1622; God: 1599.

l.39. *fond:* foolish.

l.41. *Sky-stolne:* Shie-stolne 1599.

l.42. *Thiefe:* Prometheus, who stole fire and gave it to man. Zeus had him chained naked to a pillar in the Caucasian mountains (hence the 'Ice' of *l*.43) while a vulture tore at his liver all day.

ll.43–44. This episode is described in one of Aesop's fables.

l.46. *Joves Guest:* Ixion. See *Hero and Leander*, I, *l*.114 n.

ll.47–8. The Danaids, daughters of Danaus, were punished—in one version of the legend—for the murder of their husbands—by having, in Hades, to fill pails that would not retain water.

ll.49–50. See *Hero and Leander*, I, *l*.101.

ll.51–2. Daedalus made his son wings from wax and feathers; but Icarus flew too near the sun: the wax melted and he was drowned.

l.71. *a* 1622; one 1599.

ll.77–80. *Mortall:* 1599; morall: 1622. This stanza brings together two Renaissance commonplaces. Hiram Haydn writes, in *The Counter-Renaissance*, 1950: 'This passage . . . invokes Socrates and Democritus in the identical way in which the Greek sceptics invoked them—as sceptical philosophers who maintained the futility of human learning and the ineffectiveness of human reason. Here the axiom . . . (although Davies goes on in the second part of *Nosce Teipsum* to establish a kind of knowledge he believes possible) is used as a sceptical argument in the "vanity of learning tradition" '. Davies' purpose was to refute scepticism; but he was not of course above using sceptical arguments.

l.77. *the wisest:* Socrates.

l.79. *mocking Master:* Democritus.

l.81. *things:* thoughts, attributes, true nature.

l.84. *know thy selfe:* Socrates' famous saying, as quoted by Plato, was, 'I must first know myself, as the Delphian inscription says'. But in Christian doctrine the Delphic oracle was the devil's mouthpiece.

l.95. *that clocke:* the heart.

l.102. *leech-craft:* medicine

l.105. *Is it:* Grosart: It is 1599, 1622.

ll.113–4. *Ladie faire . . . cow.* Io, a priestess of Hera, was loved by Zeus, who turned her into a cow in order to hide her from his wife's wrath.

l.130. *sluttish:* dirty; *Sprites:* ghosts 1599; spirits 1622.

l.133. *broke:* bankrupt.

l.135. *revoke:* take back.

l.139. *carry . . . mind:* take the mind away from itself.

*l.*153.   This is a reference to the incident that led to Davies' disgrace and disbarment. See Introduction, p. 34. The 'Mistresse' is Affliction.

*l.*158.   *Leas* 1622; *Seas* 1598. Lees are the sediment in wine, which work their way to the bottom.

*l.*161.   *Minerva:* Roman Goddess of wisdom.

*l.*164.   *Dame's:* Affliction's.

*l.*165.   *She:* 1598. So Bullett. *Lists:* Enclosures where tournaments are held.

*l.*166.   *list not go:* do not desire to go.

*l.*170.   *within:* with in 1598.

II

*l.*1.   *the:* 1622; this 1598.

*l.*18.   *decocts:* this probably means 'digests'; digestion was regarded as a kind of preparation of food, a cooking, in the stomach.

*l.*21.   *Martha:* patron saint of good housewives.

*l.*23.   *Dryas:* dryad: a tree-nymph.

*l.*26.   *still:* continually.

*l.*30.   *sent:* scent.

*ll.*45–76.   Bredvold compares this passage to one from Peter de Primaudaye (see Introduction, p. 39) to show how closely Davies followed *The Second Part of the French Academie:* 'Let us knowe therefore, that the eies were given of God to men to cause them to see, and to be as it were their watchtowers & sentinels, the guides & leaders of the whole body: as also they are as it were the chiefe windowes of the body, or rather of the soule, which is lodged within it . . . Therefore by good right they beare rule among the senses, and all the other members of the body, as being their guides. For they are given to man chiefly to guide and leade him to the knowledge of God, by the contemplation of his goodly works, which appeare principally in the heavens and in all the order thereof, and whereof we can have no true knowledge and instruction by any other sense but by the eies. For without them who could ever have noted the divers course and motions of the celestiall bodies? yea wee see by experience, that the Mathematicall sciences, among which Astronomy is one of the chiefest, cannot be well and rightly shewed and taught, as many others may, without the helpe of the eyes: because a man must make their demonstrations by figures, which are their letters and images. I passe over many other Sciences, as that of the Anatomy of mans body and such like . . . Wherefore seeing the bodily senses are the chiefest masters of man, in whose house the spirite and understanding is lodged and enclosed, the greatest and first honour is by good right to be given to the eies and sight. Likewise it is the first mistresse that provoked men forward to the studie and searching out of science and wisdome . . . His [God's] spirituall light hee hath infused into spirituall creatures, and bodily light into bodily creatures, to the ende that by this benefite the spirites might have understanding, and the eyes sight. So that Angelles and the spirites of men, which are spirituall and invisible creatures, are illuminated by the meanes of understanding, with that spirituall and heavenly light whereof God hath made them partakers: as the bodies of living creatures, and chiefly of man are illuminated with the corporall light of the Sunne by meanes of the eyes.'

*ll.*81–112. Cf. Primaudaye: 'For this cause the eares are not pierced outright, but their holes are made winding in, like the shell of a snayle, whose forme they represent, so that one cannot thrust straight foorth so much as a litle threede . . . over great soundes would marre the instrument of hearing, if they were not distributed and compassed according to the capacity thereof. For there must alwaies be an answerable and apt proportion between the sense, the thing subject to sense, and the meane by which the sense is made. Hereupon it falleth out often, that many become deafe by hearing over great soundes, whereof wee have experience in Smithes, amongst whome many are thicke of hearing, because their eares are continually dulled with the noyse and sound of their hammers and anviles . . . Therefore as the eyes are judge of light and colours, and by that means bring great pleasure and profite to men, so the eares judge of sounds and of the voyce, of notes, harmony, and of melodies, whereby man receiveth commoditie and delight . . . how many instruments are there of most excellent and melodious musicke, what voices and pleasant songs, framed very cunningly, and with great grace and harmonie by the arte of musicke? . . . But above all, the chiefest profite that the eares bring to men, is by the meanes of speeche, whereby they communicate one with another all their conceiptes, imaginations, thoughtes and counsailes, so that without them the whole life of man would bee not onely deafe, but dumbe also and very unperfect, as if man had neyther tongue, mouth nor speech. And on the other side, seeing man hath alwayes neede of doctrine and instruction, albeit all the other senses helpe him therein, neverthelesse, none is so fitte or more servicable to this purpose, next to the eyes, then the eares . . . After the knowledge of things is found out, and artes begunne by meanes of the sight, . . . then the sense of hearing teacheth a great deale more, both greater matters and sooner . . . etc.'

*ll.*113–20. Cf. Primaudaye: The tongue 'must first judge of tastes & discerne between good & bad meat, and between good and bad drinkes, to the end, that whatsoever is good for the nourishment of the body, may be kept, and that which is bad, rejected . . . But wee are to know this thing further, that men judge by their taste, not onely of such things as may serve to nourish them, but also of medicines . . . Nowe as hee cannot live without eating and drinking, so it is requisite that he eate and drinke with that moderation, that he take in no more meate and drinke then he ought to doe. For . . . if hee take too much, in stead of being satisfied, he shalbe burdened, and in stead of preserving his life, hee will kill himselfe . . . But the danger that commeth by not keeping a mediocrity, is a great deale more to be feared on the one side then on the other. For there are but fewe that breake not square oftener in eating and drinking too much then to litle.'

*ll.*125–32. Cf. Primaudaye: 'Neyther doe those thinges which serve for delectation, alwayes bring profite, but sometimes the contrarie, principally through their fault that knowe not howe to use them moderately. For they are so subject to their pleasures, that they can never keepe measure in anything, as wee see by experience, especially in these two senses of taste and smell. For as the ordinary meates satisfie not the delicate appetites of men, but they must have new dainties daily invented to provoke their appetite further, and to cause them to eate and drinke more then is needefull, to their great hurt: so men are not contented with naturall odours which nature bringeth foorth of it selfe, but nowe they must have muskes and perfumes, with infinite varietie of distilled waters and artificial smells, in regard of which, naturall savors are nothing set by. And yet if they were used with sobrietie, there were no cause of reprehension . . . Not to seeke far offe for examples, we have the testimonies of the holy Evangelists, as our Lord Jesus Christ himselfe, who was neither nice nor voluptuous, but the perfect paterne of al sobriety and temperance, did not reject nor condemne pretious ointments and sweete odours, but sometime permitted the use of them upon his owne person. Moreover, it is certaine, that the animal spirites in the braine are greatly relieved and recreated by those good and naturall smels that are conveyed unto them by means of the nose, and of the sense of smelling placed therein: . . . For the spirits of the head are subtile, pure, and very neate, so that sweete smelles are good for them, and stinking savors contrary unto them.'

*l.*128.   *Sith:* 1622; *Since:* 1598.

*l.*131.   *old Devotion:* ancient religion.

*l.*135.   *sinewes . . . foot:* the nervous system.

*ll.*145–52. Cf. Primaudaye: 'The Common sense is so called, because it is the first of all the internall senses of which we are to speake, as also the Prince & Lord of all the externall senses, who are his messengers and servants to minister and make relation unto him of things in common. For it receiveth all the images and shapes that are offered and brought unto it by them, yea all the kindes and resemblances of materiall things, which they have received only from without, as a glasse doth: and all this for no other cause, but that they should discerne and sever every thing according to it owne nature & propertie, and afterward communicate them to the internall senses. For although all the knowledge that is in the minde of man proceedeth not from the outward senses, as we shewed in the beginning of our speech, nevertheles they are created of God, to the end they should send to the understanding the similitudes of things without, and be the messengers of the minde, and witnesses of experience: and also to the ende they should awaken and stirre up the minde to behold and marke the things that are without it, that by considering of them, it may judge of, and correct the faultes. Wee must then observe, that the externall senses have no judgement of that which they outwardly receive but by meanes of the common sense, unto which they make relation, and then that judgeth: so that they ende where that beginneth.'

*ll.*161–4; *ll.*169–72. Cf. Primaudaye: 'This faculty therfore and vertue of the soule is called Fantasie, because the visions, kindes, and images of such things as it receiveth, are diversely framed therein, according to the formes and shapes that are brought to the Common Sense . . . Moreover this facultie of the fantasie is sudden, & so farre from stayednes, that even in the time of sleep it hardly taketh any rest, but is alwaies occupied in dreaming & doting, yea even about those things which never have bin, shalbe, or can be. For it staieth not in that which is shewed unto it by the senses that serve it, but taketh what pleaseth it, and addeth thereunto or diminisheth, changeth and rechangeth, mingleth and unmingleth, so that it cutteth asunder and seweth up againe as it listeth. So that there is nothing but the fantasie will imagine and counterfaite, if it have any matter and foundation to worke upon . . .'

*ll.*173–80. Cf. Primaudaye: 'Forasmuch as the memory is as it were the Register and Chancery Court of all the other senses, the images of all things brought and committed unto it by them, are to be imprinted therein . . . Therefore it is not without the great wisdome & providence of God, that the seate & shop thereof is in the hindermost part of the head, because it must looke to the things that are past. So that we have in that part as it were a spiritual eye, which is much more excellent and profitable, then if wee had bodily eyes there, as wee have before, or else a face before and an other behind, as the Poets fained that Janus had.'

*l.*210. *blockes:* blockheads.

THE TEXT

Nosce Teipsum first appeared in 1599, and was reprinted four times during the author's lifetime: 1602, 1608, 1619, and, together with *Orchestra* and *Hymns of Astraea*, in 1622. The 1622 text, which incorporates some corrections, is reproduced here; some variations from the 1599 edition have been noted.

175. THE 11TH: AND LAST BOOKE OF THE OCEAN TO SCINTHIA

The spelling in this poem is peculiar even by Elizabethan standards. The reason is that not only did Ralegh speak 'broad Devonshire to his dying day' (as Aubrey tells us), but also that he spelled it, too. The same kind of spelling

253

is found in his letters. 'Sun' is 'soonn' or 'soon', 'earth' is 'yearth', 'air' 'eayre', 'icicles' 'isakells' and so on. To standardize Ralegh's poem is to ruin it, and of course I have printed it as he wrote—or, doubtless more precisely, drafted—it. Wherever confusion is possible, I have added a note.

OCEAN. Ralegh's and the Queen's name for himself, arrived at thus: Walter —Water—Ocean.

l.3. *yow:* the dead joys, which he is addressing; *fancy erred:* presumably by paying attentions to Elizabeth Throckmorton instead of the Queen.

l.5. *If to the livinge.* Cynthia is dead to him.

l.6. *inhold:* enclose.

ll.7–8. 'his own passion is so repressed that it is the dead speaking to the dead' (WO).

l.17. *streames:* cf. *l.*33.

l.25. *soon:* sun, meaning 'sunny'.

l.29. *sheapherds cumpunye:* doubtless refers to Colin Clout: see Introduction, p. 45.

l.30. *renew . . . consayte:* sing his melancholy lays.

l.33. *streames:* cf. *l.*17. Songs, messages to Cynthia of the poet's sorrow.

ll.35–6. Everything on earth shrinks from his sadness—the Queen is for once deaf to his feelings—as a plant shrinks from an icy wind.

l.37. *invention:* the source of his inspiration: like the 'spurr' of the following line.

l.38. *consayte:* my view of love.

l.40. *transpersant:* transpiercing.

l.41. *adamande:* adamant: diamond-hard.

l.42. *my paynes acceptance:* as WO suggests, the 'person who accepts the results of the poet's painful toiling', i.e. the Queen.

l.49. *sythes:* sighs.

l.55. *poure:* power.

l.57. *still:* constantly.

l.58. *contrary consayte:* conflicting ideas.

ll.59–60. These lines refer to Elizabeth's habit of inspiring her favourites to perform great deeds (to bring herself, as well as them, glory) and then suddenly refusing to allow them to proceed.

ll.63–4. The Queen recalled Ralegh from a voyage in order to imprison him.

l.68. *cares:* responsibilities; *cumforts:* advantages that he might have gained from a successful expedition.

l.69. *Ize:* ice.

l.71. *mich:* much; *waynde:* weaned.

l.77. *yeven:* even.

l.78. *soonn:* sun.

ll.87–8. *with . . . addrest:* i.e he is thinking of voyaging to far-off lands.

254

*l.*88.   *of:* off.

*l.*90.   *inebrased:* embraced.

*l.*91.   *writes in the dust:* refers to the writing of this poem.

*l.*94.   *the sowle . . . departing:* returns to the first metaphor he used, *ll.*73–6, to depict his present desolate state.

*l.*95.   *the passages of olde:* his past exchanges with the Queen.

*l.*96.   *sythinge:* sighing.

*ll.*101–3.   It is interesting that when Ralegh was once again cast into desolation, in 1603, he set to work on a history of the world. These lines imply not only the bitterly difficult—impossible—nature of such a task, but also that it may none the less be most truthfully performed under such circumstances. Ralegh seems most often to have been driven to poetry by worldly disappointment.

*l.*106.   *soonn:* sun: Elizabeth.

*ll.*107–8.   *so . . . but that:* i.e. the sun has never declined in such a way that its beams were not held by his mind.

*l.*110.   *of:* off.

*l.*116.   *imbalmed:* soothed.

*l.*120.   *Twelve yeares intire.* For a discussion of the question of exactly how long Ralegh had been in the Queen's favour, see WO, pp. 21–80.

*l.*124.   *So wrate I once.* 'Of all which past the sorow onely staies' (*l.*123) occurs in Ralegh's poem 'Farewell to the Court'. As has been suggested, this poem could conceivably have formed part of the early, 'lost' *Cynthia.* PE comments: 'But this poem never starts: it is always about to relate the whole great tragedy, but then is pulled aside into a digression. Then we reach a point at which we realize that the whole story has, piecemeal, been related and there is nothing more to do except bring the poem to a close.'

*l.*125.   'My mind already predicting disaster'.

*ll.*126–7.   Marble 'weeps', 'sweats', before a storm.

*l.*128.   *att hande:* to come. Ralegh is still writing retrospectively.

*l.*130.   *under land:* already set.

*ll.*132–60.   The sense of these lines is not completed: the idea of the small, foreboding icicles, being melted into a flood by the sun is not fully worked out.

*l.*136.   *outweares:* used intransitively: wastes away, exhausts itself.

*l.*137.   *from of:* from off.

*l.*138.   *valles:* valleys.

*ll.*145–6.   Refers to Ralegh's distracted behaviour when first confined in the Tower; what the indiscreet writing was we cannot know for certain. WO suggests *The Lie,* particularly the lines 'Tell Potentates they live/acting by others action,/Not loved unless they give,/not strong but by affection./ If Potentates reply/ give Potentates the lie'. When he was refused permission to row, in disguise, near the Queen on the Thames in order to be near her, he became, according to Sir John Neale, Elizabeth's foremost biographer, 'dangerously mad': he came to blows with his guardian, Sir George Carew, and drew his dagger. It does seem as though, for a time, Ralegh's reason was affected by his imprisonment.

l.146. *scurgde myne own consayte:* [his writing] harmed his case by its extremism.

l.150. *stranger:* 'other (than my own)'; *meanest:* most trifling.

l.151. *What altered sence:* 'what sense other than mine'.

l.152. *tare:* tore.

l.161. *liveless:* lifeless.

l.162. *apalde:* grew pale.

l.166. *passed:* past.

l.174. *worlds:* 'Pronounce with a strong West Country *r* to make a dissyllable' (AL).

ll.181–92. The argument that love is subject to time holds no water for him, because the object of his heart is immortal.

l.192. *vade:* fade; disappear.

ll.193–200. As PE observes, this is a bitterly ironic interpolation, suddenly broken off.

l.201. 'Yet such immortal wonders [the poem here resumes where it left off at *l.*192] lack something if they lack compassion'. WO compares Ralegh's letter to Sir Robert Cecil: 'All wounds have scars but that of fantasy; all affections their relenting but that of womankind'.

ll.203–4. 'She will only be a commonplace woman if she abuses her virtues in this way'.

l.205. *that immortall pour:* God; *seat:* set.

l.210. *a change of fantasye:* a changeable disposition.

l.215. An admission of despair: it is of no use for Ralegh to make sure that the Queen knows of his love for her; he must now forget the past.

l.228. *the carefull charge:* the sorrowful burden.

l.230. Ralegh, by means of a pun on 'arections' (erections), compares the process of his love to the physical process of detumescence.

l.232. *thrale:* thrall.

l.237. *then:* than.

l.250. *reves:* steals, here used in the sense of 'takes': Cynthia as the moon takes light from the sun: when she diverts it from the plant to which she has been supplying it, the plant withers.

ll.257–68. It is difficult to resist WO's conclusion that this passage refers to 'the rivals who have displaced him . . . his friends once cherished for his sake, now estranged'; but is it reading the poem too literally to suggest that?

l.261. 'reads as if it refers to a particular incident, in which one of Ralegh's gifts had been used to mock him'.

*l.*271. *Bellphebes:* Belphoebe's. Cf. Spenser's letter to Ralegh prefacing *The Faerie Queene*: 'For considering she beareth two persons, the one of a most royall Queene . . . the other of a most vertuous and beautifull Lady, the latter part in some places I dooe expresse in Belphoebe, fashioning her name according to your owne excellent conceipt of Cynthia: (Phoebe and Cynthia being both names of Diana)'.

*l.*272. The conjunction of the Ocean (Sir 'Water') and Cynthia or Belphoebe is a thing of the past.

*ll.*273–4. The former Ocean-poet now merely runs 'dangerously mad'; all in him that was formerly blessed is cursed.

*l.*278. *foylde:* foiled: literally, 'third-ploughed': 'foil' meant to subject the land to a third ploughing in preparing it for sowing'. *O.E.D.* dates the first use of the word in this sense as 1616.

*l.*285. *grones:* a mark beneath this word in the MS suggests that Ralegh was not satisfied with it.

*l.*287. Cf. *As You Came From the Holy Land. . . .:* 'Love lykes not the fallying frute/From the wythered tree'.

*l.*288. *Who:* Love.

*l.*289. *hee:* Love.

*l.*295. *soune:* soon; *consayte:* conceit: fanciful notion of love. Cf. *As You Came From the Holy Land. . . .:* 'Of women kynde suche indeed is the love/Or the word Love abused/Under which many chyldysh deyres/ And conceytes are excusde'.

*ll.*297–8. 'My mind was afflicted with sorrow; I should not dare to say it was deceived except that I have decided that her part in the affair ['promise'] was deceitful.' But Ralegh has wrapped up his meaning in obscure phraseology, and could have denied this interpretation if challenged.

*l.*303. *could be:* understand 'could not be'; the construction is appropriate because it seemed that it could.

*l.*306. 'I loved Cynthia when she was giving and when she was not giving.'

*l.*308. *th'incarnat:* the pink.

*l.*312. *thos:* to whom Cynthia now sends her sweetness.

*ll.*315–18. C. S. Lewis suggested the following interpretation to WO: 'So long as he [Love] knows what he himself feels, he refuses to know—shuts his eyes to the frequent and unscrupulous perseverance of such rivals (rivals against him) not only in their deeds and manners of love, but in their statecraft and everything they have done from the first moment they came into favour'.

*l.*319. *borne:* pronounce with two syllables.

*l.*320. *the dust . . . bearinge:* the dust over which she had trod.

*l.*321. *fancy . . . nature.* Cf. Spenser's letter about the Queen's two persons, quoted above (*l.*271 n.): Ralegh loved her as Queen and as woman.

l.323.   *affection:* for the Queen.

l.325.   *improvinge:* magnifying.

l.332.   *for:* from WO. But the emendation is unnecessary: 'for' here means 'for the sake of'.

l.333.   *th'ellect:* those still in high favour at court.

l.336.   *thow:* though.

l.339.   Ralegh meant—I think—not that he had not loved his wife, but that his love for her did not in any way affect his attitude to the Queen. The poem does not at any point pretend to an amorous feeling for Elizabeth.

l.342.   The reference is to the quartering of the corpses of executed traitors.

ll.344-9.   'are a hymn of adoration to Cynthia, apparently taken from an earlier part of *Cynthia* . . . repeated here with some sarcasm' (PE). Hence the question of *l*.355.

l.356.   'She does not care for your [Ralegh's] tributes, and gets none from her current favourites'.

l.366.   *draw on rest:* promote sleep.

l.374.   *affecteth thy depravinge:* aims to drive you [Ralegh] mad.

l.378.   *her:* Love's.

l.385.   *wackfull:* wakeful.

l.391.   *tyme . . . untye:* time tries even now vainly to destroy Ralegh's respectful care (*l*.385), his ever-anxious fear of losing her (*l*.386), his memory of her favours (*l*.387), the past pleasures that he had from her.

l.392.   *perrellike:* pearl-like; inexplicably, WO says this 'seems to have little meaning here', and proposes 'perrie-like': like a casket of jewels: a bizarre suggestion.

l.404.   'If she [Cynthia] could have been subject to old age, misfortune, etc.'

l.410.   *of . . . cumpounded:* i.e. of complete integrity.

l.416.   His love persists, despite the rebuffs and scorn he has experienced.

l.417.   *medcines:* 'the *wrongs* and *scornes*' of *l*.416 (AL).

l.418.   'in other people these [wrongs and scorns] would truly cure love'.

l.420.   *sythinge:* sighing.

l.421.   *deseas:* of loving Cynthia.

l.422.   *Externall fancy:* infatuation; superficial affection.

l.426.   i.e. 'I carry the memory of Cynthia's love in my mind'.

ll.438.   *Thow:* Love; *that unhappy minde:* Ralegh's mind.

l.439.   'which being naturally worthless'.

l.440.   *to . . . kynde:* to grow a soul.

l.441.   i.e. when Cynthia's virtues began to work in the [worthless] mind.

l.462.   *thos, or thes:* simply a way of referring to all that he has been writing of: his despairs, her beauty and virtue, etc.

ll.464-5.   This is bitterly ironic (in the light of the preceding description of the integrity of his love; and yet it is also questioningly puzzled, and has the force of 'What did I do wrong, to deserve this?' 'Love', read as 'my love', in *l.465* also punningly hints that Cynthia herself was false.

ll.466–9. The sense is: 'Could all I did for love really be thought to have been planned for what I could get out of it (a berth in the Tower)?'

l.471. worren: worn.

l.473. rinde: branch. Hannah, in his edition of 1870, read thus. AL reads 'vinde' (wind), which does not make sense. Since Ralegh's *r*'s are almost indistinguishable from his *v*'s, I think the Hannah reading is the obvious one. WO naughtily claims this reading as his own thought.

l.474. geve . . . way: let destiny take its course.

l.480. harty: of the heart.

l.484. bett: beat.

l.486. of: off.

ll.493–6. Here Ralegh sounds a note of weary resignation, the logical culmination of the series of moods that he has depicted throughout the poem. *l.496* means both 'Die, and then Cynthia may then remember you' and, at the same time, that Cynthia is at least realized as an imperfect love-object.

ll.501–3. This is surely a fairly direct way of announcing that Cynthia is now prey to unhappiness and misfortune because she has repelled Ralegh's love and relies on that of others.

l.504. brast: broken.

l.517. it: his 'sowles sole love'.

l.520. meane: intermediary; mediator.

THE END OF THE BOOCKES, OF THE OCEANS LOVE TO SCINTHIA, AND THE BEGINNINGE OF THE 12TH BOOCK, ENTREATINGE OF SORROW

'The poet is abandoned by Cynthia and others have taken his place in her affections. In this rejection and new gathering, Cynthia is like the sun, which nurtures young growing things, then leaves them to die while it fosters a new brood, its own power remaining constant and unaffected by the succession of growth it both observes and causes. . . . Ralegh comes to recognize a necessary mutability in human relations; though he suffers, he must not repine—there is some order and meaning in the cycle of change' (PE). There is little to add to this apt comment. Clearly this next book was to be (or was if it ever existed in very rough form) a more resigned and less personally felt elegy. It is only a fragment, but it provides evidence enough that Ralegh was evolving towards a more objective statement than we have in the 11th book.

l.7. thes: 'dayes delights'.

ll.8–9. others . . ./. . . thos: those who have supplanted him.

259

THE TEXT

The sole textual authority for *Cynthia* is the MS, in Ralegh's own hand, which was discovered in the 1860s in Hatfield House. I have reproduced this, except that I have supplied the lightest possible punctuation: as it is, the MS would provide too many difficulties for the student. Ralegh's indispensable editor, Miss Agnes Latham, printed the poem in the four-line stanzas in which she believes it would have been written out in a final draft. I have preferred to print it here as we have it—always guided, of course, by Miss Latham's authoritative decipherment and account of the MS. The spelling is Ralegh's own, except that *i* becomes *j* where appropriate, and *u* and *v* are similarly interchanged (as elsewhere in this edition); on three occasions I have expanded *the* to *they*. Those interested in a full study of the text should consult Miss Latham's two editions.

195. PROTHALAMION

PROTHALAMION. Song sung before a wedding. Coined by Spenser, on the model of 'Epithalamion'. Greek θάλαμος: 'wedding chamber'.
l.2.   *Sweete breathing Zephyrus:* the gentle West wind.
l.4.   *which . . . fayre:* they sparkled pleasingly and temperately because modified by the West wind.
ll.5–11.   Spenser, despite the enthusiasm of the Earl of Essex, never obtained the preferment at Court that he believed he deserved. Since this was a society occasion, possibly he believed that some notable would come to his rescue, and deliver him from his Irish exile. In any case, there was poetic precedent for the insertion of such complaints.
l.12.   *rutty:* rooty. This spelling is unique to Spenser; but Chapman in his *Iliad* rendered 'wooded' by 'rooty'.
l.17.   *Against:* in preparation for.
l.25.   *entrayled:* entwined; *curiously:* carefully; elaborately.
l.26.   *flasket:* a long, shallow basket.
l.27.   *feateously:* deftly; dexterously.
l.33.   *vermeil:* bright scarlet.
l.37.   *two Swannes:* the two brides-to-be.
l.38.   *Lee:* (i) The Greenwich Lee, (ii) the Hertfordshire and Middlesex Lea, or (iii) the sheltered side of the Thames. There is no agreement among commentators on this matter. If an actual river-fête was celebrated—but this is unlikely—then the reference could be to one of these rivers; but the third meaning is the most likely.

260

ll.42–3. when . . . Leda. Jove changed himself into a Swan and raped Leda (wife of Tyndareus). She brought forth two eggs, from which emerged Castor and Clytemnestra, and Pollux and Helen.

l.55. Eftsoones: Afterwards.

l.60. Them seem'd: It seemed to them.

l.67. Somers-heat. A pun on the 'birdes' surname, Somerset.

l.78. Peneus Waters: Peneius, a river in Thessaly; and one of the River Gods of Greek mythology.

l.86. Their: the Swans'.

l.97. Sonne: Cupid.

l.100. assoile: absolve.

l.110. undersong: refrain.

l.115. see *l.*38 and n.

l.121. shend: disgrace, i.e. put to shame by her brightness.

l.128. Confirmation that Spenser was London born and bred.

ll.130–1. The reference is to the Spencers of Althorpe in Northamptonshire, a *nouveau riche* family who (with plenty of precedent) falsely claimed descent from the great family of the Despensers (Despencier): such claims cost cash, which such families had in abundance, to 'establish'.

ll.134–5. When Edward II suppressed the Order of Knights Templar, their London estate on the bank of the Thames was leased to the students of Common Law.

l.137. a stately place: Essex House, once the London home of Spenser's patron the Earl of Leicester, who had died in 1588.

l.140. Another complaint; cf. *ll.*5–11.

l.145. a noble Peer: the Earl of Essex, now at the height of his fame and success. He had just captured Cadiz. Spenser got nothing tangible for this fulsome stanza; but two years later Essex paid for his funeral.

l.169. Two . . . Knights: the bridegrooms.

l.174. Bauldricke: the Zodiac (as a jewel-studded belt).

l.177. th'appointed tyde: the betrothal ceremony.

THE TEXT

The text exactly reproduces that of the first edition of 1596.